THE EVENT AND ITS TERRORS

Cultural Memory
in
the
Present

Mieke Bal and Hent de Vries, Editors

THE EVENT AND ITS TERRORS

Ireland, Famine, Modernity

Stuart McLean

STANFORD UNIVERSITY PRESS

STANFORD, CALIFORNIA

2004

Stanford University Press
Stanford, California

Library of Congress Cataloging-in-Publication Data

McLean, Stuart (Stuart John)
    The Event and its terrors : Ireland, famine, modernity / Stuart McLean.
        p.   cm. — (Cultural memory in the present)
    Based on the author's Ph.D. thesis in anthropology, Columbia University, 1999.
    Includes bibliographical references and index.
    ISBN 0-8047-4439-4 (cloth : alk. paper)
    ISBN 0-8047-4440-8 (pbk. : alk. paper)
        1. Ireland—History—Famine, 1845–1852—Historiography.   2. Famines—
Ireland—History—19th century—Historiography.   3. Historiography—Ireland.
I. Title: Ireland, famine, modernity.   II. Title.   III. Series.
DA950.7.M38 2004
941.5081'072'DC22

                                                    2004008721

Original Printing 2004

Last figure below indicates year of this printing:
13   12   11   10   09   08   07   06   05   04

Contents

Acknowledgments

Authorship, it has been said, is necessarily a condition of indebtedness. In the course of writing this book I have incurred numerous debts, on both sides of the Atlantic. The book began life as a doctoral dissertation, submitted in the Department of Anthropology at Columbia University. I wish to thank my advisor, Mick Taussig; the members of my committee, Val Daniel, Nick Dirks, Marilyn Ivy, and Larry Taylor (of the National University of Ireland, Maynooth) for their continuing enthusiasm for the project and their always positive and insightful readings of successive drafts; Joan Vincent, for helping to foster my initial interest in Ireland; Roz Morris, for her consistent support and encouragement, and my friends and contemporaries Chris Lamping, Drew and Barbara Walker, Paul Mendelsohn, Lea Mansour, Zoë Reiter, Karin Zitzewitz, and Sean Pue. In Ireland, I thank the Head of the Department of Irish Folklore, University College, Dublin, for permission to quote from the archives of the Irish Folklore Commission, and the Departments of History and Modern Irish at Trinity College, Dublin, for admitting me as a visiting postgraduate student during the academic year 1994–1995, during the early stages of my research. Thanks are due also to an assortment of friends, colleagues, and former colleagues in Ireland, including Steve Coleman, Jamie Saris, Abdullahi El-Tom, Séamas Ó Síocháin, Colin Coulter, David Slattery, Rik Loose, Fionnula Rowley, Stephen Toomey, Stephen Winder, Lisa McCaffrey, and Jayne Enright.

The award of a postdoctoral fellowship in the Department of Anthropology at Johns Hopkins University made it possible for me to finish revising the manuscript for publication. I thank Veena Das, Gyan Pandey, and Niloofar Haeri for welcoming me to the department and for their support for my work. Patti Henderson and Aaron Goodfellow provided friendship, stimulating discussion, and a congenial environment in which to write. At Stanford University Press, Helen Tartar and Nathan MacBrien championed the book on its way to contract and beyond, while Kim Lewis

Brown kept me updated on the production process across often considerable geographical distances. The two reviewers of the original manuscript, Begoña Aretxaga and George Marcus, were generous in their enthusiasm and constructive in their suggestions. Both must share the credit for any improvements effected in the course of rewriting. Unfortunately, Begoña's untimely death prevents me from thanking her in person. I wish also to express my appreciation to the University Seminars at Columbia University for their help in publication. Material in this work was previously presented to the University Seminar on Irish Studies.

Finally, I wish to thank my mother, Margaret McLean, for her love and support, and most of all, my wife, Jennifer Sime, for more than words can possibly say. It is to her that I dedicate this book with all my love.

THE EVENT AND ITS TERRORS

Writing After the Event

Modern Historiography and the
Uses of Disenchantment

How does one give death its due? This book sets out to engage a perennially human question through the prism of a particular place—Ireland—and a particular time—the period known to posterity as the Great Famine, commencing with the potato failure of 1845. To speak of death is always to speak of the gratuitous, the excessive, at once symbol-laden and unsymbolizable, of that which simultaneously founds and threatens the ordering of the human world. It is to speak also of a certain elusive materiality, flickering at the limits of signification and discursivity, a materiality of the corpse, of nature-in-becoming, of dissolution, flux, transformation, rebirth. My concern here is with the ways in which the publicly enacted signifiers of social memory, including colonial discourses, academic historiography, and latter-day, state-sponsored acts of commemoration, can be seen to implicate the death function, to the extent that the cultural forms through which disaster, mass mortality, and social upheaval are imagined in the Ireland of the 1840s and later are obliged to predicate themselves on a notional past antecedent to symbolization, the "prehistory" from which the present struggles to detach itself, but which continues to underpin the possibility of culture-making and historical agency. The resultant drama of disavowal and return, it will be suggested, is one that has been played out with singular force and urgency under the auspices of colonial and postcolonial modernity, never more so than today, at the turn of the twenty-first century, when that same modernity's own dominant self-images have been increasingly subject to critical scrutiny and questioning.

My point of departure is not the classical punctuality of in medias res, but the more vexed and asymmetric space of hindsight. It is here, arguably, that the famine and its various legacies first appear on the horizon of historical intelligibility. Writing in 1849, the Irish-born surgeon and antiquarian William Wilde, future husband of the poet Jane Elgee ("Speranza") and father of Oscar, looked back on what he termed a "revolution" in the lives of the Irish peasantry. Starvation, sickness, and mass emigration had wiped out many rural communities. The result, he feared, would be an entirely new social order, in which long-established customs and traditions would have no place. Wilde's reflections, which were published as the preface to a volume entitled *Irish Popular Superstitions* (1852), express concern that a centuries-old, Irish-language-based oral culture, including beliefs relating to fairies, ghosts, holy wells, and miraculous cures, is fast disappearing from postfamine Ireland under the combined influence of depopulation, the establishment since 1831 of an English-language-based National System of Education, and the efforts of a reinvigorated Catholic Church. The result was, in Wilde's estimation, a cultural catastrophe: a landscape once populous with supernatural presences now appeared newly denuded, just as its human inhabitants too had been carried off by death or economic exile.[1]

What was the "great convulsion" to which Wilde referred? The appearance in Ireland, during the summer of 1845, of the fungus *Phytophthora infestans* (causing a disease known as potato murrain or potato blight), which had previously swept through North America and continental Europe? Its impact on a rural economy that, since the seventeenth century, had become increasingly reliant on the potato both as a subsistence food and, to a lesser extent, a cash crop?[2] The relief measures implemented by Robert Peel's Conservative government and subsequently curtailed under the Liberal administration of Lord John Russell?[3] A million or more dead, many of them buried where they fell in fields and ditches, with a further million having sought refuge in Britain or North America?[4]

As an employee of the commission for the 1851 Census of Ireland (the first to be conducted in the aftermath of the potato blight) and coauthor of the report accompanying the Table of Deaths, Wilde was all too familiar with what were to become the staples of future historiography.[5] Yet his account is notable for registering also a profound sense of cultural loss. In this respect, the most telling aspect of his characterization of Ireland in the wake of the potato failure is his identification of the present as a time of disenchantment. Ireland is seen as emerging into an increasingly secular world, in which the spirits, rituals, and sacred places of popular belief have given way to the more strictly regulated observances of institutionalized religion, in the guise of the Roman Catholic Church and the (Anglican) Church of Ireland.[6]

These misgivings find an echo in the (possibly apocryphal) words of one of Wilde's own informants, "Darby Doolin, an old Connaughtman of our acquaintance." The latter, as quoted in the text, has the following to say about the changes taking place in Ireland:

The good people [fairies] are leaving us fast: nobody ever hears now the tic-tac of the *leprechaun*. . . . Sure, the children wouldn't know anything about the *pooca* [a mischievous spirit often taking the form of a horse]. . . . The warning voice of the *banshee* [a supernatural death messenger, often associated with native landowning families] is mute, for there are but few of the "rare old stock" [the native aristocracy] to mourn for now; the *sheogue* [fairy] and the *thivish* [ghost] are every year becoming scarcer; and even the harmless *linane shie* [fairy lover] is not talked about nowadays.[7]

The inventory of supernatural beings set forth here takes its cue from the presumed fact of their imminent disappearance. For Darby Doolin, as for Wilde himself, the contemporary world is understood with reference to the perceived encroachment of the present on earlier modes of life, a movement associated in equal measure with the demise of popular supernaturalism and with the concomitant effacement of collective memory. It is not only the "good people" who are fast disappearing, but also the ability to tell stories about them.

Such a view had previously been a staple of romanticism's critique of the emergent industrial order of late eighteenth- and early nineteenth-century Europe. It was, moreover (as George Stocking notes), a commonplace of early Victorian social thought to conceive of the changes accompanying industrialization in terms of a polarity between, on the one hand, "the age of steam," and, on the other, an "old world" of small-scale, tradition-bound local communities, the latter thought of sometimes as spanning the entire period from early human settlement to the onset of the new era.[8] Stocking reminds us that a similar polarizing tendency was inherited by the twentieth-century social sciences. Thus, the origins of European

and global modernity have been explicated with reference to a "great transformation," defined in contradistinction to "the world we have lost" and
seen as entailing the "disenchantment" of the world (*Entzauberung*, a term
borrowed by Max Weber from the writings of Friedrich Schiller), accomplished through institutionalized Christianity's assault on popular animism
and, more specifically, through the Protestant Reformation's break with notions of divine immanence and church-mediated salvation.[9] According to
the now-familiar teleology implicit in such accounts, modernity, whether
personified by capitalism, industrial technology, or the secular political rationality of the nation state, is understood as originating at a specific moment in Europe and as spreading outward in its effects to encompass the
non-European and colonized worlds (including, in this instance, Ireland),
which are themselves seen as destined to experience, belatedly and at sec-
ondhand, the same series of transformations.

The present study aims to challenge this view. The trope of disenchantment should not be understood here as designating an established
social-historical given. Rather, my concern will be with the ways in which
such a figure contributes to the discursive perpetuation of the very realities
whose passing it purports to mark. As Wilde's account makes clear, to
point to the disenchantment of the world necessarily entails the contrapuntal invocation of a nondisenchanted world, a still-spiritualized nature,
albeit one constituted under the sign of imminent loss. Such a juxtaposition has become newly significant in the context of an early twenty-first
century present that appears to contradict many of the canonical definitions of modernity proposed by the social sciences. Thus, in place of the
often-predicted secularization of politics and the relegation of religion to
the private sphere, the contemporary world has witnessed a proliferation of
highly public and in many instances overtly politicized manifestations of
religiosity, many of them directly associated with new media and representational technologies.[10] Anthropological studies of the present point to the
contemporary persistence of phenomena such as witchcraft, once labeled
as "traditional" and moribund.[11] The concept of modernity itself is ques-
tioned or pluralized to accommodate the seeming variety of its local manifestations.[12] Ideologies of modernization are interrogated on the basis of
their links to colonial power and its historical legacies.[13] Meanwhile, scientific theories of chaos and complexity have disclosed a natural world,
which, far from being a passive object of knowledge, quietly subservient to
instrumental reason and the invariant laws of classical mechanics, appears

instead irreducibly marked by the play of chance and indeterminacy and therefore irreducible, finally, to the operations of human knowledge production.[14] These developments I take to be indicative less of a break with the past (of the kind that modernity itself was once thought to represent) than of the fact that the world has never corresponded to the official self-descriptions promulgated by theories of modernization. The opportunity that presents itself today is not, therefore, that of embarking on a new, "postmodern" epoch, but rather of thinking the history of modernity otherwise. The figure of disenchantment provides a suggestive starting point for such a task insofar as it holds together the secular and the supernatural in a relation of contrast and opposition that is also, necessarily, one of interdependence. It is to the implications of that interdependence for the writing of history in the modern period that I now turn.

Wilde's forebodings have been echoed and corroborated by many commentators in the twentieth century. The Belfast-based geographer and folklorist E. Estyn Evans, writing in 1954, described the famine years as a "watershed," marking the end of "prehistoric times in Ireland," a point he proceeded to back up with a list of vanished cultural forms, from traditions relating to fairies, ghosts, and holy wells to the practice of early marriage. More recently, Angela Bourke of the Department of Modern Irish, University College, Dublin, has characterized the 1840s as a moment of "cultural loss," marking the disappearance not only of specific practices and idioms, but of an entire corpus of orally transmitted knowledge and belief, actualized through the lived relationship between people and landscape.[15] It is striking that Wilde and his successors should situate their accounts not in the midst of catastrophe, but in its aftermath. Indeed, it appears to be a precondition for such an interpretation of the changes occurring in Ireland that the event alluded to should already have taken place. If the numinous geography evoked in the guise of popular belief offers a vision of the natural world as suffused both with a variety of nonhuman agencies and with numerous reminders of a premodern and pre-Christian past, the imputed passing of such a condition has, arguably, been a prerequisite for the construal of the 1840s in Ireland as an episode with a specifiable historical, sociological, and human significance, to which a variety of names have been retrospectively appended: the Great Famine, the Great Starvation, *An Droch-Shaoghal* (the Bad Times), *An Gorta Mór* (the Great Hunger). It is precisely the marking of such a boundary between past and present that makes it possible both to proclaim the advent of a new, "modern" historical dispensation and to construct the premodern past as an object of historical knowledge.[16] In thus positioning itself in the wake of an epochal social transformation, Wilde's account can be seen to prepare the way for a range of contemporary and later interpretations. For Assistant Chief Secretary to the Treasury Charles Edward Trevelyan, the civil servant in principal charge of the administration of relief under Russell's government, writing in 1848, the demographic disaster of the famine was an inevitable consequence of Ireland's presumed economic backwardness and overpopulation, resulting in a fatal imbalance of people and resources. For the Irish nationalist John Mitchel, writing from American exile in 1861 (following his involvement with the revolutionary Young Ireland movement of the 1840s), the famine was to be viewed rather as an artificially created event, brought about not by an absolute shortage of food, but rather by the inadequate responses of successive British governments: "the Almighty sent the potato blight, but the English created the famine." The famine thus becomes explicable, on the one hand, as a parable of forced economic modernization, or, on the other, as an episode in the larger story of Ireland's mistreatment at the hands of its then-powerful neighbor and (for Mitchel in particular) as a crucible of future resistance to foreign rule.[17]

Subsequent famine historiography has sought, variously, to negotiate between these competing views. The first book-length study to emerge from the decades following Ireland's independence was the anthology *The Great Famine*, edited by Robert Dudley Edwards and Desmond Williams of the Department of History, University College, Dublin. Conceived, initially, to coincide with the hundredth anniversary of the potato blight's first appearance, it was published, after a series of delays, in 1956.[18] The volume brought together contributions from a number of scholars, many of them trained at English universities, to offer an overview of the famine in its various aspects—administration of relief, emigration, medical history, agriculture, folklore.[19] What would later be termed its "revisionism," consisting in a deliberate eschewal of explicitly partisan stance of nineteenth-century nationalist histories like Mitchel's, has found support among a number of more recent historians who have sought to reassess the famine's significance as a social-historical watershed, along with the extent of English governmental culpability.[20] At the same time, its "value-free" approach has met with harsh criticism for its alleged sanitizing the Irish past and its unwillingness to acknowledge the continuing effects of conquest and colonization.[21] More recently, the famine's hundred and fiftieth anniversary (1995–1997) provided the occasion for a wave of new scholarly publications, many of them stressing once again the insufficiency of government relief measures, along with the famine's enduring economic, social, and cultural impact on Irish life.[22] These were accompanied by a series of commemorative events, including a lecture series cosponsored by Radio Telefís Éireann (the Irish national broadcasting network), conference proceedings, and the opening in 1994 of a Famine Museum in Strokestown, County Roscommon.[23]

The competing claims of these often divergent interpretations have been the subject of much recent academic debate.[24] It should be noted too that history, alongside historically inflected literary scholarship, continues to occupy a dominant position, not just in famine-related research, but also in the wider field of Irish studies, with the result that the problematics thus generated have tended to set academic agendas across a range of disciplines.[25] It is not my intention here, however, to review the competing claims of rival historiographical schools, but rather to consider their shared (if sometimes unacknowledged) conditions of possibility. The supposed evacuation of the physical landscape of forces and presences construed as anterior to human intentionality and the epochal break thus constituted have been the prerequisites not only for the characterization of modernity as a process of disenchantment, but also for the institution of modernized forms of historical consciousness and historical knowledge, a development that has entailed a fundamental reconfiguration of the relationship between past and present. During the European eighteenth century, this transition assumed the form of a nascent ethos of human progress combining earlier, Christian conceptions of time as a one-directional movement from Creation to Last Judgment with newer, secular notions of rational predictability.[26] The result would later be characterized by Walter Benjamin as the "homogeneous, empty time" of capitalist modernity and, as Benedict Anderson has further suggested, of the modern nation-state.[27] For Hegel, notably, the modern state, understood as the vehicle of purposive self-consciousness and human progress, was the sine qua non of history, insofar as the state alone was deemed capable of furnishing both the appropriate subject matter for historical knowledge and the documentary records necessary for its preservation and transmission.[28] Such a view of history presupposes not only a specific form of sociopolitical order (normatively construed here on a western European model) but also a specific type of human subject as the agent and interpreter of history thus defined. Whether conceived of as an individual, a nation, or a class, the modern subject has been consistently placed at the center of the historical process, which has, in turn, been understood as the project of human agents engaged in the active reshaping of their world.

Jean-Joseph Goux finds the prototypical expression of the modern subject in Oedipus' answer to the Sphinx's riddle: "Man." The gesture of "anthropo-centering" (Goux's term), in which powers formerly attributed to supernatural agencies are recognized as human projections and correspondingly withdrawn, is seen as cognate with a distinctively modern experience of subjectivity: "Oedipus is emblematic of the movement by which the human subject, recognizing itself as the source and agent, withdraws what it had projected onto the external world, with the result that in a single and two-sided gesture of de-projection, the subject discovers the world as an object (rather than a sign) and situates himself as a subject."[29]

In Goux's account, the modern subject, like modernity itself, is born of a process of disenchantment, aimed at dispelling the presences hitherto thought of as investing the material universe by incorporating them into itself. A newly autonomous and self-enclosed subjectivity (subsequently to find one of its most influential elaborations as the Cartesian *cogito*) confronts a material world that is no longer to be propitiated or identified with, but possessed and mastered.

The hubristic and ultimately self-destructive aspect of the modern project, Goux believes, derives from its assumption that the attempted realignment of self and world can be accomplished without residue, that it does not entail the repression of a component of the self that facilitates or seeks out external identifications. It is for this reason, he suggests, that modern philosophies of the subject continue to be assailed by their discarded antiselves. The counterclaims of these superceded regimes of knowledge are attested both by Oedipus' crimes of patricide and incest (which Goux relates to his encounter with the Sphinx) and, latterly, by modern philosophy's own ambivalent reappraisal of alterity: the Hegelian dialectic's positing of negativity as an inescapable moment in the unfolding of truth and presence, Nietzsche's invocation of the Dionysian powers of disorder and disintegration, or, no less strikingly, the Freudian Unconscious, which Goux (like Freud himself) identifies as the internalization of historically suppressed modes of symbolizing and relating to the world.[30]

Wilde's remarks on Ireland before and after the potato failure serve as a reminder that modern historical time-consciousness has been no less reliant on a founding appeal to a contrapuntally defined image of the premodern past. The landscape of which he writes is conceived of as one that until recently had been densely marked by traces of such a past—stories, seasonal observances, and physical geography affording the medium through which that past was enabled to manifest itself, intermittently, within the present. If the twentieth-century social sciences have, similarly, made much of the divergence between this foregrounding of cyclicality and repetition and the linear, one-directional time of modernization, progress, and social change, they have, characteristically, had less to say about the way in which the positing of such a break itself serves to prepare the conceptual ground for formulations of modernity as a project of societal and finally global transformation, defined in contradistinction to a fast receding era of tradition, in which humans tilled the soil, gathered to hear stories, and trafficked with ancestors and spirits.[31] Yet it is from just such a retroactively imagined split that both the modern subject and modern conceptualizations of history can be seen to have sprung. History, as the ideological self-knowledge of history-making human subjects, has sought to subsume other configurations of temporality and subjectivity by recasting them as its own retrojected antecedents, bygone moments in a teleology of human advancement that would, so it was claimed, subsume pockets of seeming backwardness both on the margins of European societies and in their burgeoning overseas empires.[32] In doing so, however, it has also testified to its own continuing preoccupation with those same antecedents, repeatedly invoking the past as a foil against which the knowledge-claims of the present are staked.

Dipesh Chakrabarty reminds us that the alternative visions of the past from which modern historical scholarship has sought to distance itself have characteristically included those associated with populations variously labeled as "primitive" or "premodern"—peasants, tribal peoples, colonial and postcolonial subjects.[33] In the case of Ireland, David Lloyd has argued that numerous histories of the post-Independence period have downplayed the significance of various forms of popular protest, including the agrarian movements of the late eighteenth and early nineteenth centuries, on precisely the grounds of their "nonmodernizing" character, frequently religious or millenarian, and their consequent failure to accord with the linear, developmental logic enshrined in the Irish postcolonial state, with its (lately, increasingly enthusiastic) embrace of market economics and global capital.[34] Nor do these omissions seem likely to be rectified by current trends. Certainly, recent historical scholarship, including research on Ireland, has shown an increased concern with groups traditionally absent from mainstream accounts of history, fueling an upsurge of interest in "history from below," working-class history, women's history, minority histories.[35] Nonetheless, the pasts of such groups, Chakrabarty suggests, have gained admission to the historiographical canon only on condition that they meet its own institutionalized criteria of rationality—that is, that they be capable of being narrated from a "rationally defensible" standpoint.[36] Versions of the past that fail to accord with canonical formulations of historicity, for example, those that explain the causes of a peasant rising with reference to the intervention of a god, or a crop failure by way of disturbances in the spirit world, are apt either to be dismissed or to be recast in other terms.[37] The challenge posed to historicism by these "subaltern" pasts (to borrow a term from the recent historiography of India) can be seen to consist not only in their divergence from the "facts" established by conventional historical scholarship, but also in their seeming invocation of a time other than that of history, a time of magic, transformative flux, and promiscuous trafficking between the human, natural, and supernatural realms. As such, they invoke a world seemingly resistant to secularization and disenchantment and yet disconcertingly contemporaneous with the present from which theories of modernization have sprung. It is perhaps the contemporary persistence of nonhistoricizing visions of the past, with their disregard of instituted boundaries between past and present, that, as much as any discrepancy of contents, has constituted the greatest scandal for academic historiography. Hence the imperative to explain, rendering the unfamiliar discursively knowable in academically appropriate terms. The alleged involvement of supernatural agents in a peasant rising in India is glossed as an instrument of political mobilization.[38] Witchcraft practices in contemporary South Africa are explicated as the expression of disjointed social relationships, or as a response to the ongoing disruptions occasioned by economic globalization.[39] What appears to remain inadmissible, even to the most democratically minded historian, is not only the suggestion that supernatural beings might have any direct influence as historical agents in human affairs (although one is likely to wait a long time for an academic history couched in such terms), but also the possibility that such an "unhistorical" rendering of events might carry its own explanatory power, capable of instructing or modifying the procedures of historical or anthropological inquiry. These exclusions, at once political and epistemological, are one means by which professional historiography, including much historical anthropology, secures its own institutional boundaries. The disjunction at issue here is not only the now-familiar one between dominant and subaltern histories, but also between what appear as distinct and perhaps incommensurable modes of engaging the past.[40]

In the same way, for all their professions of nostalgia and regret, the accounts of Wilde and later commentators, along with subsequently composed histories of the famine, whether nationalist, revisionist, or counterrevisionist in bent, are obliged to recapitulate the very inaugurating gesture of modern historiography, which takes wing only when the human subject, secured against incursions of alterity, is enshrined as the sole and self-begetting agent of the historical process. It is only when the spirits and ancestors (among them the million or more dead) have been definitionally deprived of their voices that the events of the past, including the famine years, are rendered available as an object of historical scrutiny.

However, modern historical scholarship also reveals that the dead are not so easily dispensed with. If the trope of disenchantment that grounds Wilde's and other accounts seeks to exorcize the dead as contemporary presences by consigning them decisively to a superceded past, it cannot but confirm also their continuing implication in contemporary formations of historical knowledge. Michel de Certeau has written of the modern historian's "bizarre relation" to death. On the one hand, the historiographical recuperation of the past appears founded on a loss of belief in the presence of the dead in the guise of ancestors or indwelling spirits; on the other, it affirms, at the same time, the impossibility of "getting over" such a loss, insofar as the dead remain the indispensable referent for the writing of history.[41] Chakrabarty makes an analogous point with regard to the multiple temporalities disclosed by the continuing coexistence of the time of gods and spirits with the time of "secular" modernity, a coexistence given one of its most forceful expressions in the guise of the anticolonial resistance movements labeled by an earlier generation of historians as "prepolitical." Although the writing of history in the modern period has tended to insist on the irrevocable pastness of the past, including the varieties of peasant belief and the spirit pantheons seen as informing such movements, the historiographical enterprise itself is nonetheless enabled, Chakrabarty suggests, by the very persistence within the time frame of modernity of those same elements: "It is because we already have experience of that which makes the present non-contemporaneous with itself that we can actually historicize."[42]

The writing of history, for all its conceptual investment in linear chronology and the homogeneous, empty time of progress, is made possible only by the continuing (if unrecognized) interinvolvement of pasts and presents, of the living and the dead. Perhaps, however, even more is at stake. Is the contemporary availability of the present-past simply a source of the empathy, which is a prerequisite of historical research and writing? Does it not appear, rather, that the very logic of historical understanding, including its evidential criteria and its claims to establish a register of knowable facts, actively presupposes the contrapuntal imagination of a different temporal order, a truly other-time in which human actors mingle with animate nature, spirits, and the dead? Images of such a time before time (before historical time, that is) might be sought, equally, in the origin-myths of so-called primitive peoples or in the vernacular animism of European popular belief that provided so much grist to the mill of Victorian folklore scholarship.[43] Historiography would therefore constitute (as de Certeau puts it) "a labor of death and a labor against death."[44] Unlike other techniques of remembrance, however, such as spirit possession, through which societies in other times and places have organized their relationship to their own dead, modern historical writing has tended not to affirm but to dissolve the implication of death-in-life by making death discursively knowable under sign of pastness and thus, at the same time, installing the dead in a place distinct from that of the living.

The historian's ambivalence toward death presupposes, too, a condition of assumed belatedness in relation to the proposed object of historical inquiry. It was against just such a condition that Nietzsche railed when he exhorted the historians of his own day to perform some "great and mighty deed" in order to justify their admission to the feast at which they, inevitably, arrived last.[45] Following Nietzsche, a variety of labels have been appended to that which is perennially eluded by the constitutive unpunctuality of historical discourse. Georges Bataille writes of the "sovereign moment" as one of pure expenditure and loss, puncturing the logic of futurity and means and ends. In doing so, it offers the fleeting promise of return to a lost order of "intimacy," of undifferentiation between self and world, which has been negated with the advent of human self-consciousness and the positing of a world of things, of utilitarian objects, conceived in contradistinction to a no less instrumentalized human subject.[46] Jacques Derrida has pointed, more recently, to the contradictory relationship between the gift (which is also "another name" for death) as an "impossible" gesture of uncalculated generosity and the circuit of economic exchange (whether of goods, money, or linguistic signs) that it both punctures and sets in motion.[47] Maurice Blanchot writes of the disaster, which is "outside history, but historically so," as the gift, waiting before and after language, debarred from signification, yet haunting its borders as a constitutive absence.[48] Jean-Francois Lyotard invokes the "event" as pure singularity, recalcitrant to historiographical recuperation insofar as it affirms the impossibility of grasping the present in the moment of its self-presentation, thus testifying that "the self is essentially passible to a recurrent alterity."[49] Each of these more or less provisional (and by no means identical) formulations points both to the limits of contemporary historical knowledge and to the ways in which a sense of the impossibility of mastering death under the sign of pastness might inform a mode of engagement with the past oriented explicitly toward the present and future. Among Wilde's contemporaries, however, the recalcitrance of the event is nowhere more succinctly evoked than by the poet James Clarence Mangan. Mangan, who was to die of starvation in the fever sheds of Dublin's Meath Hospital in June 1849, produced a number of apocalyptically phrased works dealing explicitly with themes of hunger and destitution.[50] The poem "The Coming Event," published in the *Dublin University Magazine* in February 1844, the year before the potato blight's first appearance in Ireland, gestures prophetically toward a catastrophe that is yet to occur. Mangan's poem looks forward to an unspecified future, identified as a time of judgment ("the Final Probation") in which present certainties will be swept away:

> Darken the lamp, then, and bury the bowl,
>   Ye Faithfullest-hearted!
> And, as your swift years hasten on to the goal
>   Whither worlds have departed,
> Spend strength, sinew, soul, on your toil to atone
>   For past idleness and errors;
> So best shall ye bear to encounter alone
>   The Event and its terrors.[51]

If the precise character of the Event is never spelled out, this serves only to make its approach appear all the more ominous. Given the circumstances of Mangan's own death, it is, inevitably, tempting to identify the coming disaster with the impending failure of the next year's potato harvest. Yet it is perhaps more instructive to consider Mangan's evasiveness here not simply in the context of the eschatological bent characteristic of much English and Irish writing of the famine period (what literary critic Christopher Morash has termed "a very Victorian apocalypse"), but, equally, as indicative of the historiographical dilemma that the textual referent "famine" helps to crystallize.[52] Whether located in the past or in the future, the Event itself seems to remain similarly ungraspable. In this sense, the terrors it evokes may be precisely what the historian struggles to hold at bay, substituting the academic protocols of analysis and explanation for the encounter with death that nonetheless provides the unspoken charter for the historiographical enterprise.

Allegory, Natural History, Death

To recognize that the relationship between the modern and its designated precursors is neither straightforwardly sequential nor oppositional is to acknowledge also the possibility of a different recounting of the history of modernity. Could the trajectory from an animate to a mute and disenfranchised nature charted by theories of modernization enable, at the same time, a rendering of the past that would take death as its acknowledged precondition, eschewing the elaboration of explanatory grand narratives to dwell instead upon their silences and ellipses, the remnants and *disjecta* of history construed as a unified and uninterrupted teleology of human progress? Walter Benjamin, in a study that has often been taken as his foundational statement on the question of modernity, argued that the silencing of nature furnished also the historical precondition for allegory, at least in its seventeenth-century, Baroque form, as exemplified in the German *Trauerspiel* (play of mourning). Benjamin distinguished allegory from symbolism on the basis of the latter's one-sided attempt to redeem of a now "fallen" nature.[53] The symbol (understood as an aesthetic misapprehension of an originally theological notion) sought to achieve the transfiguration of nature and the arrest of time under the auspices of eternity through the momentary fusion of form and content. In contrast, allegory showed itself to be indelibly marked by the passage of time and the presence of death. Allegory was born of "a strange combination of nature and history," whereby history had "passed into the setting," becoming legible in fragmentary guise through natural forms and details of landscape. The history thus revealed, however, was not a triumphalist account of progress and human advancement, but partook rather of defeat and dejection, a combination of attributes finding its most poignant expressions in the ruin, positioned ambivalently between the human and natural realms, and the death's head, evocative of the inescapable interinvolvement of death and life. Nature, meanwhile, appeared in the guise not of permanence, but of decay and transience, a condition disclosing, at the same time, the actual historicity of the seemingly natural and its consequent incapacity to serve as a stable ontological ground. Unlike the symbol, allegory was understood by Benjamin to have both a destructive and a redemptive aspect. On the one hand, it confirmed the muteness of fallen nature, which was capable of signifying only insofar as the allegorist assigned meaning to it.[54] On the other, the allegorical enterprise itself undertook to redeem nature precisely by bestowing significance on it.[55]

The *Trauerspiel* study anticipates successive variations on the theme of nature-history elaborated in Benjamin's later writings. The storyteller, in the essay of 1936, as the exponent of premodern oral narration (in contrast to the print format of the novel and the newspaper), is characterized by a concern for and intimacy with both death and the data of natural history, extending to the subterranean realm of rocks and minerals as the "lowest stratum" of created things: "Death is the sanction of everything the story-teller can tell. He has borrowed his authority from death. In other words it is natural history to which his stories refer back."[56] Later essays project these concerns into the present by developing a theory of "non-sensuous correspondences" and of the mimetic faculty ("the once powerful compulsion to become or behave like something else") as a capacity existing both in nature and in forms of human practice, including language, a capacity whose latter-day reemergence has been further associated with the rhythms of technological modernity via the new representational media of photography and film and the phantasmagoric commodity culture of late nineteenth- and early twentieth-century capitalism.[57]

In the case of Baroque allegory, the potential resurgence of material nature was linked explicitly to an unresolved tension between past and present. Benjamin saw the Baroque as characterized by a conflict between a vision of fallen nature awaiting allegorical resuscitation and a contrasting vision of a purer *natura deorum* (nature of the gods), embodied in those vestiges of the pagan pantheon recast as devils by medieval Christendom, and subsequently as fleshly emblems of virtue and vice by the Renaissance and Baroque. The emblematic reading of classical divinities was understood by Benjamin as a gesture of containment, indicative of a continuing anxiety that maleficent forces might linger in the vestiges of their cult.

Such an anxiety had found an earlier basis in the medieval identification of the material and the demonic in the figure of Satan, whereby multiple pagan powers were condensed into one theologically defined Antichrist, whose assigned sphere of influence was precisely the realm of matter. It was the possible resurgence of devilish powers from earth's depths that marked the limits of the allegorist's capacity to assign meaning to fallen nature: "Just as earthly mournfulness is of a piece with allegorical interpretation, so is devilish mirth with its frustration in the triumph of matter."[58]

Devilish laughter challenged allegory because it appeared to offer an alternative means through which the muteness of matter might be overcome—but not by being subsumed under the aegis of intelligibility. It was just such a resurgence of nonsignifying materiality that the allegorizing mode of interpretation at once enabled and sought to avert by imposing humanly assigned meaning upon its subject matter. The allegorist's attempt to compose meaning from fragments can thus be seen not as a definitive subjugation of the material world, but rather as a protracted struggle involving the constant risk of subversion. The mutually reinforcing silence and mournfulness of nature in the Baroque indexed not only the postlapsarian condition of the natural world, but also the countervailing possibility that silenced nature might reappear from unforeseen directions to reclaim its voice.[59] If Benjamin tended in the *Trauerspiel* study to view such a prospect with suspicion, regarding it as indicative of the allegorist's continuing beguilement at the hands of an ahistorical and mystified "demonic" nature, the motif of satanic laughter, its force redoubled by theological interdiction, can nonetheless be read as anticipating the more positive engagement with questions of natural history and the creaturely to be found in his later writings.[60] It affords, too, a telling vantage point from which to reflect upon the epistemic protocols of contemporary historicism—a theme Benjamin himself was to take up in his "Theses on the Philosophy of History" of 1940.[61]

Behind the pieced-together forms of Baroque allegory, there lurked the threat of an insurgent and potentially uncontainable materialism, its precondition in the supposed fall of nature being analogous to that of modern historiography, which is obliged, similarly, to posit a disenchanted nature as its designated theater of action. If the Baroque allegorist, in Benjamin's recounting, confronts the recalcitrance of matter in the guise of devilish mirth, so too the modern historian risks conjuring the specter of "alternative" pasts, which remain opaque to the operations of historical understanding, but which are nonetheless the indispensable counterpart to the knowledge the latter affords. These alternative pasts conjure up a world in which supernatural and nonhuman agents continue to play an active role in both nature and human events, a world that appears disconcertingly at odds with the modern conception of a sovereign and self-authored human subject. The modern subject, as history's self-designated agent and interpreter, attempts, always unsuccessfully, to foreclose alterity, because the event, conceived of as pure and ungraspable singularity, necessarily represents, in Lyotard's words, "the formula of non-mastery of self over self," revealing the knowing subject to be incapable of taking possession and control over what is.[62] If the ruminations of Wilde and his successors conjure a supposedly lost world in which the human realm remains permeable to other presences and agencies, the significance assigned to the famine by these commentators is, inevitably, all too human. Nevertheless, as Benjamin's discussion of Baroque allegory and the ruminations of generations of historians and folklorists serve to remind us, such conceptual boundary marking depends on the simultaneous invocation and repudiation of an altogether different mode of being-in-the-world, conceived of as prior to any such originary sundering between past and present, life and death, spirit and matter. It is just such a vision that continues to haunt the modern historical imagination, albeit under the sign of disavowal. If Benjamin (at least in his earlier writings) was apt to dismiss these subaltern visions of a supernaturally endowed nature and history as so many instances of mystification, their contemporary persistence remains as both an affront and a largely unanswered challenge to existing theories of modernization, including, arguably, Benjamin's own.

If both the Baroque allegorist and the storyteller (in Benjamin's later essay of that name) are obliged, on the basis of an accredited and constitutive relationship to death, to confront the possibility that the human may itself be precariously interwoven with these definitionally excluded realms, the modern historiographical orientation to the past as an object of scholarly scrutiny seems calculated rather to forestall any such realization. It is for this reason that the modern framing of historical knowledge has been destined to repeat endlessly its own inaugurating gesture, whereby the past is at once distinguished from and folded into the present.

This book takes as its starting point the view that historical knowledge, at least in the modern west, is founded on the silencing and sublation of other ways of knowing, including communion with spirits and the dead.

It is not, however, a critique of historiography as such. It is, rather, a quest for a different mode of engagement, one that does not seek to render the past in terms of explanatory foreclosure, but to dwell instead on the silences and evasions of historical discourse as contemporary presences, a provocation to reconceive the here and now. Suggestions for such a mode of engagement will be pursued across a range of sources: through the stories told by eyewitnesses and survivors of the famine and by their descendants, through philosophy, poetry and fiction, and, above all, through a renewed attentiveness to the irreducible materiality of historical sites— bodies, landscapes, texts, archives—as simultaneously inviting and resisting discursive appropriation.

My aim, however, is not to disparage the achievements of contemporary historical scholarship, on which much of what follows necessarily relies. It is, rather, to urge an awareness of three things:

1. The modern discipline of history, as numerous anthropological studies of recent decades have demonstrated, is the product of a specific attitude toward the past, including the dead of previous generations—an attitude not necessarily shared in other times and places.[63]

2. The modern configuration of the past as an object of historical knowledge is indelibly marked by its own unacknowledged indebtedness both to these same dead and to the "unhistorical" renderings of the past from which it purports to distance itself.

3. If an alternative historiography of the modern is to become critically cognizant of its founding exclusions, it must confront the imposture of its own origins in the guise of the specters of the nonmodern—the intransigent materialities, the "subaltern pasts" resistant to historicization, the metamorphic interchanges among history, nature, and the supernatural—haunting its self-designated perimeters.

It is in pursuit of some of these specters that the remainder of this study proposes to embark.

2

This National Disaster

The Irish Folklore Commission
and the Famine

If the historian, as Nietzsche alleges, is a perennial latecomer to the scene of death, a similar condition of belatedness has surely characterized the retrospective recuperation of the notionally premodern past in the guise of folklore, especially under the tutelage of the modern nation-state.[1] It has become a commonplace to assert the ubiquity of the nation-state as a model of social and political organization in the modern world.[2] Equally remarkable, however, is the degree to which the nation-state, in purporting to embody the values and aspirations of a national community, has remained invested in images of the premodern past. Nowhere has this been more apparent than in the state-sponsored collection and study of folklore during the nineteenth and twentieth centuries. Like the nation-state itself, the concept of folklore has a genealogy comprising diverse elements, including early modern antiquarianism, Enlightenment travel writing, Indo-European philology, the concepts of *Kultur* and *Volksgeist* elaborated by Johann Gottfried von Herder and the German Romantics, and the anthropological theory of "primitive survivals" developed by Edward Tylor.[3] During the nineteenth century, these influences contributed to a view of folklore as the repository of a "national" past, finding its purest expression among isolated rural dwellers and other populations considered to have been minimally subject to outside influence. The study of folklore came to assume particular importance both for national independence movements (in Europe and elsewhere) and for the new nation-states to which they gave rise. By asserting the antiquity of the national traditions that the new state claimed to represent, folklore established a link between modern political forms and the authority of a remote ancestral past, even as the state's own beginnings represented a (sometimes violent) break with the more recent past.

In Ireland, as in many other newly independent polities of the early twentieth century, it was preeminently the rural poor, the same section of the population who had been most severely affected by the potato failures of the 1840s, who were to be conscripted as the assigned bearers of a timeless national essence. Diarmuid Ó Giolláin has traced the development of folklore scholarship in Ireland from the work of eighteenth- and early nineteenth-century antiquarians such as Charles Vallancy, Charlotte Brooke, Thomas Crofton Croker, and William Wilde through the self-proclaimed "rediscovery" of Gaelic past by W. B. Yeats, J. M. Synge, and other English-language writers associated with the Anglo-Irish literary revival, to the explicitly nationalist agendas invoked by linguistic revivalist organizations such as the Gaelic League and by scholars such as Douglas Hyde, later to become the first president of an independent Ireland.[4] The Gaelic League, established in 1893 and still active today (as Conradh na Gaelige), sought to revive Irish as a spoken and written language by establishing a national network of branches, served by traveling teachers, by the promotion of Irish music, dancing, and other cultural activities, and by sponsoring the publication of Irish-language texts.[5] Tom Garvin has suggested that the League played a decisive role in educating those who would later occupy positions of power in the post-Independence Irish state, estimating that at least half of government ministers and senior civil servants during the first fifty years of independence were members of the League in their youth.[6] Hyde, who served also as the League's first president, identified the study of folklore explicitly with the project of "de-Anglicizing Ireland," to be achieved through the deliberate cultivation of neglected traditions and cultural forms taken to persist in fragmentary guise among the contemporary Irish peasantry.[7] In the wake of national independence, when Ireland came under the sway of the new political class whose sensibilities the League had helped to shape, such a vision was to be given institutional expression in the form of a national folklore archive and a state-funded body—the Irish Folklore Commission—charged specifically with the task of recording and preserving Irish folk tradition.

The existence of the Irish Folklore Commission and its archive (currently housed in the Department of Irish Folklore at University College, Dublin) is almost coextensive with that of the Irish nation-state. The Anglo-Irish Treaty, ratified in January 1922, marked the end of the war of independence (or "Anglo-Irish war") waged by the Irish Republican Army against British forces from 1919 to 1921. The treaty established the twenty-six-county Irish Free State (later the Republic of Ireland) as a self-governing dominion within the British Commonwealth; the six counties of Northern Ireland remained a province of the United Kingdom. The ensuing Irish Civil War, fought between pro- and antitreaty factions of the Irish Republican movement, lasted until May 1923, when antitreaty forces declared a unilateral cease-fire.[8] Four years later, 1927 saw the establishment of An Cumann le Béaloideasa Éireann (the Folklore of Ireland Society), along with its journal *Béaloideas* (Folklore), which continues to be published in association with the Department of Irish Folklore.[9] The first edition featured a bilingual editorial address by the president of the society, Séamus O Duilearga (James Hamilton Delargy, 1899–1980), a native of County Antrim, who had studied at University College, Dublin, where he was later to be appointed lecturer in Irish and, subsequently, professor of Irish Folklore. The Society's aim was to build on the earlier revivalist efforts of organizations such as the Gaelic League, founded in 1893. The program set out by Ó Duilearga would combine the romantic nationalism of Herder and his successors with an approach to the ordering and classification of material derived from the more recent work of Swedish scholars.[10] The editorial defined the aim of An Cumann as being "to collect what still remains of the folklore of our country."[11] Ó Duilearga appealed to his readers to record and submit folklore manuscripts, taking care that the latter be transcribed verbatim, along with details of the reciter's name and the provenance of the material. In 1930 the Institúid Bhéaloideas Éireann (Irish Folklore Institute) was established by the Irish government, also under the directorship of Ó Duilearga, with the specific aim of collecting and recording folklore. In 1935 it was replaced by a larger and better-equipped organization—the Coimisiún Béaloideasa Éireann (Irish Folklore Commission)—intended to take responsibility for the collection, preservation, classification, and study of all aspects of Irish folk tradition and supported by an annual grant-in-aid from the Irish government. Ó Duilearga, who by this point occupied a post at University College, Dublin, was appointed honorary director. Finally, in 1971 the Coimisiún was replaced by the Department of Irish Folklore and incorporated into University College, Dublin, where its archive remains situated today.[12]

The materials comprising the folklore archive derive from a number of different sources: material donated by private collectors, field trips carried out by Commission's indoor staff, and material brought together by specially employed full- and part-time collectors stationed in various parts of Ireland, mostly working within the vicinity of their homes. The latter, all men (no women were employed directly as collectors by the Commission), accounted for the majority of the material collected. They were sent usually to Irish-speaking districts equipped with an Ediphone recording machine. Recordings were made on wax cylinders and later transcribed into standard notebooks, which were then bound and housed in the Commission's archive. Because of limited funds, many of the cylinders were then erased and reused.[13] These sources comprise the so-called Main Manuscript Collection, totaling 1,735 volumes at the time of the Commission's incorporation into University College, Dublin. In addition, the Commission's archive houses the Schools' Collection, consisting of material collected between 1937 and 1938 from children in the majority of National Schools in the twenty-six counties of the Irish Republic and comprising a further 1,127 volumes and copy books.[14]

Both the Main Manuscript Collection and the Schools Collection contain remembrances of the famine years in both English and Irish. From the outset, guidelines issued to collectors had included reference to such materials. *A Handbook of Irish Folklore* produced by the Commission's archivist, Seán Ó Súilleabháin, and published in Irish in 1937 and in an expanded English version in 1940, listed a number of topics related to the famine, including alternative foodstuffs resorted to in the absence of potatoes, the provision of famine relief, instances of proselytism (offers of food made conditional on the recipient's conversion to Protestantism), emigration, and evictions.[15] The booklet, *Irish Folklore and Tradition*, produced in 1937 for the use of pupils and teachers in National Schools, includes among its various headings "Famine Times" and suggests the following questions:

Have the old people stories about the great famine of 1846–7? Did it affect the district very much?

Was the district very thickly populated before that time? Do people still point out sites of houses then occupied and now in ruins?

How did the blight come and the potato crop fail? Did the potatoes decay in the ground or afterwards in the pits?

Are there any accounts of seed potatoes for the following year? Were they sown broadcast like grain?

What food had the people instead? Did government relief reach the district? Did people die in great numbers there? Did great sickness follow the hunger?

Do people talk about other periods of famine and distress due to the failure of the potato crop?[16]

The booklet concludes: "Great importance is attached to the writing down by the children of events which occurred locally during the famine years, as in these short and apparently trivial stories the background of this National Disaster is clearly pictured."[17]

In addition to the regular activities of its full- and part-time collectors, the Commission distributed more than a hundred specialized questionnaires, dealing with such topics as furniture, milk, transport, holy wells, music, and the Danes in Ireland. These were answered by private individuals, who in many cases, in addition to their own knowledge, made use of material collected from friends and neighbors. A questionnaire, dealing with the famine and its effects, was issued in 1945, on the hundredth anniversary of the potato blight's first appearance.[18] The responses furnish the source for Roger McHugh's essay "The Famine in Irish Oral Tradition," first published in the 1956 volume *The Great Famine*.[19] More recently, they have provided, along with other famine-related materials collected by the Folklore Commission, the basis of two anthologies of famine folklore in Irish and English, published in association with RTE Radio (the Irish national broadcasting network) to mark the famine's hundred and fiftieth anniversary.[20] Of the respondents to the famine questionnaire, one in four lived in the westernmost province of Connacht, two in five in Munster (southwest), and one in five each in Leinster (east) and Ulster (north, the majority of respondents being from County Donegal). Approximately two-fifths of the material collected is in Irish.[21]

The collection and archiving of materials relating to the potato failure and its aftermath by the Irish Folklore Commission formed part of a larger vision of folklore studies as a project of national-cultural retrieval, a vision endorsed by Eamonn de Valera's Fianna Fáil party governments of the 1930s and 1940s and of which Ó Duilearga was to become a leading academic exponent.[22] In his later writings, Ó Duilearga would place increasing emphasis on Irish-language folklore as the repository of an ancient Gaelic past, antecedent to conquest and colonization, and surviving to the present only among isolated rural populations on the westernmost fringes of the modern Irish nation-state.[23] Already, in his editorial address of 1927, he had affirmed the importance of collecting and thus preserving what were presumed to be rapidly disappearing traditions.[24] The schools hand-book of 1937 reiterated the same message in the context of an explicit appeal to Irish nationhood:

The collection of the oral traditions of the Irish people is a work of national importance. It is but fitting that in our Primary Schools the senior pupils should be invited to participate in the task of rescuing from oblivion the traditions which, in spite of the vicissitudes of the historic Irish nation, have century in, century out, been preserved with loving care by their ancestors. The task is an urgent one for in our time most of this important national oral heritage will have passed away for ever.[25]

For the (uncredited) authors of the booklet, the importance of recording and thus preserving Ireland's folklore heritage was twofold. First, it offered the possibility of understanding more fully both Ireland's own past and its relationship to the rest of Europe through the decipherment of supposed pagan, early Christian, and medieval vestiges in contemporary oral tradition. Second, it was an opportunity to observe and record a world perceived as being on the verge of extinction—that of the "Irish country people," identified as the authentic repository of the "historic Irish nation." With this latter point in mind, pupils and teachers were reminded that "In writing down these traditions, the standpoint should be taken that this is the first time, and perhaps the last time, that they will be recorded."[26] The project of folklore collecting was thus defined with reference both to the latter-day retrieval of the national past and to the promulgation by the post-Independence Irish state of a vision of national identity distinct from that of the former colonizing power and taken to reside in those parts of contemporary Ireland assumed to have been least subject to English linguistic and cultural influence.

If the 1930s, which marked the beginnings of the state-sponsored collecting, transcribing, and archiving of folk tradition in Ireland, were identified by Ó Duilearga and others as a time of rapid change, tending toward the ultimate dissolution of their proposed object of study, folklore scholarship in Ireland since the mid-nineteenth century had been no less inclined to view the period following the 1840s as one in which the potato failure, starvation, sickness, and mass emigration, combined with the long-term effects of such British governmental initiatives as the workhouse system and English-language education, had sealed the fate of many rural communities.[27] The famine and its aftermath have thus been construed repeatedly as a cultural moment analogous to that of the 1930s, which gave birth to the Irish Folklore Commission and its successor body. For Ó Duilearga, Ó Súilleabháin, and their colleagues, however, what distinguished their own time was the possibility of creating a comprehensive and enduring record of the repertoire of popular belief and practice that William Wilde and others had earlier feared was being expunged before their very eyes. If the customs, beliefs, and remembrances of the Irish country people were destined by a seemingly inexorable historical logic to vanish from everyday usage, they might nonetheless be conserved, in transcribed and textualized guise, in the newly instituted national archive.

Storytelling in the Archives

Benjamin famously described the experience of modernity in terms of a transition from the world of the storyteller, of face-to-face oral narration, to an era of information, characterized by an ethos of instant intelligibility and exemplified in the print format of the novel and newspaper, a transition linked to the diminished communicability of experience in a world of continuous sensory bombardment.[28] Benjamin's account of the disappearance of the storyteller appears at first glance to coincide with the widespread social scientific characterization of literacy as a development enabling the growth of bureaucratization and state power, reaching its culmination in the formidable apparatus of surveillance and control that is the modern state.[29] Orality would thus, by contrast, be relegated to the realm of the "traditional" or the "primitive," those definitionally indispensable margins of the modern, whose assigned fate is to be subsumed by the onward momentum of "progress."[30] It is, however, worth remembering that, for Benjamin, the figure of the storyteller is exemplified not in an anonymous and illiterate peasant narrator, but in the work of the Russian writer Nikolai Leskov, a nineteenth-century commercial traveler, whose writings sought to incorporate and imitate the local traditions encountered in the course of his journeying.[31] Leskov's work thus constructs an interface between the oral and the written, through which the stories of the artisan and peasant class are transcribed and refashioned for an urban bourgeois readership. It is by this means that the vanishing world of peasant cultivators, along with its accumulated remembrances and its attendant forms of verbal and gestural communication, becomes incorporated into the cultural repertoire of an emergent modernity.[32]

The archive of the Irish Folklore Commission constitutes another such interface. Predicated on the presumed disappearance of the cultural world of the Irish country people, the activities of the Commission aimed nonetheless to secure the latter's perpetuation in textualized and transfigured guise as part of a self-designated national patrimony.[33] The folklore archive is the site of intersection between a nostalgically invoked world of oral performance and place-centered narration and an emergent national history seeking to transcend the specificities of the local in the name of an overarching appeal to nationhood. The "imagined community" of the nation (in Benedict Anderson's now-familiar phrase) as the privileged referent of nation-state ideology, reveals itself to be an entity composed of heterogeneous fragments that, in the process of transcription, become detached from their previous contexts and recast as evidential tokens of a presumptive national-cultural whole.[34] The undertaking testifies powerfully to the duality inherent in the cultural logic of the modern nation-state, to what Homi Bhabha has termed the "double time" of national narration, characterized by a constant oscillation between the performative present of nationalist ideologies (as evidenced, for example, in the Commission's remit and in the guidelines issued to folklore collectors) and the archaic time of origin, here exemplified by the traditions and beliefs of rural Ireland, which they seek to resuscitate in the name of collective belonging.[35] Nowhere is this ambivalence of national time more evident than in the volumes relating to the famine years. If, by 1945, the writings of generations of folklorists had constructed the 1840s as a moment of cultural catastrophe and loss, the accounts themselves serve at once to confirm such a view and to mitigate the perceived loss through the narrative recuperation of persons and places. The following description of rural life before the potato failure was supplied by Michael Corduff, of Rossport, County Mayo, one of the Commission's sometime collectors, and refers to the isolated coastal region of northwest Erris:

As already pointed out, there was little or no intercourse from this remote area with towns owing to lack of means of communication. There were no country shops. Women used to peddle some goods through the country from Belmullet which was the nearest town and instead of money received eggs, wool, yarn, stockings etc. for their sales and took these goods back to the town where they received cash for them, or a fresh supply of wares to sell. Cash transactions were not frequent, and in the dealings of the people with one another, there was much barter. For instance, a man might give a sheep or a number of days' labor in exchange for a hundred of fish or a few "creels" of potatoes or some "barths" of oats. The black-smith, the tailor, the boat builder, even the priest etc. were all paid mostly in kind. Local resident landlords were similarly paid their rents to a great extent, supple-mented by labor. There was scarcely any wage earning excepting the employees of the "big houses" who were more or less permanent staff. There might be an occa-sional turn of casual labor such as on building operations when the daily wage was about six pence without food. I was told of a man who worked on the erection of a protestant church as a laborer, who got only four pence a day. Fortunately for the people, they were self-reliant and hard-working and though their methods of earn-ing their livelihoods from farming were very wanting as regards system judged by present day standards, they managed to maintain and sustain a strong, hardy healthy population.[36]

The account marshals all of its descriptive resources to invoke a van-ished world, enumerating the people's living conditions, habits, and means of livelihood. At the same time, one is forcibly reminded that the commu-nities depicted are no longer physically present, having been laid waste by starvation, disease, or emigration. The intermittently nostalgic tone of the description confers upon these scenes the status of a phantasmal aftertrace, discernible only in the moment of its own disappearance.[37] Such, indeed, appears to be the very precondition of archival resurrection. Other ac-counts make explicit reference to changes taking place in Ireland since the mid-nineteenth century, including the forgetting of oral traditions and the disappearance, in many localities, of the Irish language as a medium of everyday communication:

Of course, the population, generally, was double what it is now. I have been, re-cently, shown places where 12, 20, and 40 families lived in a restricted locality of 20–30 Ir. Acres. I can't even imagine how they existed under these trying circum-stances of uneconomic living. Life then in those places must have been active and gay, and with the general use of the Irish language, and the practice of our Gaelic habits and traditions. The typical Irish countryside of those times must have pre-sented a striking contrast to the present day with its depopulated areas and dena-tionalized inhabitants.[38]

It would be extremely difficult now to get in touch with someone of the older generation who would still have some recollection of stories of the past told round the fireside in childhood days—stories of the Great Famine, say. Such a person could only be found living in a lonely cottage on a remote hillside or on a bye way far from the main road. But these conditions do not exist in the Ards, where the bus runs, not only on the main roads, but across country and along lit-tle roads which were lonely enough thirty or forty years ago. Motor carts and bread carts frequent the boreens [small roads], and there is hardly a house that is not in touch with the great world of traffic and noise and confusion.[39]

The status of such descriptions parallels that of another Benjaminian topos: the ruin, which in the *Trauerspiel* study furnishes both the raw material of allegory and the form in which history is understood to manifest itself to the gaze of the Baroque dramatist. As Stefania Pandolfo has observed in the very different context of present-day Morocco, the ruin acquires its contemporary poignancy insofar as it appears to bear the fragmentary traces of a prior disaster, unrepresentable in that it has always already taken place, sundering the link between sign and referent, and with it the possibility of a transparent and unmediated knowledge of the world. The precondition for the rehabilitation of fragments and the elaboration of new meanings that Benjamin himself identified with allegory's redemptive aspect thus remains an always bygone moment of originary loss.[40]

Ruins feature directly in many of the accounts of the famine and its aftermath collected by the Folklore Commission. The following was submitted by Ned Buckley of Knocknagree, County Cork, another sometime collector:

The poor were everywhere in those days, as the remains of whole streets of "bohawn" or mud houses show today even, and such little ruins or little fields or "haggards" were very noticeable sixty years ago. A little paddock attached or by the side of each little ruin.

In the townland of Shanballa, between the bog road and the boreen that used in those days to be the only road, dozens of these little ruins are to be noticed today. I have often stood by these and considered their positions.[41]

Like Michael Corduff's description of northwest Erris before the potato failure, the remains of fields and houses here become charged with significance because they mark a conspicuous absence that comes to assume the status of a surrogate presence, recollection substituting, in written form, for a cultural world, the presumed disappearance of which seems the very precondition of its own retrospective recounting. The significance of these ruined structures derives precisely from their capacity to invoke an otherwise vanished past. This space of vanishing characterizes the work both of the archive and of the nation-state to which its history is inextricably tied.[42]

Given the distinction between allegory and symbol central to Benjamin's argument, it may appear that the historiographical and folkloric rehabilitation of the "national" past should be understood with reference to the symbol as the preferred vehicle of romantic nationalist imaginings, the synthesis of pasts and presents being invoked to underpin and guarantee the timeless unity of people and place on which the national community is supposedly founded.[43] Yet the example of folklore scholarship in twentieth-century Ireland reveals too an inescapably allegorical dimension to the nationalist enterprise. The latter-day appropriation of the national past appears to presuppose a moment of prior loss, against which both the claims of nationhood and the project of folklore studies must be staked. The covert affinity between symbol and allegory (which Paul de Man has elsewhere elucidated with reference to the rhetoric of European romanticism) appears, in this instance at least, to be no less a feature of the self-imagining of the modern nation-state, evoking a foundational absence that both enables and undermines the possibility of symbolic articulation.[44]

The archival rehabilitation of an ostensibly lost world reveals the state's cultural self-legitimation to be analogous to a feat of necromancy, seeking to transmute the vestiges of a foregone past into a redemptive vision of national persistence and renewal. This project necessitates both the positing and the attempted overcoming of a prior moment of cultural loss. It is not enough for the nation-state simply to assert the antiquity of its ancestral pedigree; for its claims to be culturally persuasive, it is necessary that these imputed primordial beginnings be reiteratively summoned and deployed in the present. The creation of a national folklore archive, established within decades of national independence, can be understood as the attempted recruitment not only of popular memory, but also of the national dead (newly classified as such), including the victims of the famine, as an authenticating presence within the political ideology of the post-Independence state.[45] Nonetheless, this summoning of the dead for purposes of national legitimation cannot help disclosing the interimplication of the symbolic and allegorical modes, and thus the radical contingency investing all ideological formations, their seeming predication on a moment of originary rupture, which is here retrospectively reconstituted as an episode in the nation's historic struggle toward self-realization.[46] The social and demographic disaster of the famine, along with its attendant legacy of political recrimination, takes its place beside the violence of the war of independence and the civil war following in its wake, which immediately preceded the establishment of folklore studies in twentieth-century Ireland. Each of these emotively interlinked episodes comes, in turn, to epitomize the intersection of worlds

marking the troubled birth of a certain political, technological, and epistemological modernity. At the same time, the covert persistence of seemingly
archaic vestiges within the epistemic stronghold of the modern, at once preserving and repudiating the memory of originary incompletion, appears to
hold out the possibility of subsequent reformulations, and thus, by extension, of alternative pasts and futures.

In this respect, the wax Ediphone cylinders, on which the voices of
so-called tradition bearers were recorded, many of them later to be erased
to make way for the work of further recording, might be taken as emblematic both of the relation between the folklore archive and the materials it
purports to conserve, a relation involving the simultaneous invocation and
effacement of a vanished (or vanishing) world of orality, and of that between the modern nation-state and the vernacular cultures that furnish one
of its principal sources of ideological support. The folklore handbook prepared by the Commission for the use of pupils and teachers in National
Schools throughout Ireland identifies the "country people" both as a source
of rapidly disappearing traditions and as the repository of the "historic Irish
nation," an entity presumed to antedate the creation of an independent
Irish state, and whose historical eclipse might be further understood as an
unspoken precondition of the latter's ascendancy. Hence pupils and teachers are reminded that the traditions of the Irish country people, if not
recorded immediately, risk being lost forever.[47]

The same point has been made more forcefully by the Connemara-
born writer, literary scholar, and language activist Máirtín Ó Cadhain
(1905–1970), one of the most forthright critics of institutionalized folklore
studies in twentieth-century Ireland. In a succession of writings (including
his celebrated Irish-language novel *Cré na Cille*), Ó Cadhain attacked the
way in which both twentieth-century folklore scholarship and the post-
Independence state had insisted on regarding the Irish language as the
repository not of lived experience, but of a dead past, to be revived only by
way of a discourse on national identity framed and controlled by politicians, academics, civil servants, and other nonnative speakers of Irish. The
effect of this approach, as he saw it, was to repudiate the *Gaeltacht* (the
community of Irish speakers) as a contemporary presence, relegating it instead to the status of an antiquarian curiosity, bereft of any influence in national political life. Instead, Ó Cadhain argued that the revival of Irish as a
national language could best be brought about by providing jobs for Irish
speakers through the redistribution of agricultural land and the industrial-

ization of *Gaeltacht* areas.[48] Ó Cadhain's writings offer a scathing critique both of the stated aims of the Irish Folklore Commission and of the work of scholars like Ó Duilearga, for whom the collecting of folklore was primarily a salvage operation, rather than a means of documenting the contemporary conditions of life in Irish-speaking communities. Nonetheless, the status of the folklore archive itself remains in my view a more problematic one. Irrespective of the intentions of its compilers, the heterogeneous materials that the archive assembles and thus transmits to posterity afford, at the same time, a potential basis for contesting the very national narratives they have so often been invoked to support.

The folklore archive, for all the material bulk of its accumulated volumes, stands in the relation of a ghostly remainder to the world it pur-ports to preserve, marking the moment of the latter's presumed disappearance. Yet at the same time, and arguably for the same reasons, it affirms that the cultural-ideological appeal of the modern (and modernizing) state hinges on its capacity to posit, and thus to offer the promise of access to such a lost object, what Žižek has memorably termed the "national thing," the obscure but indispensable referent of nationalist ideologies.[49] What must be deemed originary here is neither the vanished world of peasant cultivators, nor its retroactive reconstitution at the hands of various state-sponsored institutions and discourses, but rather the gesture of definitional bipartitioning that establishes the relationship between these avowedly distinct but strangely interdependent realms. The nation-state, as the quintessentially modern form of social and political organization, seems fated to straddle this split. The nation-state is obliged to posit itself as an entity existing in the homogenous, empty time of secularism and progress, yet its projects of cultural self-legitimation, including folklore, point to the copersistence of multiple temporalities (that is, of the premodern and nonmodern) and thus pose a potential challenge to this official chronology. The status of the folklore archive is therefore a profoundly ambivalent one. Its very existence appears to sustain a split between orality and textuality, living and dead, modernity and tradition, even as it testifies to the inevitable and ongoing transgression of such classificatory boundaries as the past is repeatedly summoned to sustain the claims of the present.

The materialization of the past in the form of the archive testifies too to a necessary incommensurablity between what Chatterjee has termed the nation and its fragments, between the synthesizing ambitions of nation-state discourses and the recalcitrance of the locally based cultural forms they seek to coopt.[50] The failure of official nationalisms to subsume their heterogeneous constituent parts is registered through the insurmountable temporal ambiguities of nationalist discourse. The persistent invocation of a titularly national past, in rendering that past contemporaneous with the present, threatens to shatter the totalizing claims made on the present's behalf and thus, potentially at least, to enable the articulation of alternative histories and political projects. The ambivalence constitutive both of the folklore archive itself and of its contemporary functioning is summed up in the words of one of Irish folklore scholarship's most celebrated informants. Seamus Ó Duilearga first encountered Seán Ó Conaill, a septuagenarian farmer and fisherman, living at Cillrialaig, an isolated hamlet clinging to a hillside overlooking the sea in the barony of Iveragh, County Kerry, during the summer of 1923, when Ó Duilearga himself was newly graduated from University College, Dublin. It was a time, he later noted, when the landscape still bore the traces of the recently ended civil war, with bridges broken and roads in poor condition. Having received no formal education, Seán Ó Conaill spoke only Irish and was unable to read or write. However, he possessed a prodigious fund of oral learning. Ó Duilearga paid a number of subsequent visits in the years before Ó Conaill's death in 1931, during which he recorded tales, songs, proverbs, riddles, prayers, anecdotes, and traditions, all of which his subject had been engaged in memorizing since his boyhood. The result was a four-hundred-page volume (*Leabhar Sheáin I Chonaill*) appearing in Irish under the imprint of the Folklore of Ireland Council in 1948 and in English translation in 1981.[51]

In his foreword to the published volume, Ó Duilearga was to credit Seán Ó Conaill with providing the initial inspiration for his own lifelong researches in Irish folk tradition.[52] Seán Ó Conaill himself was no less punctilious a recorder of the stories and sayings of his friends and neighbors, although the only means of storage at his disposal was his own capacious memory, spurred by a sense that much of the material imparted to him since childhood was otherwise in danger of being forgotten. Ó Conaill himself thus became an intermediary between an orally transmitted vision of the past and the contemporary world of state-funded folklore scholarship, with its very different apparatus of transcription and classification. The book that bears his name testifies to the archival persistence of that same past and, further, to the extent to which modernity's own transformative project, in Ireland and elsewhere, has been sustained through the reiterated summoning of its own antecedents, fast-forwarding the before-time of the ancestral dead into the now of the living, and in the process belying the self-proclaimed unity and unidirectionality of official and "national" histories. The position of the storyteller and of the national archive as interface between orality and textuality, past and present, "modernity" and "tradition" is nowhere better summed up than in Seán Ó Conaill's own words:

So that is the way I went through life, busy at my work during the day, and in the company of old people beside the fire at night during the long nights of winter and through a portion of spring, listening to their talk about the world they had known and picking up from them all that I could bring with me. Many though the tales be which I have given you, I have forgotten as many more. The world has changed greatly since then. Wherever there was a company of old people, it is there we used to be, but the old people who had tales and anecdotes to tell are all gone now, and we shall follow them when the call comes. It was a quiet peaceful world we lived in in old times; but it was at times a lean and hungry world, especially before my time when people died of hunger on our doorsteps and on the roads and footpaths and elsewhere. I do not remember it but many are the tales I heard of it.[53]

An Irish Journey

How does one approach the unspoken conditions of historical knowledge other than by way of a series of detours—an interminable circling-toward whereby one's goal retreats even as it appears to draw nearer? Rather than the shortest distance connecting fixed points, such a journey implies an open-ended curiosity regarding what lies in between (and thus, perhaps, a fascination with travel for its own sake, not as a means to any preconceived end). It has, arguably, been the fate and privilege of history, ethnography, and certain forms of travel writing to occupy just such interstitial spaces between counterpoised realms—documentary and fiction, orality and literacy, the primitive and the modern, the familiar and the far away. Here we join one such independent-minded traveler at the commencement of a journey threading together scenes from two adjacent islands—from the bustle of the port of London to the open spaces of West Donegal and back again to the commercial hubbub of Glasgow—an itinerary composed, equally, of a concatenation of often jarring visions— of urban prosperity and agrarian destitution, of narrative realism and waking dreams, of social progress and social breakdown—each trailing the other as its shadowed antithesis and indispensable counterpart. As such, it is equally, a journey into the subterranean spaces of memory, where death, as always, waits in multiple guises.

The Scottish essayist and historian Thomas Carlyle (1795–1881) had, he later recalled, no particular desire to visit Ireland during the summer of 1849 but was impelled "as by the point of bayonets at my back" by a sense of morbid curiosity concerning the state of the country in the wake of the recent and successive failures of the potato crop. More than that, Ireland might offer, he thought, a microcosm of the current condition of British society, as though, by a process of circuitous divination, the colonial fringe would yield up the secrets of the metropolitan center: "Ireland really *is* my problem: the breaking point of the large suppuration which all British and European society now is. Set down in Ireland, one might at least feel, '*Here* is thy problem: In God's name what wilt thou do with it?'"[1]

As such, it was a voyage undertaken more as a duty than a pleasure, and begun in ill humor and poor health (the dyspeptic condition that plagued Carlyle throughout his life as the result of his own irregular eating habits) on a "close damp sunny morning" at the end of June, as he took leave of his wife at Cardogan Pier and boarded the Chelsea steamer.[2]

Carlyle had previously visited Ireland in September 1846, shortly after the adjacent island had experienced one of its periodic changes of government, Robert Peel's Conservative administration having been replaced in 1846 by Lord John Russell's Liberals. Carlyle traveled first to Belfast, then south to Drogheda, and, finally, Dublin, where he had met and talked with members of Young Ireland, a group of militant Irish nationalists associated with the journal the *Nation*.[3] At the time of Carlyle's first visit, it had appeared that the relief measures instituted under Peel were be continued if further crop failures ensued, but the greater reluctance of Russell and his supporters to interfere in the workings of the free market had led, by 1848, to the closing of public works and government food depots. The Poor Law Extension Act, passed in the previous year, had sought to transfer the funding of relief from national to local level, through a poor rate levied on landed property. The new legislation had included the controversial "Gregory" or "Quarter Acre" clause, introduced by William Gregory, a member of Parliament for Dublin who held estates in Galway. The clause stipulated that no one occupying more than a quarter of an acre of land was eligible to receive relief either inside or outside the workhouse. One of its immediate results had been a wave of evictions at the hands of landlords wishing to rid themselves of financial responsibility for impoverished tenants (poor rates being payable on land valued at £4 or less), thus adding further to the numbers of destitute roaming the countryside. In addition, an unsuccessful armed rising the previous summer, organized by members of the Young Ireland faction, resulted in the imprisonment, conviction, and transportation of many of those Carlyle had met on his earlier visit. Charles Gavan

Duffy, who was to act this time as Carlyle's guide, was released on bail pending his own trial. Meanwhile, the return of the potato blight in the autumn of 1848 had imposed a further strain on the already overstretched resources of Poor Law unions, which were now expected to provide the majority of funding for relief. Many unions, particularly in the south and west, had already exhausted their funds or were in debt, and poor rates were often difficult to collect because of the insolvency of local proprietors. In the face of objections from the treasury and from members of his own party, Russell had undertaken in February to make available a further £50,000 from government funds for the relief of Irish distress, and when that sum was exhausted (as it was by April), to introduce a system of rate-in-aid, or temporary taxation (6d on the pound levied on all ratable property in Ireland) as a means of relieving financially overstretched unions.[4] It was during the summer of 1849 that the number of workhouse inmates in Ireland reached its peak at 222,329. Along with a further 784,370 receiving outdoor relief (that is, outside the workhouse), this brought the total number in receipt of relief to more than a million.[5]

Carlyle's own attitude to the political economy that held sway in British parliamentary circles, as revealed by his writings of the 1830s and 1840s, had been an ambivalent and by no means uncritical one. At times, he had written in nostalgic terms of a vanished era of feudalism, with its ties of custom, rank, and obligation, in contrast to the (supposedly) more fragile nexus of contract and cash payment that characterized his own day. At others, he had responded more positively to contemporary changes, calling upon "Captains of Industry," as the new wielders of power in the ascendant capitalist order, to assume, alongside members of the aristocracy, a moral responsibility as leaders of the laboring masses (freedom for the latter consisting in "the right of the ignorant man to be guided by the wiser").[6] In a series of articles published during the spring of 1848, Carlyle had raised many of the same concerns with specific reference to Ireland. An essay published in May in the *Examiner* had warned of Ireland's vulnerability to the revolutionary movements then sweeping Europe (his fears were, seemingly, to be confirmed by the Young Ireland rising of that summer). Also in May, Carlyle published two further articles on Ireland in the *Spectator*, in the first of which, "Ireland and the British Chief Governor," he had ridiculed the efforts of the Lord Lieutenant (the senior British official in Ireland), Lord Clarendon, to remedy discontent by encouraging the more widespread registration of Irish voters, at a time when much of the population was without sufficient food. Carlyle's own solution, set out in his second essay ("Irish Regiments of the New Era"), characteristically emphasized strong leadership and the regeneration of agriculture rather than democratic enfranchisement or economic liberalization. Instead, he argued for the formation of organized regiments of otherwise unemployed Irishmen, to be given the task of reviving Ireland's economy both by cultivating the land and by instilling in the rest of the population an ethic of self-discipline and hard work that was otherwise, he thought, sadly lacking.[7]

It was this Janus-faced vision, at once reformist and backward looking, that was to inform Carlyle's professed fact-finding mission. In the event, by his own admission, his expedition appears, even in its initial stages, to have yielded little in the way of certainty, the familiar sights of London and the British coast being viewed as though through a distempered haze. His memory of the journey south was of a "blank nightmare" until arriving at the wooden platform to the north of London Bridge, where he called for a boatman to take himself and his luggage to the steamer *Athlone*, lying "in a kind of greasy sleep" at Alderman Stairs.[8]

At ten o'clock the bell rang, the steam mechanism rumbled into life, and the journey began. Landscape and climate were to prove decisive influences in Carlyle's recounting of his voyage, and already the topography of the Thames estuary offered a foreshadowing of things to come.[9] The journey down the Thames passed, he recalled, in a hallucinatory blur—"a dim *tint* of green-green country and spectral objects rushing past me." The Thames mouth itself was "a wild expanse of shoals and channels," while of Broadstairs, Ramsgate, and Deal "nothing but a tremulous cloudy shadow remains."[10] After Southampton and Portland Bill, the *Athlone* followed the coasts of Dorset and Devon with their caves, gnarled promontories, and rocky inlets, a landscape dotted with "trim houses and no fields, no human creature visible: a silent English Sabbath country—like the dream of a Sabbath." Finally, the Plymouth lighthouse came into view in the thickening dusk, and the steamer rounded the breakwater at around ten o'clock to pass the night in the harbor.[11]

After putting in at Falmouth, the *Athlone* rounded Lizard Point, the southernmost tip of Britain, and headed toward Land's End, "the wildest and most impressive place I ever saw on the coasts of Britain." A solitary lighthouse nestled among ragged skeletal rocks, the effect resembling a "cathedral," while inland could be seen isolated mining villages scattered along the promontory. With the sky darkening and the wind rising, the

Athlone headed out to sea, making toward the Tuscar Light on the adjacent coast of Wexford, 130 miles off.

The following morning brought the first glimpse of Ireland in the form of Tuscar. Wexford itself was visible only as a "black line on the coast," although the outline of the Wexford and Wicklow hills could be made out, calling to Carlyle's mind a bygone (and, as he saw it, characteristically futile) episode of Anglo-Irish history—the defeat of the 1798 rising of the United Irishmen: "one of the ten times ten thousand fruitless 'battles' this brawling, unreasonable people has fought,—the saddest of distinctions to them among peoples!"[12]

Wicklow Head, Wicklow Town, and Bray Head went by in turn, and in the late afternoon, the *Athlone* entered Dublin Bay. Disembarking in Dublin, Carlyle made his way to the Imperial Hotel in Sackville Street. His time in Dublin passed in a blur of social calls and dinner invitations—"I have *quite* forgotten the details." The city itself depressed him, with its "vapid-inane" looking streets, which seemed to lack all traces of commerce or prosperity: "sad defect of wagons, real *business* vehicles or even gentlemen's carriages; nothing but an empty whirl of street cars, huckster carts and other such 'trolley'"—a panorama of seemingly profitless activity, conducive to no discernible end. He was visited at his hotel by Duffy, and together they planned a route, taking in the south and west coasts and ending in Derry, where Carlyle was to board a steamer for Glasgow.[13]

The following Sunday, Carlyle set out, traveling alone at first, from Dublin to Kildare—"one of the wretchedest wild villages I ever saw." Kildare was the scene of a different kind of profitless clamor, in the guise of the numerous beggars who crowded about the worshippers as they exited the local church: "a harpy swarm of clamorous mendicants, men, women, children:—a village winged, as if a flight of harpies had alighted in it! In Dublin I had seen winged groups but not much worse than some Irish groups in London that year; here for the first time was 'Irish beggary' itself!" The scene appeared both quintessentially Irish and, at the same time, foreign and exotic, "like a village in Dahomey."[14]

"A Drunk Country"

Journeying on by coach to Carlow, Carlyle boarded a train for Kilkenny, where Duffy was waiting to meet him. Together they proceeded south by rail to Thomastown, and then by private car to Waterford. From

Waterford, they journeyed south along the coast in the direction of Cork: "carts met, some air of real trade, alas! If you look it is mostly or all meal sacks, Indian corn sacks,—poorhouse trade."[15] Beyond Cork, in the direction of Blarney Castle, the countryside became "barer, wilder." Specific features were hard to recall: "Remember next to nothing of the country; hedgeless, dim—moory, tilled patches in wilderness of untilled; heights in the distance, but no name to them discoverable, nor worth much search."[16]

At the same time, as he journeyed south and west, indications of famine became more striking. Millstreet, where he alighted for lunch, appeared, viewed from a distance, a pleasant village, but close up revealed itself "one mass of mendicancy ruined by the famine."[17] Approaching Killarney, in the adjacent county of Kerry, the carriage passed huge numbers of people camped by the wayside, waiting for outdoor relief to be dispensed at the local workhouse. Entering the town itself, the carriage was surrounded by beggars "like ravenous dogs, storming round carrion."[18]

Carlyle was most dismayed by the apparent absence of cultivation. Pockets of agriculture were swallowed up in a surrounding mass of wet, flat countryside, swept by almost continuous rain. Indeed, the landscape around Killarney seemed to match and reinforce the idleness and apathy he had noted in its inhabitants—"like a drunk country fallen down to sleep in the mud."[19] As Carlyle skirted the southern tip of Ireland and headed northward, through County Galway toward Westport in County Mayo, the impression was progressively reinforced—"Watery fields, ill-fenced, rushes, rubbish; country bare and dirty looking; weather rather darkening than improving"—and always rain.[20] At intervals could be glimpsed ragged, emaciated figures, passing to and fro with no discernible purpose. The yielding, spongiform softness of the landscape seemed to absorb all human effort and volition.

Carlyle's characterizations of people and landscape echo those of numerous earlier writers. For the late twelfth-century Anglo-Norman cleric, Giraldus Cambrensis (Gerald of Wales), writing in the wake of the invasion and settlement of Ireland carried out under the English King Henry II, Ireland was a land of monsters and marvels, occupying the westernmost edge of Christendom.[21] Its human inhabitants were classed as uncivilized forest dwellers (*gens sylvestris*) leading a life akin to that of beasts, having not yet progressed from pastoral living to settlement and agriculture.[22] Gerald's portrayal, which remained influential throughout much of the Middle Ages, was later to be given a religious and sectarian inflection by the Reformation policies pursued under Henry VIII and Elizabeth I, the imputed proclivities of the Irish being viewed as indicative both of their backwardness and of a lack of loyalty to the English crown.[23] The Elizabethan poet-diplomat Edmund Spenser, in his *A View of the Present State of Ireland*, composed in the early stages of the Nine Years' War (1593–1603), depicted the native Irish as a race of bloodthirsty and scantily clad savages, by turns indolent and violent, the stark antithesis of English civility.[24] Such a vision, reiterated by many of Spenser's contemporaries, was reinforced during the seventeenth century by the events of the Confederate War (1641–1653) and by Oliver Cromwell's campaigns in Ireland.[25]

It was not until the later eighteenth century that English portrayals of Ireland and the Irish began to soften. The construction of roads and the extension of administrative control in remote districts brought with it a revaluation of those features of landscape—mountains, forests, moorlands—that had inspired most unease in earlier writers. The accounts of successive English travelers began to evince both an aesthetic appreciation of wild and mountainous scenery, and a more benign view of the Irish themselves, regarded no longer as savages, but as embodiments of an ideal simplicity. This shift in perception found support in the newly fashionable concept of the "sublime," disseminated initially through Boileau's translation of Longinus, and subsequently given one of its most influential formulations by the Dublin-born Edmund Burke. The latter's *An Inquiry into the Origin of our Ideas of the Sublime and Beautiful* (written around 1750 and published in 1757) defined the sublime in terms of "terror," "obscurity," "power," "vastness," "infinity"—concepts that furnished a ready vocabulary for the description of rugged and sparsely populated country and that were accordingly soon taken up by many writers on Ireland, including the English agriculturalist and traveler Arthur Young.[26]

By the time of Carlyle's visit, however, a number of factors had intervened to qualify this picture: the rising of the United Irishmen of 1798; ongoing agitation for repeal of the Act of Union, which had followed, in response to the rising, in 1800, formalizing Ireland's incorporation into the larger British polity; the unsuccessful Young Ireland rising during the summer of 1848; and a succession of reports in the British press emphasizing the state of Ireland in the wake of the potato failure. Against this backdrop, English portrayals of Ireland and the Irish tended to reaffirm earlier rhetorics of racial differentiation, newly suffused with the language of nineteenth-century science. The Irish came increasingly to be classified, alongside other colonized populations, both as physically distinct from their English rulers and as occupying a lower stage of civilization.[27] As such, their imputed primitivism was apt to appear too as a potential threat to Britain's own continuing advancement, a view Carlyle himself had advanced in his earlier writings on the Irish question.

Carlyle's own encounter with the landscapes of Ireland's west coast thus appears, if anything, a travesty of his more aesthetically inclined predecessors. If, for Burke's best-known reader, Immanuel Kant, the experience of sublimity, similarly associated with vistas of vastness and immensity, issued ultimately in affirmation of the human imagination's capacity to form a conception of the sublime, Carlyle (notwithstanding his own immersion in German literature and philosophy) was unable to wrest comparable reassurance from the waterlogged expanses through which he traveled.[28] In the face of productive labor and economic initiative, the west of Ireland's landscape of mountain and bog appeared to present the constant threat of reversion to a state of primordial chaos that the bulwark of (English) civilization strained to hold at bay. Even so, the appearance of such an unsolicited resurfacing of the remote past was itself intimately related to a range of contemporary transformations.[29]

Of Bogs, Bodies, and the Data of Prehistory

From the late eighteenth century onward, the reclamation for agricultural and commercial use of the peat bogs occupying much of the midlands and west coast was facilitated by a program of road building throughout Ireland, linking remote areas to ports and market towns and thus adding to the potential value both of existing agricultural land and of adjacent areas of as yet undrained bog.[30] As a result of these developments, during the early decades of the nineteenth century, the reclamation and commercial exploitation of Ireland's bogs came increasingly to be viewed as a matter of concern to politicians and landowners, a point illustrated by the setting up in 1809 of a government-appointed Bogs Commission to inquire into peat bogs and their uses. The commission's reports, published between 1810 and 1814, included details of the formation, morphology, and vegetation of bogs, along with maps, drawings, and advice on drainage.[31] Reclamation of wastelands was frequently proposed as a means to stimulate the expansion of agricultural production in Ireland and thus to provide for a growing population. The reports of the Bogs Commission had estimated that 1.4 million acres could be reclaimed for tillage, and a further 2.3 million for pasture. The Devon Commission (1843–1845), set up under Peel's administration to inquire into the land question in Ireland, further publicized these findings. The chair of the commission, the Earl of Devon, served also as head of the Irish Waste Land Improvement Society (founded in 1842) and continued to urge government support for its activities during the famine years. Russell himself attempted to introduce a Waste-Land Reclamation Bill as a remedial measure in 1847, at the height of the famine, but was blocked by members of his own party, who regarded it as an interference with the free trade in land. In subsequent decades, the project of reclamation was to be taken up too by Irish nationalists through the Land League, established in 1879 to campaign for the rights of tenants. The League's founder, Michael Davitt, the son of an evicted farmer from Mayo, advocated a wasteland reclamation scheme, financed by a land tax, as a means not of fostering the development of capitalized large farming, but of settling agricultural laborers as peasant proprietors.[32]

Alongside such schemes, and the continued harvesting of peat for domestic fuel, the nineteenth century also witnessed an increasing awareness of bogs as material repositories of the past, a development directly linked to the ongoing transformation of the landscape. In Ireland, as elsewhere in nineteenth-century Europe, the drainage of bogs and wetlands resulted in the uncovering of increasing numbers of buried or submerged artifacts, fueling an upsurge of amateur and scholarly interest in wetland archaeology.[33] Nor were inanimate objects the only finds associated with drainage and reclamation projects. In Ireland, as throughout northern and western Europe, bogs were a plentiful source of human remains, preserved below the surface in the acidic, oxygen-free waters by a process analogous to tanning. These bog corpses, often interpreted as human sacrifices or as victims of execution, have since found wider fame through the writings of the Danish archaeologist P. V. Glob and latterly through the poetry of Seamus Heaney (of whom more below). Although the best known of them (the "Tollund Man," the "Grauballe Man") hail from the vicinity of Jutland in southern Denmark and take their names from local parishes, Ireland has produced more than eighty bog people in the years between 1750 and the present. As Ireland's population and with it the extent of agricultural encroachment on boglands increased during the early decades of the nineteenth century, so did the frequency of such finds. The best preserved was found at a depth of nine and a half feet at Gallagh, near Castleblak-eney, County Galway, in 1821 (and is described in accounts by archaeologist George Petrie and others). Having been disinterred several times for the benefit of visitors, it is now displayed in Dublin in the National Museum of Ireland.[34]

The scenes that Carlyle identified with the sullen intransigence of unreformed nature were, therefore, at the same time, the repository of an altogether human history, the bringing to light of which was a direct correlate of the social and economic transformations taking place in rural Ireland. Seldom has the resurfacing of the archaic past under the auspices of modernity been more attentively theorized than in the writings of Walter Benjamin. For Benjamin, however, the imaginings of a resurgent past conjured in the wake of modernization pertained less to a specific historical epoch than to a chronologically unlocatable vision of originary flux and formlessness that could appear by turns threatening and potentially emancipatory. In his essay on Goethe's *Elective Affinities* (written between 1919 and 1922 and first published in *Neue Deutsche Beitrage* in 1925), it is the former aspect that is underscored. Benjamin identifies the novel's protagonists as unwittingly in thrall to a retrogressive "mythic nature," identified with telluric forces, inscrutable fate, and the power of matter, a power that manifests itself all the more surely to the degree that human beings assume themselves to have transcended its reach.[35] In the later essay "Franz Kafka" (1932), it is the bureaucratic apparatus of the modern state that, insofar as it appears to promise deliverance from the world of myth and implacable fate, furnishes the medium through which these archaic forces are enabled to manifest themselves in the present. Kafka's world is thus one in which the archaic and the modern are interfolded to disconcerting effect: "Kafka did not conceive of the world in which he lived as an advance over the beginnings of time. His novels are set in a swamp world."[36]

The swamp world, or "prehistoric world" (*Vorwelt*), corresponds to the "hetaeric" phase of human development described by the nineteenth-century Swiss jurist and amateur antiquarian Johannes Bachofen (whom Benjamin cites). Bachofen identifies the hetaeric as a stage of primitive promiscuity, prior to the institution of marriage, in which human life remains subservient to the "law of matter," "the unbidden wild growth of mother earth, manifested most abundantly in the life of the swamps."[37] Humanity's emergence from such a condition is taken by Bachofen to signal its liberation from the primeval past and thus the beginning of history proper.

For Benjamin, in contrast, the realm of prehistoric is not to be straightforwardly conflated with the domineering power of mythic nature. Prehistory,
construed as a state both antecedent to and contemporaneous with modern
society and its radically individualized human subject, is credited with the
power to evoke not only the threat of dissolution, but also the utopian
promise of a classless society (and with it the prospect of redemption for a
now fallen world). In Kafka's novels, it is precisely those characters not yet
fully emerged from the "womb of nature," the "unfinished" ones, the "as-
sistants," for whom, uniquely, there appears to be hope.[38]

Following Benjamin, the bringing to light of submerged pasts—
both individual and collective—can be taken to define the task both of the
archaeologist and of the contemporary cultural critic, concerned with ex-
cavating the buried traces of European modernity's prehistory, along with
the sedimented layers of collective (mis)representation that have accumulated atop these retrojected contents.[39] Anna Stüssi stresses the degree to
which this view rests upon the presumed interimplication of pasts and
presents, such that the former continue to impinge, sometimes obscurely,
on the latter:

> For Benjamin, the past never lies merely "behind"—it has not been disposed of—
> but rather "below" in the depths. In the present it lies subliminally contempora-
> neous . . . the city still stands in whose ground its own past lies hidden. The pres-
> ent-day city transforms itself in the light of remembrance into an excavated one
> that bears testimony to the time of the past. Archaeology takes its place on the
> showplace of modernity.[40]

The archaeology of the forgotten entails the recognition and decipherment of veiled continuities within the form of the new, an enterprise
made possible by the anachronistic resurfacing of the ancient past within
modernity as a direct result of modernity's own developmental logic. Turning once more to nineteenth-century Ireland, however, one is confronted
by the problem of transposing Benjamin's insights (formulated principally
with reference to the sedimented prehistory of the modern metropolis) to
areas located on the fringes of industrial development. Where the forces
transforming both human society and the natural environment are themselves actively engaged in bringing the traces of the buried past to light—
as was demonstrably the case with the drainage and clearance of the Irish
boglands—what remains for the critic, other than to note these developments as concomitant with the realignment of patterns of production, labor, and social organization? Here, as Carlyle and generations of archaeol-

ogists were to discover, the past Benjamin expended such pains to recover keeps thrusting itself upon the observer, as though in a show of tellurian exuberance short-circuiting the need for analytic retrieval. In this respect, perhaps a more congenial guide to the landscape through which Carlyle journeyed may be found in the work of Ireland's most recent Nobel laureate.

Seamus Heaney's poetry reveals an abiding fascination with Ireland's bog landscapes, both as repositories of the past and as the medium through which that past is able to obtrude, to disturbing effect, upon the present. In the early poem "At a Potato Digging," it is the famine dead themselves who are fleetingly resurrected through the sight of newly dug potatoes, evoking, in a mimetic flash, "live skulls, blind eyed" and thus recalling too the skeletal forms of the starving, soon to rot in the earth alongside the blighted potato crop.[41] A no less explicit alignment of landscape, memory, and death is to be found in a series of later poems from the 1975 collection *North*, which apostrophize not only the peat-bog corpses of Ireland and Scandinavia (the "Grauballe Man," the "Bog Queen," her hollow intestines threaded by aquatic plants, the "teenage adulteress," garroted and cast into the dark waters), but also the bog itself as a nurturant preserver of persons and objects, which it finally regurgitates both as the stuff of poetry and as an unsettling yet secretly familiar presence among the living:

> Earth-pantry, bone-vault,
> sun-black, embalmer
> of votive goods
> and sabred fugitives.[42]

Crucially, historical agency here is the assigned prerogative of the earth itself (the poet casting himself elsewhere in the role of "voyeur"), as though the jettisoning of bodies and artifacts from these amorphous depths were also the sporadic reassertion of another temporality, antedating the humanly constructed timescale of chronicles, calendars, and clocks. It is precisely by virtue of their prior ingestion by the earth that the bog bodies of which Heaney writes acquire a new historical legibility, their reemergence into the present enabling not only the scholarly decipherment of Iron Age sacrificial and mortuary practices, but also the drawing of analogies across the intervening centuries between these and the state and paramilitary violence besetting the poet's native Northern Ireland in the mid-1970s. This voluptuous and, finally, gratuitous disgorging affirms at once the historicity latent in seemingly unreclaimed nature (and thus the covert persistence within the present of its own buried antecedents) and the continuing implication of that same nature in processes of historical transformation and renewal. The intersection of nature and history to which Benjamin gestured in his study of the German *Trauerspiel* is rendered disconcertingly literal by the submerged but all-too-palpable presence of bodies and artifacts, fueling the dreams of both developers and antiquarians, along with the poet-voyeur's own troubled glance over the shoulder into the obscure recesses of personal and collective remembrance.[43]

The Acme of Human Swinery

For Carlyle, it was the region around Westport, County Mayo, including the boglands of Erris, that offered the most vivid exemplification of Irish destitution. The desolation of landscape and climate appeared to him mimicked and reproduced in the degradation of the people themselves. Of the workhouse in Westport, he wrote,

Human swinery here has reached its *acme*, happily: 30,000 paupers in the union, population supposed to be about 60,000. Workhouse proper (I suppose) cannot hold above 3 or 4000 of them, subsidiary workhouses and outdoor relief the others. Abomination of desolation; what *can* you make of it! Out-door quasi-*work*: 3 or 400 big hulks of fellows tumbling about with shovels, picks and barrows, "leveling" the end of their workhouse hill; at first glance you would think them all working; look nearer, in each shovel there is some ounce or two of mould, and it is all make-believe; 5 or 600 boys and lads pretending to break stones, can it be a *charity* to keep men alive on these terms? In face of all the twaddle of the earth, shoot a man rather than train him (with heavy expense to his neighbors) to be a deceptive human *swine*.[44]

An ever-growing number of paupers, constrained to a life of profitless activity: at once a mocking parody of productive labor and a microcosm of conditions Carlyle had observed elsewhere in Ireland. Even so, the building, filled to overcrowding, did not succeed in containing destitution within its walls. Outside, those unable to gain admission to the workhouse thronged the streets of Westport. A local Catholic priest to whom Carlyle had been given a letter of introduction claimed to be beset by beggars each time he showed his face out of doors—an extravagance of scarcity fast becoming an all-too-tangible threat. The Westport Poor Law Union was receiving at the time £1,100 from government funds, the nearby Castlebar Union £800. Poor rates in the district were scarcely collected, and rents were long overdue. There was minimal stock left and little cultivation. As a result, many landlords were left without income—"living on the rabbits of their own park." Carlyle was moved to reflect, despairingly, that the result could only be an all-consuming implosion of hunger: "Society is at an *end* here, with the land uncultivated and every second soul a pauper.—'Society' *here* would have to eat itself, and end by cannibalism in a week, if it were not held up by the rest of our empire still standing afoot."[45]

Nonetheless, in Carlyle's view, the struggle against the Irish wilderness of moorland and bog, for all their seeming recalcitrance, remained eminently worth waging. Passing Lord Lucan's estates near Castlebar (County Mayo), he noted approvingly the evidence of agricultural improvements in the form of drainage and land clearance, new building, and planting. If these had been achieved at the cost of numerous evictions (as Lord Lucan's former tenants readily pointed out), the price seemed an acceptable one for what amounted to a victory of human will and initiative over intransigent nature. It was in these terms that he described the fruits of Lord Lucan's husbandry: "Gigantic drain; torn thro' a blue *whinstone* range of knolls, and neatly fenced with stone and mortar; drippings of the abominable bog (which is all round, far and wide, ugly as chaos), run now through it as a brown *brook*. Abominable bog, thou *shalt* cease to be abominable, and become subject to man!"[46]

If the bog was to be drained and subdued to human purposes, the only viable agents of its subjugation, in Carlyle's view, were not the Irish themselves, but the English and Scottish settlers who had acquired farms in the region. He was especially fulsome in his praises of Lord George Hill, who held estates near Dunfanaghy in County Donegal, and who acted as Carlyle's host and guide during his stay in the locality. Lord George had fenced and drained, and he insisted that his tenants consolidate their holdings in a single enclosure, with access to a road, rather than the scattered strips that had previously been the norm. In addition, he had engaged the services of a number of outsiders to the region—Aberdeen and Ulster men ("solid, clever")—as tenants and managers. Carlyle accompanied the chief manager, an Aberdeen man, to the farmhouse he was building for himself, surrounded by newly laid out fields—"he really is subduing the moor." Carlyle was confident of his success.[47]

In contrast, the local population appeared to have been vanquished by their environment, as though a lifetime spent amid the black, muddy moors and gray, rugged mountains had drained them of energy and volition, just as the moors themselves absorbed the near-continuous rain. On the road between Letterkenny and Dunfanaghy, he passed a "foolish old farmer" at work in a peat stack, employing packhorses instead of carts to transport the peat—"a scandal to behold."[48] Most puzzling to Carlyle was the people's stubborn and seemingly irrational clinging to subsistence cultivation and their reluctance to work as wage laborers. Visiting the coastal village of Bunbeg, he noticed on the road the figure of a "winged scarecrow" breaking stones. This man, he was informed by Lord George's managers, the tenant of another "scandalous ragged farm," when his potato crop had failed, had lived on the charity of relatives and had only taken to working for wages when he had exhausted their supplies as well as his own.[49] Attempts to encourage other means of livelihood had, it appeared, proven similarly unsuccessful. Lord George had tried to establish a fishery at Bunbeg, but the people were unwilling to fish, despite being given lobster pots and taught how to use them. At present the only income from the fishery was due to another Aberdeen man, an "excellent clear-eyed, brown-skinned, diligent sagacious fellow."[50]

It was in the example of these newcomers that Carlyle discerned the only hope for the region. Otherwise, the locals were "lazy, superstitious, poor and hungry." In some cases, they had actively resisted the changes introduced by Lord George. Carlyle was told how, with the encouragement of the local Roman Catholic parish priest, the people had torn down fences and refused to pay rents, how they had no concept of working by the day, turning up at any time from eight o'clock to eleven o'clock and complaining when the manager insisted on paying them by the hour. In these circumstances, he could only fear for the success of Lord George's improvements. Rents, although not raised since the initial failure of the potato crop, continued to be paid only sporadically. Drainage and enclosures had made only a slight impression on the surrounding landscape of moorland, such improvements being "all swallowed in the chaos," which remained chaotic still.[51] Meanwhile, there remained the insurmountable and seemingly inbred indifference of the locals themselves. For Carlyle, it was a struggle not merely between man and nature, but between distinct races and customs: "Lord George and his Aberdeens versus Celtic nature and Celtic art."[52] As Carlyle boarded a ferry along the coast to Derry, for the final leg of his journey, the final outcome remained undecided.

Approaching the city of Derry, on the northern coastline, the countryside appeared to change once more, and for the better. If the terrain of north Mayo and Donegal had seemed to threaten the resurgence of primordial chaos, Derry suggested, in contrast, a landscape successfully subdued and domesticated by human effort. The countryside, Carlyle noted, was dotted with forts, occupied by artillerymen, and although otherwise bare as before, wore "a scotch aspect, rather than Irish, beggary and rags having become quite subordinate." It was as though these visible tokens of the British presence were themselves sufficient to hold at bay the threat of dissolution, which had hitherto seemed all too real. Derry itself was "the prettiest looking town I have seen in Ireland." The adjacent River Foyle was well supplied with ships, and Carlyle noted approvingly the presence of linen and flax mills, together with a coal yard, giving "the appearance of real trade."[53] During his stay, in the company of the London agent of the Fishmongers' Company, he visited the Templemore Agricultural School (founded in 1826 by the Northwest of Ireland Agricultural Society, on land belonging to the Grocer's Company). A "Mr. Campbell," another Scotsman, managed the school. Carlyle applauded the quality of the teaching (which included, in addition to agricultural methods, such subjects as surveying, civil engineering, and land stewardship), but was less impressed by the pupils, who were, for the most part, Catholic and "very ugly."[54]

On Monday, August 6, Carlyle boarded the steamer for Glasgow. On the quays he was assailed by the noise of "wild men and cattle," an indication of "the general tumult of (Irish) nature not yet ended."[55] It was not until the Scottish coast came into view, passing the Mull of Kintyre, that he was able finally to note, "Much improved prospects . . . comfortable fenced crop fields; comfortable *human* farms."[56] The steamer landed in the early hours of the morning at Glasgow, where Carlyle passed the night at a nautical inn in fitful sleep, punctuated by the pulsing of nearby iron furnaces. In this case, however, the disturbance was not an unwelcome one. Indeed, Carlyle found his sense of the real comfortingly restored by Glasgow's familiar sights and sounds. The following morning, he took time to walk around this "Commercial Capital of Britain," taking in the reassuring evidence of thriving industry and commerce, before boarding the train home to Scotsbrig the next day: "The sight of fenced fields, weeded crops, and human creatures with whole clothes on their backs,—it was as if one had got into spring water out of dunghill and puddles; the feeling lasted with me for at least several days."[57]

4

The Most Difficult People
in the World

Ireland and Political Economy

What sort of discipline could be pitted against the spongiform wilderness of mountain and bog, not to mention the intransigence of "Celtic nature and Celtic art"? Unlike, for example, Bataille's visions of excess, conjoining human expenditures with the elemental extravagances of starbursts and surging cataracts, the political economy promulgated in nineteenth-century Ireland was, by its own definition, a sober and sobering science. Ignorance of its principles was among the most frequently attributed causes of Irish "backwardness," fueling a concern on the part of successive British governments with fostering economic development in Ireland in order that the industrial and commercial progress of the rest of the then–United Kingdom should not be impeded. Beginning in 1821, a succession of national censuses, undertaken at intervals of ten years, sought to gather information pertaining to levels of poverty, the landholding system, agricultural development, population size, and the reliance of large sections of the population on the potato both as a subsistence food and, to a lesser extent, a commercial crop. The 1841 census report, the last to be compiled before the blight made its appearance, drew attention to each of these factors and observed, moreover, that Ireland appeared not to be undergoing a transition to industrialization, the percentage of the labor force involved in industry having declined (from 43 percent to 28 percent) since the 1821 census.[1]

Among the most frequently cited reasons for Ireland's failure to industrialize was the supposedly congenital indolence of the Irish themselves. That the Irish poor took a perverse pleasure in degradation and squalor had long been a commonplace of English accounts. During the famine years, such a view was to be reiterated many times by both conservative and liberal commentators. An article appearing in *Frazer's Magazine* in March 1847, following the second successive failure of the potato crop, makes use of an explicitly racialized vocabulary to contrast the idleness of the Irish poor with the diligence and industry of the English working class:

The English people are naturally industrious—they prefer a life of honest labor to one of idleness. They are a persevering as well as energetic race, who for the most part comprehend their own interests perfectly, and sedulously pursue them. Now of all the Celtic tribes, famous everywhere for their indolence and fickleness as the Celts everywhere are, the Irish are admitted to be the most idle and fickle. They will not work if they can exist without it. Even here in London, though ignorant declaimers assert the reverse, the Irish laborers are the most difficult people in the world to deal with.[2]

The (unnamed) correspondent asserts that there is only one solution to Ireland's present difficulties: "She must be civilized"—a process seen to entail the reformation of all sections of Irish society, including spendthrift and profligate landlords.[3]

In characterizing the Irish and the English as distinct races, descriptions like these express, at the same time, a palpable dread of contamination occurring across the divide thus posited. The Irish are depicted as a race apart, yet they seem capable at the same time of infecting the English working class with their bad habits by virtue of the simple fact of contiguity. Such a possibility was no less a source of concern to Friedrich Engels in his study *The Condition of the Working Class in England*, written between 1844 and the early months of 1845, on the eve of the initial potato failure. Engels remarks on the increase in Irish immigration into British cities in response to the rapid expansion of British industry, an expansion itself made possible by the existence of a large and impoverished reserve population in Ireland. There were, as he noted, already more than a million Irish in Britain, with a further fifty thousand arriving each year. Having, as he considered, grown up accustomed to poverty and unsanitary living conditions, these people brought with them standards and expectations conspicuously lower than those of the English working class among whom they settled. They gravitated toward the worst slums of Britain's industrial cities—like the "Little Ireland" district of Manchester, which furnished much of the material for Engels's study—where they lived whole families to a single room, their living quarters shared with the pigs they habitually kept and with filth and garbage deposited directly outside the door.[4] In these surroundings, amid a large and densely concentrated mass of people, disease, squalor, and drunkenness were enabled to flourish to a degree not possible in the more thinly populated expanses of the Irish countryside. The consequences of this influx of Irish were, as Engels saw it, twofold: first, being accustomed to only the barest level of subsistence, Irish laborers were willing to work for less than their English counterparts, and their presence in large numbers thus had the effect of driving down wages; second, they might communicate their habits of uncleanliness, intemperance, and improvidence to the English working class, whose own level of "civilization" had hitherto been higher: "For when, in almost every great city, a fifth or a quarter of the workers are Irish, of children of Irish parents, who have grown up amid Irish filth, no one can wonder if the life, habits, intelligence, moral status—in short, the whole character of the working class, assimilates a great part of the Irish characteristics."[5]

The pessimistic scenario outlined by Engels is notable for its temporalizing of ethnic and cultural differences. By virtue of being less advanced than the English industrial masses, the Irish are further from developing what Engels and his sometime coauthor, Marx, would later theorize as revolutionary class consciousness. In the context of the early 1840s, however, it is striking that the denizens of Manchester's Little Ireland should embody, for Engels, the threat of reversion to an earlier phase of economic and historical development, as though the mere fact of their physical presence in large numbers in Britain's centers of industry and commerce were enough to upset the chronology of civilizational progress and send it spinning into reverse. The past of agrarian savagery and unrule from which these Irish immigrants appeared to have stepped might thus, it is implied, become the future of the English industrial proletariat, assuming the tide of immigration remains unchecked.

"The Rags and Wretched Cabins of Ireland"

If Engels's principal concern was Irish immigration to Britain, many writers had long viewed the growth of Ireland's domestic population as an equally alarming prospect. Among the first to address the implications of Irish population growth in the context of its potential effect on the living standards of the English working class was Thomas Malthus, who, in an article written for the 1824 supplement to the *Encyclopaedia Britannica*, noted that Ireland's rate of population increase since 1695 had been among the highest in Europe, despite "the frequent pressure of great distress among the laboring classes."[6]

Although little specific mention is made of Ireland in the 1798 version of the *Essay on Population*, the revised and expanded 1803 edition, published in the wake of the 1798 rising and the Act of Union, draws selectively on sources relating to Ireland, including Arthur Young's two-volume travelogue of 1780. The *Encyclopaedia Britannica* article "A Summary View of the Principle of Population," subsequently republished as a pamphlet in 1830, draws on data collected by the 1821 census of Ireland, while two articles commissioned by the *Edinburgh Review* and appearing anonymously in 1808 and 1809 deal expressly with Irish subject matter.

Catherine Gallagher has pointed to the importance of Malthus's first (1798) *Essay on the Principle of Population* in reconceptualizing the social and economic significance of the human body. Earlier eighteenth-century thinkers such as David Hume and Adam Smith, although cognizant of the dangers of population increase, had tended to reiterate a two-millennia-old tradition of seeing the individual body as an indicator of the health or sickness of the larger social body—population increase being viewed as an inevitable correlate of societal well-being. Hume claimed in his essay "Of the Populousness of Ancient Nations" that "Every wise, just and mild government . . . will always abound most in people."[7] For Malthus, in contrast, it was precisely the healthy and therefore reproducing body that posed the threat of social catastrophe. Given his much-cited dictum that populations increased geometrically while food production and food stocks, even under optimal conditions, could only increase arithmetically, Malthus could foresee no other outcome of the unchecked human urge to procreate than the generation of a potentially disastrous imbalance of people and resources. The vigorous, sexually active body, far from betokening a well-ordered society, was viewed as the harbinger of a society overrun by emaciated, diseased bodies, placing impossible demands upon a comparatively underdeveloped subsistence base. It was on these grounds, famously, that he argued for the phasing out of the Speenhamland system of poor relief then operative in England.[8] Instead, he suggested that the "punishment of want" could be invoked to check the "immorality" of those who entered into marriage without the means to provide for their children.[9]

At the same time, as Gallagher notes, the worker's body was for Malthus the primary locus of production and thus of economic value. It was this identification that led him to take issue with Adam Smith for "representing every increase of the revenues or stock of a society as an increase in the funds for the maintenance of labor." Smith's error, according to Malthus, consisted in his failure to distinguish between increases in revenue resulting merely from the products of labor, including manufactures, and those increases that might be converted into a proportional quantity of provisions. For Malthus, it was only the latter, the stock of working-class food destined for consumption by working-class bodies, that provided an index of society's capacity to sustain and support population growth.[10]

Malthus's censure of Smith amounted to a critique of the labor theory of value for abstracting from the physical particularity of the individual human organism to propose an equivalence between, for example, a bushel of corn and a piece of lace in terms of the relative quantity of labor embodied in each. In doing so, it made it possible to overlook any connection between production and the subsistence needs of producers themselves. In contrast, Malthus's argument implies a hierarchy of commodities, whereby those products that contribute directly to the maintenance of producers are to be valued above those that do not. The latter might include foodstuffs not destined for consumption by the working population, such as butcher's meat. Malthus disparaged the conversion of arable into grazing land as an overall diminution of human subsistence, despite any advantages it might offer in terms of market price. Thus (in the first version of the *Essay on Population*) he writes that a fattened beast may be considered as an unproductive laborer, who consumes resources without himself adding to the general stock.[11]

The image is a telling one in that it conflates two contrasting visions of the human body, which are both, nonetheless, profoundly implicated in Malthus's thinking. On the one hand, the working body is identified as the indispensable producer of value, whose continued sustenance is deemed both legitimate and necessary; on the other hand, the same body is, potentially, an unproductive consumer of resources and capable of further adding to the strain on society's subsistence base through the procreation of similarly unproductive offspring. In the 1803 version of the *Essay* and in the two articles on Ireland, published anonymously in the *Edinburgh Review* in 1808 and 1809, the fatted, unproductive beast finds a disturbing analogue in the overzealously reproductive bodies of the Irish poor. Malthus introduces the subject of Ireland in the revised (1803) version of the *Essay* in discussing a proposal by Arthur Young to the effect that poor relief should everywhere be limited to the provision of potatoes, rice, and soup. Malthus endorses Young's suggestion with the proviso that these items should not then be introduced as the staple food of the poorer classes, because this would, he argues, have the effect of lowering wages and thus of condemning English laborers to "the rags and wretched cabins of Ireland."[12]

In an accompanying footnote, Malthus refers directly to Young's account of his Irish tour and disputes his claim that the Irish peasantry are protected from want by their abundance of potatoes, suggesting that, had Young visited Ireland during the first years of the nineteenth century, his impression would have been different.[13] Book 3 of the revised *Essay* further elaborates on the disadvantages of the potato and the deleterious effects on the Irish poor of the low price of food. The ready availability of subsistence food in Ireland is cited as a principal cause of population increase: "The Irish laborer paid in potatoes has earned perhaps the means of subsistence for double the number of persons that could be supported by the earnings of an English laborer paid in wheat, and the increase in population during the last century has been nearly in proportion to the relative quantity of customary food awarded to the laborers in each."[14]

The cheapness and abundant yield of potatoes were seen to result, equally, in higher rents and an increase in the price of other produce and commodities. Thus, any surplus food produced by the Irish laborer went but little way, it was claimed, toward the purchase of food, lodging, and "other conveniences." The resultant situation, as Malthus saw it, was one in which the Irish poor had become progressively habituated to squalor and were capable of envisioning no better life for themselves.

In the first of his essays for the *Edinburgh Review*, published in July 1808, Malthus reviewed two recent works on Ireland—Thomas Newenham's *Statistical and Historical Inquiry into the Progress and Magnitude of the Population of Ireland* and a pamphlet by the Reverend H. Dudley, an Anglican clergyman, calling for the repeal of the anti-Catholic penal laws then still in force. Newenham's book drew attention to the "extraordinary phenomenon" of the rapid increase of Ireland's population, which, in Newenham's estimation, had quadrupled since the beginning of the preceding century. Malthus contrasted the circumstances of this increase with the "wise institutions" and "increasing demand for labor" laid down by Smith and Hume as causes of population growth. Instead, as in the 1803

Essay, he proposed that the prevalence of the potato as a subsistence food was the principal factor accounting for the increase. Similarly, high rents were attributed not to the rapacity of landlords or the preponderance of middlemen, but to the fact that only a small portion of land was needed to support those engaged in potato cultivation. In Malthus's view, the result of these factors, along with the low monetary value of the potato, was that Ireland's burgeoning population, predicted by Newenham to reach 20 million by the end of the century, was likely to consist largely of paupers.[15]

Turning to Dudley's essay, Malthus supported its call for Catholic emancipation as a means to avert the hostility of a disaffected and ever-growing Catholic majority in Ireland. The difficulties of governing such a "prodigious mass" might otherwise, he feared, prove insurmountable: "In the present state of the country, the increasing strength of Ireland is the increasing weakness of England. . . . each passing year, while it adds both to the disposition and power of Ireland to resist the wrongs she suffers, diminishes in a still greater proportion the capacity of England to enforce them."[16]

The threat posed here by a proliferation of Irish bodies is political and military as well as economic. As a solution, Malthus proposes the dismantling of remaining legal distinctions between Catholic and Protestant, in order that the Irish might take their places as full citizens of a united Britain.[17] Such a course, he argues, might yield, in place of an insurrectionary mass, a ready supply of healthy adult males to be profitably employed in the armies of the British Empire.[18]

Malthus's second *Edinburgh Review* essay, appearing in April 1809, addressed itself to another of Newenham's works, *A View of the Natural, Political and Commercial Circumstances of Ireland*, which had been published the previous year. In the context of the Napoleonic Wars, Malthus again reiterated the importance of tying Ireland more closely to Britain through the repeal of anti-Catholic legislation, a move that would similarly have the effect of elevating the moral condition of the Irish peasantry and thus allowing them to better their living conditions. They might then, he thought, be capable of exercising the kind of moral restraint he had previously urged on the English poor and thus of becoming valuable producers rather than feckless procreators. This time, however, he emphasized the importance of the contribution that Ireland, with its richly fertile soil, might make to British agriculture. With the introduction of new farming methods and the eradication of the pernicious potato monoculture, Ireland, far from imposing a demographic and financial burden on its neighbor, might, he suggested, contribute greatly, even disproportionately, to their general funds for subsistence.[19]

A Poor Law for Ireland

The disciplining of Irish paupers and the inculcation of habits of thrift and industry had been a primary objective in the framing of an Irish Poor Law. Before 1838, Irish poor relief had been supplied entirely from private charity, a situation that, in the aftermath of the Napoleonic Wars, had increasingly become a source of governmental concern, intervention in Irish affairs being argued for on the grounds that an influx of Irish paupers into Britain would reduce the living standards of the British working class (a concern shared too by Engels). Between 1825 and 1837, no fewer than seven Poor Law Bills for Ireland were introduced, unsuccessfully, into the House of Commons. Finally, in 1833, a Royal Commission, chaired by the Anglican Archbishop of Dublin Richard Whately (who had previously occupied the Drummond Chair of Political Economy at Oxford), was appointed by Viscount Melbourne's Liberal administration to inquire into the condition of the poorer classes in Ireland. After conducting interviews with 1,590 people over a period of three years, the Commission concluded that around 30 percent of Ireland's population required some form of assistance for at least part of each year and recommended the adoption, not of a variant of the English Poor Law (implemented to replace the earlier Speenhamland system of poor relief), based as it was on relief in the workhouse, but of a series of economic development schemes, along with a program of land reclamation, the development of fisheries, and assisted emigration. The Commission's advocacy of public spending was widely criticized by, among others, the economist Nassau Senior (Whately's friend and former student) and Lord John Russell (then Home Secretary), who attacked the commissioners for exceeding their remit, which had been simply to consider the question of destitution. Russell argued that the solution lay instead in the assumption of greater responsibility by landlords, a view later to inform the framing of the Poor Law Extension Act of 1847, which sought to make the provision of famine relief entirely dependent on locally collected poor rates.[20]

For politicians of both parties, the adoption of an Irish Poor Law appeared to offer an opportunity of forcing a transition from a subsistence economy to one based on capitalist farming.[21] In 1837, a second Commission of Inquiry was established under the chairmanship of George Nicholls, who had served as one of the English Poor Law commissioners. Nicholls's report, submitted within three months of his arrival in Ireland, argued that the English Poor Law was indeed applicable to Irish circumstances, because the function of a Poor Law was to relieve only the truly destitute, amounting, in his view, to just 1 percent of the population. Nicholls advocated the adoption of a workhouse system as a means of facilitating the desired social changes (consolidation of holdings, wage labor, energetic landlords) as well as of improving "the character, habits and social conditions of the people."[22]

Nicholls was asked by Russell to prepare his report for submission to Parliament as a bill. However, the death of William IV occasioned a delay, making it possible for Nicholls to make additional visits to Ireland and to compile a further report. Nicholls's second report (1837–1838), which served as the basis of the bill finally submitted to Parliament in December 1837, concluded that Irish distress was worse than he had previously thought, although beneficial change might be achieved if the workhouse system were stringently administered. He suggested making each district responsible for its own poor, thus forcing landlords to take an active interest in their estates. This recommendation aroused particular opposition when the bill was presented to the House of Lords, where one in four peers owned property in Ireland.[23] The Irish Poor Law, as introduced in July 1838, showed a number of divergences from the English model, making no provision whatsoever for "outdoor" relief (as distinct from relief within the workhouse) and no automatic "right" to relief, which was, rather, discretionary and dependent on available workhouse places and locally collected rates. A further departure from the English system was the absence of a Law of Settlement. Irish paupers could receive relief at any workhouse, irrespective of their usual place of residence, destitution being the sole criterion for eligibility. In England, in contrast, paupers who had not worked in a particular district for a period of years could be forcibly removed to the parish of their birth, a provision subsequently to be invoked against Irish paupers attempting to settle in England, Wales, and, after 1846, Scotland. In most cases, such individuals were not returned to their own districts, but simply offloaded at the nearest port, provoking strenuous protests from the Dublin and Belfast Poor Law Unions.[24]

As in England, the administration of the new Poor Law was in the hands of the Poor Law Commission, a nonparty body working through intermediaries at the Home Office and the Executive at Dublin Castle, except during the famine years, when the treasury (under Trevelyan) took over as the main agency of government.[25] Ireland was divided into one hundred thirty new administrative units, or "unions," each consisting of a group of electoral divisions, which were made units of taxation in an attempt to localize the collection of rates. There were various sizes of union, the largest being found mainly on the west coast, the smallest in the east and Ulster. Each union was equipped with its own workhouse, situated near a market town and under the supervision of a board of guardians comprising a mixture of elected and ex officio local men. Admission to the workhouses was conditional on a means test. Whole families, rather than individuals, were to be admitted, but once inside, families and sexes were to be strictly segregated. Work, according to a directive of the commissioners, was to be of an "irksome" nature, to deter malingerers, and the food provided was to be of lower quality than the diet of independent laborers, or, where this was not possible, as in the poorest areas, was to be deliberately monotonous.[26]

It had been Nicholls's recommendation that the workhouses should be equipped to hold approximately 1 percent of the total population (approximately 100,000 people). In the event, one hundred thirty workhouses were built, varying in capacity from two hundred to two thousand places. Before the potato failure of 1845, few of these were full, although they were later to prove unable to accommodate all those in need of relief, amounting sometimes to half the total population of a given district. By Nicholls's own admission, the system was not equipped to deal with large-scale destitution, being intended, rather, for seasonal scarcity, from June through August, between the exhaustion of the old potato crop and the harvesting of the new one. Poor harvests in 1839 and 1842 had already raised the question of whether the provisions of the Poor Law should be extended in the event of unforeseen scarcity. In both cases, central government had left the decision to the Poor Law commissioners themselves, who determined that their role should remain restricted to the provision of relief within the workhouse. Individual instances of distress were met with combination of local voluntary efforts and subscriptions and central government funds. Relief officials were instructed to stress that government intervention was intended to supplement rather than to replace locally based efforts.[27]

Potatoes, Providence, and Protestantism

The Irish temperament had long been cited too as one of the principal reasons for Ireland's "failure" to embrace the Reformation (for example, by David Hume in his *History of England* of 1778).[28] Arguments for political economy as a means of reforming the Irish character often portrayed Roman Catholicism, Ireland's majority religion, as implicitly antieconomic, entailing, so it was claimed, the repression of individuality and an uncritical reliance on institutional authority—a view coinciding with that held by many members of the Church of England. Catholic priests were often held responsible for prorepeal agitation, despite the officially antirepeal stance of Vatican. In its most extreme form, anti-Catholicism led to a view of the potato failure as a form of divine punishment, visited on Ireland for the combined sins of heresy and sedition.[29] On May 12, 1848, the Dublin-based *Protestant Watchman* published a letter addressed "To the Right Hon. Lord John Russell," in which Ireland's sufferings, like those of Israel as recounted in Hosea 4, were held to be the result of "superstition and idolatry." The letter ended by urging Russell to combat "popery" by having "the word of God taught and preached in every village in Ireland."[30]

The extent to which the potato failure was interpreted as an instance of divine intervention is illustrated by a National Day of Fasting held on Wednesday, March 23, 1847. A sermon preached on the occasion by the bishop of London at the Chapel Royal, in the presence of the Queen Dowager, the Duke of Cambridge, and "several members of both houses of Parliament," argued that famine should be understood as a punishment for national sin, albeit one visited on only one part of the nation, and that atonement should be made by all to prevent the spread of calamity, in the form of sectarian strife or armed insurrection. In Westminster Abbey, at a service attended by Russell, Peel, Home Secretary Sir George Grey, and other senior politicians, the preacher, the bishop of Saint Asath, affirmed that recent events in Ireland were an instance of direct intervention by God in human affairs, and not an "accident." In this case, the "sin" of the British nation was identified as national pride, along with a failure to employ prosperity toward the spiritual enlightenment of those who continued (like the Irish) to dwell in ignorance and poverty. The sermon went on to invoke the collapse of previous civilizations—Babylon, Nineveh, Rome—and to urge the congregation to repent before suffering a similar fate.[31]

The providentialist interpretation of the famine found perhaps its most influential expression among the group of prominent Protestant evangelicals that included Trevelyan and Charles Wood, chancellor of the exchequer under Russell. Both Wood and Trevelyan regarded the blight as potentially beneficial in its long-term effects, irrespective of the short-term suffering it might cause, insofar as it would enable Irish agriculture to move from potato-based subsistence to the commercial cultivation of grain, with a resultant increase in prosperity and employment. The potato failure could therefore be regarded both as the visitation of a higher power, occasioned by Ireland's present social and economic malaise, and as a prospective remedy for present abuses. Wood and Trevelyan shared the view that the financial burden of relief should fall principally not on central government, but on Irish landlords, whose perennial shirking of their responsibilities they considered one of the principal causes of Ireland's distress. Their insistence on this point brought them into sporadic conflict with the more moderate liberal Anglican Russell, who showed at times a greater willingness to countenance government expenditure to meet the immediate shortfall in Ireland's food supply.[32]

A somewhat different convergence between Protestantism and political economy is to be found embodied in the discipline's best-known proponent in nineteenth-century Ireland: Richard Whately, Anglican archbishop of Dublin and former holder of the Drummond Chair of Political Economy at Oxford. Whately propounded a vision of free-market providentialism stressing the coincidence of individual and group interests, the market being seen as instituted by God for the general benefit of humanity. Although Whately rejected interpretations of the famine as an instance of divine retribution for "National Sin" (a view he condemned in his "Address to the Clergy and Other Members of the Established Church" of 1846), he nonetheless confided to the economist Nassau Senior, his former student, the hope that the teaching of political economy in national schools might help wean the Irish populace away from Roman Catholic "superstition."[33] In addition to his Episcopal duties, Whately had served as one of the original commissioners on national education and had been a long-standing member of the Board of National Education. He also established and funded a chair of political economy, bearing his own name, at Trinity College, Dublin, was actively involved in the foundation of the Dublin Statistical Society (serving until his death as its first president), and published a school textbook, *Easy Lessons on Money Matters*, which became one of the nineteenth century's best-selling works on economics.[34]

For Whately, the excesses of the Irish character that political economy aimed to curb pertained no less to language than to temperament.
His views reiterated a familiar contemporary characterization of the Irish as
an "oral" people, who were, therefore, peculiarly susceptible to displays of
oratory, particularly those of campaigners against the Act of Union like
Daniel O'Connell.[35] Schools inspectors frequently reported that pupils'
oral answering was better than their written and were severely critical of the
style of teaching employed in schools run by Catholic religious orders,
such as the Christian Brothers, where there was a strong reliance on learning through oral repetition.[36] Whately himself, in his *Elements of Rhetoric*,
described the "language of savages" (including, presumably, many of the
native Irish) as "highly rhetorical" and calculated to incite passion at the
expense of reflection. In contrast, he saw the discourse of political economy
as appealing not to the emotions, but to reason, and thus as serving to foster the development of that faculty. Writing in 1833 in the *Saturday Magazine*, he expressed the view that were the lower orders of society in Britain
and Ireland to be instructed in political economy, they would not be "as
now, liable to the misleading of every designing demagogue" and would be
rendered more "provident" in their ways.[37]

Whately and many of his contemporaries viewed political economy
both as a means of inculcating the habits of thrift and self-reliance deemed
necessary for the economic transformation of Irish society and as an alternative to national consensus based on religion or political affiliation. With
the establishment in 1832 of a state-sponsored system of elementary education, political economy came to occupy a privileged place as a form of ostensibly value-free knowledge, claiming universal applicability irrespective
of locality or circumstance. Social harmony, it was argued, might be
achieved through the enlightened cultivation of individual self-interest.
Hugh Hamill, a schools inspector for County Cork, declared in 1833, "I believe that, next to a good Religious Education, a sound knowledge of Political Economy would tend as much to tranquilize this Country, if not
more, than any other Branch of Knowledge that can be taught in
Schools."[38]

With the same end in view, Richard Barrington, a Dublin merchant,
established a trust in 1834 to fund lectures in political economy, aimed in
particular at workers, in towns and villages throughout Ireland. Barrington
claimed to be struck by the "ignorance of their own true interests which
the workmen displayed, and he thought that if they had been better informed they would not have entered into unwise combinations to regulate

wages."[39] In 1849, the running of the lectures was taken over by the Dublin Statistical Society, founded two years previously in 1847, for the express purpose of "promoting the study of Statistical and Economic Science."[40] The Statistical Society was thereafter responsible for appointing lecturers in accordance with the "Regulations Respecting the Barrington Lectures in Political Economy," which stipulated that every lecturer should "abstain in his lectures from all allusions to party politics or religious polemics."[41] Senior, Whately's successor to the Drummond Chair of Political Economy at Oxford, published a series of articles in the *Edinburgh Review* in which he lamented Ireland's economic "backwardness": the absence of capital and a tripartite division of labor (landlords, tenant farmers, laborers), along with the lack of an established middle class.[42] Senior, like Whately, argued that social conflicts in Ireland might be resolved through the harmonization of individual and factional interests (in this case in a capitalized, large-farm society, where land would be treated as an investment rather than a source of subsistence). It was, however, their sense of Ireland's economic underdevelopment that led both Senior and Whately to oppose the 1847 amendment to the Poor Law, with its attempt to shift the burden of famine relief onto locally collected poor rates. Both shared Malthus's skepticism concerning the capacity of Ireland's existing resources to sustain the proposed changes. Senior argued that Ireland lacked both the market institutions and a sufficient wages fund for the transition from subsistence to capitalist farming to be completed in a single step. Like Malthus, he considered that the Irish poor, unlike their more "advanced" English counterparts, could not be relied on under present circumstances to choose higher living standards over the urge to reproduce.[43]

Russell and many of his supporters, considered, contra Malthus, that Ireland's resources were indeed sufficient to support the desired changes. It was to this end, and to shift responsibility for relief from national to local level ("Irish property must pay for Irish poverty"), that the revision of Peel's relief measures was undertaken.[44] The Temporary Relief Act passed in February 1847 was intended as a preliminary step. Pending closure of the public works (ordered by the treasury in March of that year), it provided for direct relief to be supplied through soup kitchens established for the purpose. These were to be funded, eventually, by local poor rates, although central government was willing to advance sums to meet the initial cost, to be repaid from the rates at a future date. It was the 1847 amendment to the Poor Law that was intended to accomplish the decisive transition from national to local-level funding. Under the terms of the 1838 Poor Law Act, relief under the Poor Law was limited to workhouse inmates, outdoor relief being expressly forbidden. The new legislation established a separate Poor Law administration for Ireland, with the authority to provide outdoor relief at its own discretion. The amendment further recognized the right of certain categories of persons to receive relief either inside or outside the workhouse—for example, the elderly, sick, or disabled, and destitute widows with two or more (legitimate) children dependent on them. Otherwise, outdoor relief, usually in the form of cooked food, could only be provided to the able-bodied as a last resort or in the absence of available workhouse places and was limited to a period of six months. The so-called Quarter Acre clause further stipulated that anyone occupying more than a quarter of an acre of land could not be considered destitute and was therefore ineligible for relief either inside or outside the workhouse. Its stated aim was to facilitate the consolidation of holdings by encouraging impoverished tenants to give up their land in order to qualify for relief. An accompanying act aimed at the curtailment of vagrancy made begging punishable by thirty days' imprisonment.[45]

In the view of Trevelyan, Wood, and other members of their circle, the relief measures instituted under Peel had already had the effect of raising the expectations of the Irish poor with regard to employment and money wages. It therefore became the responsibility of the administration to consolidate these changes by breaking both peasants and landowners of the habit of relying on government handouts.[46] If public works schemes had served, in the first instance, as a means to accustom the Irish poor to buying food, the closure of the works during 1847–1848 could be seen as representing a further stage in this educational process. In Trevelyan's estimation, it was the potato monoculture above all that was to blame for Ireland's distress. Writing anonymously in the *Edinburgh Review* in January 1848, he posed the question, "What hope is there for a nation that lives on potatoes?" The non–labor intensive character of potato cultivation, along with the possibility of obtaining an abundant yield from poor soils, had, as he saw it, created a population habituated to idleness and unwilling to work to better their conditions of existence. It was in this sense that the potato failure could be represented as a providential occurrence, effecting "a salutary revolution in the habits of a nation long singularly unfortunate" and thus bringing "permanent good out of transient evil."[47] Previously, in a letter to the *Times* printed on October 12, 1847, Trevelyan had spelled out what such a revolution might be expected to entail: "The change from an idle, barbarous, isolated potato cultivation, to corn cultivation, which enforces industry, binds together employer and employed in mutually beneficial relations, and, requiring capital and skill for its successful prosecution, supposes the existence of a class of substantial yeomanry who have an interest on preserving the good order of society, is proceeding as fast as can reasonably be expected under the circumstances."[48]

Here it is suggested that starvation and mass mortality might accomplish decisively what successive British governments had attempted, with only limited success, to achieve through legislation and educational reform: the eradication of subsistence agriculture and the creation of a new class of Irish subjects schooled in the lessons of political economy.[49]

Political Economy and Colonial Difference

Comparison between the distinctly anti-Malthusian optimism of Trevelyan, Wood, and (with certain reservations) Russell, and the more cautious approach advocated by Senior and Whately, reveals that alongside calls for economic and political assimilation, there persisted a stubbornly recalcitrant sense of Irish difference. Nowhere is this more apparent than in the writings of Malthus himself, which provided a diagnostic model of Ireland variously invoked and challenged by later writers. Here, the massed bodies of the Irish poor are figured as a site of procreative excess at once threatening and necessary to the well-being of British society. If the Irish could not be turned into loyal British subjects, an alternative solution, Malthus thought, was to reduce their numbers by means of a program of assisted emigration. Testifying in 1826 before a Parliamentary Committee on Emigration from Britain, he warned that "It is vain to hope for any permanent and extensive advantage from any system of emigration which does not primarily apply to Ireland, whose population, unless some other outlet be opened to them, must shortly fill up every vacuum created in England or Scotland and reduce the laboring classes to a uniform state of degradation and misery."[50] Despite Ireland's still recent incorporation into the British polity, the growing mass of Irish bodies is perceived here not as a resource to be harnessed for the general good, but as the threat of a debilitating alien incursion into the English social body.

Ireland confronted Malthus, in insuperably graphic form, with the paradox inherent in his own conceptualization of the productive (and reproductive) body. On the one hand, he had affirmed the possibility that the reproductive capacity of individual bodies might outstrip the social body's capacity to produce sufficient food for its own needs; on the other, he had argued that the individual laboring body (presumably in all its reproductive vigor) was also the indispensable raw material enabling the circuit of economic production and exchange to be set in motion. The productive and reproductive body was thus posited as simultaneously integral to and dangerously disruptive of economic progress and as contributing toward and undermining the health of the larger social body. In the same way, for Malthus and for later writers, (including Engels), the Irish themselves were apt to appear simultaneously inside and outside the British polity: included under the terms of the Act of Union of 1800, yet at the same time a foreign and potentially polluting presence, credited with the alarming capacity to overrun their hosts.

As a set of discourses and practices aimed at the regulation of bodies, including work practices and sexual behavior, and the formation of new subjectivities, political economy exemplifies the logic of what Foucault famously termed modern *biopower*.[51] It serves to establish the relation between the Irish (and more particularly the Irish poor) and the British polity as one of simultaneous inclusion and exclusion.[52] Given the idiom of political economy through which it finds articulation, it is instructive to consider this relation with reference to the anthropological and philosophical figure of the gift. In Marcel Mauss's classic account, the gift was defined by its combination of seemingly contradictory attributes, "apparently free and disinterested, but nonetheless constrained and self-interested."[53] It is this juxtaposition of altruism and self-interest that has been seized on by later theorists such as Georges Bataille, and, more recently, Jacques Derrida, for whom the gift constitutes an impossible gesture of pure expenditure or loss, enacted without the expectation of a return, which is understood as the simultaneous negation and precondition of all forms of economic calculation or balanced exchange. According to Derrida, even to name the gift as such is to annul it by placing it within a preexisting horizon of expectations. The "pure" gift, if such a thing can be imagined, must go unrecognized and unacknowledged by both donor and recipient. Yet if the gift exists outside any system of calculus or reckoning, it is nonetheless indispensable to such a system as the inaugurating gesture that sets in motion the regulated play of forces within any "economy," not least the purchase and sale of commodities.[54]

If for Heidegger (whom Derrida cites) the gift represented the perennially unthought-of western philosophy, exemplified in the *es gibt* of Being, through which the earth's self-occlusion opened itself to the counterpoised world of human thought and practice, Christopher Bracken has drawn attention to the gift's significance as a figure of colonial discourse, marking the definitional limit of a distinctively western, capitalistic economic rationality.[55] Writing of the practice of ceremonial distribution of property among the native peoples of British Columbia that came to be known by the Chinook term *potlatch*, Bracken argues that Euro-American accounts of that institution, which tended to find in it an unstable and undecidable mix of gratuitous expenditure and economic calculation, performed a double gesture of differentiation and incorporation, establishing both a racialized Other of economic reason and a condition of definitional interdependence such that this disruptive exteriority was precariously folded into the logic of capitalism's own self-imaging. The assembled ethnographic and legal documents pertaining to the potlatch are read as an exemplary colonial case history, affirming the interimplication of self and other in a cultural and geographic setting where the representatives of the west at once encountered and sought to subsume the limits of their own self-constituting project.[56]

It is also worth recalling that, centuries before the arrival of the first European settlers in North America, Ireland had frequently been taken to mark the westernmost limits of Christendom, and, later, Europe. If, by the eighteenth century, this derogatory image had been modified, in part by the burgeoning cult of the sublime, with the result that Ireland's inhabitants could be viewed as "wild" human counterparts to a newly aestheticized landscape of mountain and moorland, such a move (facilitated, ironically, by the expansion of communications between urban centers and remote districts) could only reinforce perceptions of Ireland's anomalous status in relation to the orthodoxy of economic reason that was gaining ground in a swiftly industrializing Britain.[57] This tension provided the impetus for the elaboration of an image of Ireland and the Irish as both economically backward and temperamentally resistant to the universalizing claims of political economy. It enabled too the articulation of a range of transformative projects aimed at the progressive annulment of Irish difference through the forcible inculcation of economic principles. If such initiatives aimed to bring a recalcitrant Ireland within the purview of a globally encompassing, context-free rationality, it was equally the case that the alleged economic irrationalism of the Irish national character furnished a necessary foil to the arguments of political economy. Political economy's aspirations to universal applicability were therefore tied to the very resistances and local specificities that the discipline promised to eradicate. As in the Canadian northwest, Britain, as the then-vanguard of empire and capital, found itself already embodied in an ostensibly alien society against which its claims to self-definition were inextricably staked.

Derrida understands the gift as the affirmation of just such a condition of indebtedness. In being recognized as indebting the recipient, the gift necessarily annuls itself as gift in favor of the closed circuit of exchange and reciprocity, yet in doing so it suggests that economic exchange is itself indebted to such an "impossible" gift, thus pointing to "the madness of economic reason."[58] The status of Ireland in the writings of early and mid-nineteenth-century political economists is a similarly paradoxical one. In offering an ideologically charged image of idleness, waste, and profligacy, an image finding its most striking exemplification in the fecklessly procreative bodies of the Irish poor, Ireland furnished both a conceptual limit and a definitional counterpoint to English political economy and the institutions through which it was promulgated. This dual status served further to fuel English anxieties regarding Ireland's economic backwardness and the threat it was seen to pose to England's own prosperity. The economic irrationalism imputed to the Irish constituted both an axis of ethnic and political differentiation and a pretext for overcoming differences through education, ameliorative legislation, and the attempted building of rational consensus. In order for such claims to be persuasive, however, it was necessary that the threat posed by the growing number of Irish bodies, the threat of subversive encroachment on the English body politic, be perceived as an all too real one. Hence the profound and unresolved ambivalence investing the accounts of Malthus, Whately, Senior, and others: the Irish are both an integral part of the British polity, needing only to be weaned from their ignorance and backwardness in order for their productive potential to be realized, and an alien and inassimilable mass, whose proclivities and way of life appear insurmountably distinct from those of their English neighbors.

The posited contrast between Britain and Ireland in the writings of mid-nineteenth-century political economists was combined with an implied relationship of contiguity and doubling, such that what Britain discovered in Ireland was an image of its own disavowed past transposed uneasily into its present and given fleshly substance in the massed bodies of the Irish poor. This juxtaposition threatened to derail the chronology of economic progress on which the future of both Britain and colonial Ireland had been staked. The spectacle of Irish destitution both grounds and menaces the contrapuntal fashioning of an emergent British modernity. Political economy proclaims the necessity of overcoming Irish backwardness, but in order for such an assertion to carry authority, it is imperative too that Ireland in the present should remain resistant to the project.[59] What British commentators on Ireland confront, in the guise of Irish reproductive excess and productive lassitude, is the aporia on which their own ethos of economic rationality is founded, the uncancelable debt implicating the circuit of exchange in the eruptive exteriority of the gift. It is the same unacknowledged compounding of selves and others that informs, equally, the elaboration of identity claims around and across the colonial and geographical divide, with the result that the "madness of economic reason" comes to appear strangely ubiquitous.

Wild Hunger

> But hunger is an evil foe
> It striketh truth and Virtue low,
>   And Pride elate.
> Wild hunger, stripped of hope and fear!
> It doth not weigh, it will not hear
>   It cannot wait.
> —"C.S.," "The Famished Land" (1847)

Scene of Origin/Scene of Contamination

What, if anything, appears as antecedent to the always-after-the-fact inscription of events as moments in a narrated teleology—of progress, modernization, resistance, national renewal? If these and other recountings of the famine years aspire to map the trajectory of a knowable historical process, what of the singularities coopted as the empirical ground of such retroactive elaborations? Surely it is the potato blight itself, the seemingly unassailable materiality of infestation, disease, and decay, that furnishes the most vexed intersection between nature and symbolization, the nodal point at which their relationship might be most strangely and suggestively theorized. This directs us to a scene of origin, which is also, in its very presumed originarity, a scene of contamination across received categories.

Phytophthora infestans first manifests itself as a whitish, downlike growth on the leaves of the potato plant. Viewed under a microscope, it consists of a network of radiating filaments, each one ending in a conical swelling. These thread their way through the leaves, draining the tissues of moisture, until the plant turns black, withers, and dies. The spore containers at the end of each tube continue to grow until wind or rain carries them to other plants, or washes them below ground to the tuber, where the same process of destruction is repeated. The spores germinate, sending fungus tubes into the flesh of the potato, which finally collapses in a pulp. In damp weather, contamination of the tubers can occur during harvesting, when the potatoes are showered with live spores, only the smallest amount of water being required for them to germinate. Within weeks, a once seemingly healthy crop is reduced to a mass of putrefaction.[1]

According to John Mitchel, "the Almighty sent the potato blight, but the English created the famine."[2] The negligence of Westminster politicians is blamed for transmuting a presumed fact of nature into a social catastrophe claiming the lives of more than a million individuals. For Trevelyan, Wood, and others of their contemporaries, the blight was to be understood rather as a providential occurrence, curtailing centuries of uneconomic cultivation.[3] For all their differences, both interpretations maintain a clear distinction between the outbreak of a hitherto unknown crop disease and the social relationships and institutions by which the effects of such a visitation are mediated.[4] This conceptual demarcation of the "natural" from the "social" has been an organizing principle of modern regimes of knowledge: the natural sciences on the one side, the social and historical sciences on the other.[5] Nonetheless, if both Mitchel's and Trevelyan's formulations depend on just such a contrast, their assertions, if examined closely, serve to make its terms appear highly problematic. In order for the famine to be construed as the product either of a doctrinaire indifference to the loss of Irish lives (as it was for Mitchel), or of economic backwardness exacerbated by a national disposition toward idleness (as it was for Trevelyan and others), the blight itself as a presumed fact of nature must be distinguished clearly from the social contexts in which its effects are felt. The positing of such a distinction, however, creates not only a contrast, but also a point of articulation between the opposed terms, whereby that which is ostensibly set apart from the social realm continues to impinge upon it as a point of reference and comparison. Political and sociological readings of the famine (from whatever standpoint) therefore remain implicated in the natural order from which they purport to separate themselves. Indeed, it is just such a slippage between the conventially natural and the conventially social that many contemporary and later accounts of the famine can be seen to enact.

How is this folding of retrojected nature into society's second nature accomplished in latter-day remembrances of the famine years, like those collected by the Irish Folklore Commission? Here, the scene of contamination is played somewhat differently. In the absence of alternative explanations, climatic and meteorological factors become central. The first appearance of the potato blight, in the summer of 1845, is recalled as being preceded by an abrupt change in the weather. July 1845 began dry and hot. Within a few days, however, the temperature dropped, and the remainder of the month saw incessant rain with bouts of fog. The arrival of the blight is remembered as being heralded by freak storms, or else by fog, creeping in from the sea in coastal areas and clearing to reveal fields of potato stalks turned black overnight.[6]

In contrast, the years immediately preceding 1845 are usually remembered as a time of abundant harvests. Potatoes, it is said, were so numerous that growers were confronted with a surplus and had to devise methods for its disposal. Potatoes were taken to market, or, if they could not be sold, were thrown into ditches or stacked in the corners of fields.[7] The Commission's informants sometimes expressed the view that the potato blight was a form of divine punishment for the abuse of plenty.[8] Sometimes, however, other forms of supernatural intervention were invoked. During the first decade of the twentieth century, Lady Augusta Gregory, amateur folklorist and sometime collaborator of W. B. Yeats, was told by tenants on her estates at Kiltartan, County Galway, that the initial appearance of the blight had been accompanied by the sound of fairy armies clashing in the sky and calling out, "Black potatoes, black potatoes, we'll have them now!"[9] Walter Yeeling Evans-Wentz (future editor and translator of the *Tibetan Book of the Dead*), conducting research toward his doctoral dissertation during the same period, encountered a "seer" who claimed to have seen these fairy hosts waging their battles over Galway City and Knock, in the adjacent county of Mayo.[10]

It is instructive to consider these differing interpretations as highlighting an unresolved (and perhaps irresolvable) tension between the seeming randomness of the potato failure considered as a fact of nature and subsequent attempts to situate it within a horizon of historical intelligibility. The passage between these contrasting visions, accomplished in the form of story and reminiscence, testifies equally to their continuing and inescapable interimplication, as attempts to explain the blight and its consequences are obliged to posit as their own precondition the very arbitrariness of the natural order they seek to transcend. The gift of death (to borrow Derrida's phrase) lingers uncannily within the economies of signification by which its presence is at once masked and revealed.[11]

The swiftness of the ensuing transition from superabundance to scarcity is rendered through stories of families foraging all day to save enough potatoes for one meal, of farmers with once fertile plots now facing destitution, and of the alternative foodstuffs resorted to in the absence of potatoes. These included turnip tops, nettles, and other roadside plants.[12] Blood let from cattle was mixed with oatmeal and made into "relish cakes," which were then fried. Sheep and pigs were killed off. Milk was boiled and the curd eaten.[13] In coastal areas, shellfish, seaweed, and even frogs were eaten, as were the carcasses of diseased animals.[14]

The fate of those who failed to discover alternative means of sustenance is widely attested. Stories tell of corpses found by the roadside, their mouths stained green from eating the grasses and wild plants with which they had attempted to satisfy their hunger.[15] Those who died unattended in this way were themselves likely to end up as food for ravenous animals:

One day Stephen Regan met a dog dragging a child's head along. He took the head from the dog and buried it and set a tree over it. The family to whom the child belonged were getting relief for the child and for that reason did not report its death.[16]

The forms of sustenance resorted to by the starving reveal the dismantling not only of the now-familiar structuralist distinction between the raw and the cooked, but, equally tellingly, of distinctions between the food of humans and that of animals. Just as desperate people devour the carcasses of beasts, so the bodies of the famine dead themselves provide nourishment for rats and stray dogs. Hunger comes to appear as a condition of exile from the social world, whereby the starving person risks reabsorption into the natural realm, whether as an indiscriminate scavenger or as carrion.

The terms deployed to evoke the plight of the starving and dispossessed are resonant too with echoes of the more distant past. In early Irish literature, grasses and wild plants were among the characteristic foods of the *geilt* or madman, a figure associated with the Wild Man of the Woods of medieval European tradition. The condition of *geltacht* typically involved a sojourn in the wilderness, dressing in rags, traversing large distances, and eating wayside plants and other raw foods. For the *geilt*, however, this sojourn in the nether-spaces of forest and outfield was usually a temporary one, ending, variously, in religious illumination or in a return to society, often with one's status enhanced by the intervening absence. Suibne (Sweeney), the eponymous protagonist of *Buile Shuibne* and arguably the best-known literary geilt, continues to lead the life of a wanderer, but does so under the guidance of the *sacerdos* (holy man) Moling. King Nechtan, whose story is recounted in the Irish *Life of St. Fintan of Corcra Duibne*, having spent seven years in the wilderness, is restored to sanity and his kingdom after his reconciliation with the saint, whose curse had led to his initial exile. In contrast, famine victims, particularly the un-housed and displaced, who are often portrayed as having assumed an analogous position of liminality in relation to settled society, appear to be denied the prospect of reintegration. As such, their very existence comes to constitute a threat to the world they have left behind.[17]

With evictions adding constantly to their numbers, the houseless and dispossessed were a source of increasing unease both to government officials and to those concerned with the administration of relief at local level. In 1847, the Cork Auxiliary Committee wrote to the Central Relief Committee of the Society of Friends in Dublin, complaining of a continuous influx of rural poor into Cork city and expressing concern about their likely effect upon the settled populace: "Country paupers continue to flock in, and our streets present a deplorable appearance. Many imposters are also taking advantage of the excited sensibilities of the charitable; and it is to be feared, the habits of mendicancy will be so confirmed in multitudes of the people, even after the famine shall have passed away, that nothing but a vagrancy act can effectively suppress it."[18]

Labeled as idlers and indigents, the newcomers are seen as likely to contaminate the urban poor with their habits, a fear similar to that expressed by many writers—Engels included—regarding the presence of the Irish in Britain's industrial cities. The correspondent's concern pertains equally to the threatened blurring of a distinction central to the theory and practice of Victorian philanthropy—that between the "deserving" and "undeserving" poor.[19] It was precisely the latter whose activities the Irish Poor Law of 1838 had been intended to curb, the report of the Commission of Inquiry of 1833 having expressed particular concern both about the preponderance of begging or "vagrancy" in early nineteenth-century Ireland and about the practice of seemingly indiscriminate alms-giving indulged in by many sections of the population. If bogus mendicants and other imposters were permitted to infect others with their habits, the reformist efforts of the Poor Law commissioners were likely, it was feared, to prove futile, with the result that Irish society risked collapsing into an indiscriminate mass of pauperism, the very prospect at once dreaded and persistently invoked in the writings of Whately, Senior, and their contemporaries.[20]

At the same time, it was precisely the homeless who were most vulnerable to the effects of the potato failure. James Harvey and Thomas Grubb, in their report "To the Auxiliary Relief Committee of the Friends of Limerick" of February 22, 1847, drew attention to the plight of squatters in the coastal parish of Kilmurry. These "homeless wanderers," many of them ejected tenants, had been drawn to the area by the free trade in seaweed manure. No attempt had been made to check their influx, with the result that one neighboring townland of 46 acres now contained more than three thousand people. The failure of the potato crop had been followed by the collapse of the seaweed trade. The itinerants had no food and no means of procuring any. Their plight was compounded by the fact they were strangers to the locality, unable to draw on either public charity or the assistance of friends and neighbors: "As they are unrecognized by any landlord, they are not considered as tenants of the soil; and hence there is no one bound to them by ties of interest, or upon whom they can urge a legitimate claim for support."[21]

The predicament of the displaced and dispossessed is metonymic of a more generalized disruption of categories. Accounts such as these offer both a reversal and a disconcerting parody of prefamine abundance, as radical scarcity finds issue in a riot of mendicancy and misdirected consumption. It is, however, an extravagance that appears fraught with the risk of collapse: the collapse of order into anarchy; of custom into biology; of the human into the nonhuman. For many contemporary English observers, there was all too evident a possibility of movement between these categorical slippages and the more tangible threat of social disintegration. The anxieties provoked by such an association yielded a rich vein of cultural fantasy through which Ireland was cathected as a site of monstrous and excessive privation, imbued with a character at once palpable and hallucinatory. These imaginings found perhaps their most vivid articulation in accounts of conditions on Ireland's west coast during the year 1847 (afterward referred to as "Black '47"), when famine mortality was widely considered to have reached its height.

Skibbereen

Conditions in Skibbereen, County Cork, close to Ireland's southernmost tip, were made known to the British reading public during the winter of 1846–1847 in part through the writings and illustrations of James

Mahony, a Cork-born artist, employed by the *Illustrated London News* to report on conditions in his native locality. The first of these "Sketches in the West of Ireland" appeared on February 13, 1847. An accompanying editorial piece, apparently anxious to preempt charges of exaggeration, claimed that, because Mahony was a native of the district, he "must already have been somewhat familiar with such scenes of suffering in his own locality (Cork), so that he cannot be supposed to have taken an *extreme* view of the greater misery at Skibbereen."[22] Mahony alighted first in the area of Bridgetown, where "I saw the dying, the living, and the dead, lying indiscriminately upon the same floor, without anything between them and the cold earth, save a few miserable rags upon them." The dead, he observed, were often left to lie next to the living for several days before their bodies were removed. At Ballidichub, in the parish of Aghadoe, in a cabin formerly occupied by one Tim Harrington, he found four people who had been dead for six days, and a fifth dying. The latter made an attempt to rise when the visitors entered but collapsed in the doorway. The living were unwilling to bury the dead, Mahony wrote, for fear of fever. He was struck too by the hopeless insufficiency of existing relief measures in the face of a numerous and largely destitute population. At nearby Schull he recalled seeing "three to four hundred women," money in hands, attempting to buy food, while a few government officers doled out Indian meal to each of them in turn. The meal itself was distributed in small quantities at "famine prices," and it was often necessary to wait all day to receive one's share. Supplies of meal had arrived by water in a sloop, accompanied by a government steamship for protection—a total quantity of just fifty tons for a population of more than twenty-seven thousand people.[23]

Schull provided Mahony too with a specimen of "in-door horrors" far worse than the predicament of those who were at least able to afford the price of meal. In the second of his "Sketches" (published on February 20), he gave a description and sketch of the hut of a man named Mullins, "who lay dying in a corner upon a heap of straw, supplied by the Relief Committee, whilst his three wretched children crouched over a few embers of a turf fire, as if to raise the last remaining spark of life."[24] Mullins, it turned out, had buried his wife some days previously. He himself had been found in a state of unconsciousness by the local Protestant clergyman, whose efforts had succeeded in prolonging his life by a few days. In the accompanying illustration, the children crowd around the fire with their backs turned. Mullins himself lies center-right, his face partially averted and his eyes closed. A child, clad in rags appears in a doorway to the right, its hand extended. However, the most prominent figure is that of a man (presumably the artist), in hat and coat, seated on a chair, surveying the scene of destitution before him. As a footnote, there appeared the following editorial comment: "Our Artist assures us that the dimensions of the hut do not exceed ten feet square; adding that, to make the sketch, he was compelled to stand up to his ankles in the dirt and filth upon the floor."[25]

Readers of the *Illustrated London News* had further opportunity to learn about conditions in west Cork through the medical diaries of the Skibbereen physician, Dr. Daniel Donovan, reprinted from the *Cork Southern Reporter*. Although for a medical practitioner, called upon daily to attend the sick and dying, such scenes inevitably took on a familiar character, Donovan himself admitted to being disturbed by his patients' acceptance of, even longing for, their own imminent demise:

Twenty-two strangers, who came into Skibbereen to beg, had taken up their abode in a house in Bridge Town; illness broke out amongst them and I was sent for to see five who were sick of the fever. The appearance of this lazaretto, when a bit of bog was lighted, to show me the patients, baffles description. Four bare walls and an old straw roof constituted the habitation, and there was not in it a single pound of straw for bedding; a shower of liquid soot was falling from the thatch and a foetid fog was rising from the filthy wet rags that constituted the only clothing of the inmates. I prescribed for my patients, and was about to leave them, when my attention was attracted to a group in the opposite end of the house, who were zealously engaged about an old woman and child who were lying on the ground.[26]

One of the party told him that her child was dead and her mother dying, and asked, would he give the latter a drink? The dying woman thanked him, and then thanked God that she would not be in need of his drink much longer. She then asked him, would she live until morning? He replied that he expected her to live no more than an hour—"this assurance seemed to give her the greatest satisfaction"—and she then asked him to arrange for her and her child to be buried in the abbey graveyard at Skibbereen. He promised to do so, but in the hurry of business, he forgot his promise. Returning to the house several days later, accompanied by "an artist from the *Illustrated London News*" (that is, Mahony), he was shocked to find the bodies in the same spot and the same position in which he had left them.[27]

Reports about Skibbereen had been appearing with increasing frequency since the autumn of 1846. In early December, two Protestant clergymen from the district, the Reverend Caulfield and the Reverend Richard Townsend (whose bulletins concerning conditions in the district had been published in newspapers in both Britain and Ireland) had traveled to London to meet with Trevelyan. They had informed him that the government relief schemes were failing, that no "practical and responsible persons of property and respectability" had come forward to form a relief committee, and that in consequence, no subscriptions had been collected. The committee, now in a "state of suspension," was unable to take effective action. The only employment in the district was on public works, which, at 8 pence a day, was insufficient to feed a family. Caulfield himself had been dispensing soup at his own house each day to between sixty or seventy people, who would otherwise have starved. Trevelyan was asked to send emergency supplies of food, but none were sent. On December 15, the commissioners of the Board of Works had written an official letter to the British government, giving notice of the extreme destitution at Skibbereen. Trevelyan responded by writing to his commissary general, Sir Randolph Routh, advising him that he should not send emergency supplies, in the absence of an effective relief committee at local level, because to do so would deplete government stocks; nor was he to consider the purchase of further supplies from overseas, thus interfering with the trade of local merchants. Appeals for Skibbereen received an official response in the form of a treasury minute, written by Trevelyan on behalf of the lords of the treasury, on January 8, 1847:

It is their Lordships' desire that effectual relief should be given to the inhabitants of the district in the neighborhood of Skibbereen . . . the local Relief Committees should be stimulated to the utmost possible exertion; soup kitchens should be established under the management of those Committees at such distances as will render them accessible to all destitute inhabitants and . . . liberal donations should be made by Government in aid of funds raised by local subscriptions.[28]

As a result, Skibbereen received no emergency supplies of food, although two soup kitchens were started with privately collected funds after the visit of a commissariat officer, Richard Inglis, on December 17.[29]

By this point, horror stories in the local and national press had begun to multiply, spinning out a mythology of chaos, death, and destitution that seemed to gain in intensity with each successive retelling. According to the *Cork Examiner*, the death rate in the Skibbereen workhouse had, by January, reached a hundred forty a month, with as many as eight dying in a single day. Dr. Donovan, addressing a public meeting, asserted that people were "dropping in dozens." The Reverend Robert Traill, Church of Ireland rector of Schull and chairman of the local relief committee, claimed that there were fifteen thousand persons destitute in his district, five thousand being entirely dependent on "casual charity." There had been fifty deaths from famine, while "hundreds" were reduced to the point where neither food nor medicine could restore them.[30]

The seeming ubiquity of death and disease suggests that Skibbereen had come to occupy an increasingly well-defined fantasy space in the imaginations of observers and commentators, perhaps as a heightened microcosm of conditions in Ireland as a whole, perhaps, more disturbingly, as a black hole of fathomless and all-consuming scarcity, in which order and intelligibility, including the lucid precepts of political economy, were pulverized into nonexistence.

By April 1847, with the worst depredations of the winter over, the picture seemed complete. The following report (again reprinted from the *Cork Southern Reporter*) appeared in the *Illustrated London News*:

The climax of mortality and misery has arrived. The peasantry are literally rotting off the surface of the earth. The living are swept off in the south western baronies by pestilence, and the dead lie unburied, melting away in this warm season where they drop and die . . . the highways, dykes and cabins of the south and west are darkly dotted with corpses blackening in the sun, or filled with masses of reeking putrefaction.[31]

The description suggests, if anything, the aftermath of catastrophe, invoking a strangely still landscape, already strewn with corpses and shrouded in the stench of decay. Human society appears to have vanished, while the casualties of its passing linger only to rot back into the soil, which waits to reclaim them.

Northwest Erris

English imaginings of famine Ireland unfolded in terms of a fantasy geography bounded, on the one side, by Skibbereen's spatial condensation of squalor and destitution and on the other, by the primitivist expanses of Ireland's northwest coast. If Thomas Carlyle had found in Westport, County Mayo, the "acme" of "human swinery," other commentators uncovered worse horrors in nearby Erris. Alexander Somerville, journalist and free-trade advocate, reporting from Ireland for the *Manchester Examiner* during the summer of 1847, singled out Mayo as "at once the most magnificent and the most mean of Irish shires."[32] On the one hand, like his eighteenth-century predecessors, he eulogized the beauty of its islands and lakes, its mountains and cliffs rising from the depths of the ocean floor to upward of a thousand feet in height, along with the traces of prehistoric habitation strewn across this ancient landscape—cairns, stone circles, tombs, and ring forts. On the other, he described the population as "the most wretched, and in the present season of famine, the most destitute of any people I have yet seen in Ireland."[33] For James Hack Tuke, visiting the region on a fact-finding mission for the Central Relief Committee of the Society of Friends during the autumn of the same year, the most extreme instances of Irish destitution were to be found in the far northwest of Mayo, in the town of Belmullet and throughout the Erris peninsula, an area of bogland with a small belt of fertile land surrounding Belmullet itself.[34] In Erris, a population computed in the previous year at twenty-eight thousand had been reduced by almost a third. Two thousand people had emigrated, principally to England, lacking as they did the funds to continue to America, and more than six thousand had died from starvation, dysentery, or fever. Of the remaining twenty thousand, Tuke estimated that at least half were on the verge of starvation, subsisting on a diet of turnip tops, sand eels, and seaweed, a situation that was doubly shocking because it existed "within forty-eight hours journey of the metropolis of the world."[35] Many of these ten thousand or so wretched individuals— evicted tenants or the landless poor—were housed in makeshift dwellings cut into the bog itself:

One may indeed occasionally imagine oneself in a wilderness abandoned to perpetual barrenness and solitude. But here and there, patches appear unexpectedly where no other sign of man presents itself to you; as you walk over the bog, and approach nearer to the spot, a curl of smoke arises from what you suppose to be a slight rise in the surface. To use the graphic language of a late continental visitor: "Let the traveler look where he is going, however, or he may make a false step, the earth may give way under his feet and he may fall into—what? Into an abyss, a cavern, a bog? No, into a hut, a human dwelling-place whose existence he has overlooked, because the roof on one side was level with the ground, and nearly of the same consistence. If he draw back his foot in time, and looks around, he will find the place filled with a multitude of similar huts, all swarming with life." Of what is this human dwelling-place composed? The wall of the bog often forms two or three sides of it, whilst sods taken from the adjoining surface form the remainder, and cover the roof. Window there is none; chimneys are not known; an aperture in front, some three or four feet in height, serves the office as door, window and chimney: "light, smoke, pigs and children all pass out through this same aperture."[36]

A landscape seemingly empty of human habitation is revealed by the traveler's unwary tread to be honeycombed with subterranean life, the unhoused having quite literally sought refuge in the ground beneath their feet. According to William Bennett, another representative of the Society of Friends, who toured Mayo in company with his son during 1847, there were numerous families "squatting" on these otherwise unoccupied lands, a cabin being easily thrown up with the assistance of neighbors. Many of these "cabins," like the ones described by Tuke, were no more than holes dug into the bog and covered over with a layer of peat, with open doorways and no chimneys or windows. Furnishings were minimal, comprising, usually, a chest and a few tin or earthenware vessels. Bennett visited a number of such hovels. As he did so, he was followed about by an ever-growing retinue of paupers, who hung back only at those dwellings infected with fever, usually perceptible by the stench. The occupants of most cabins were "wild and all but naked, scarcely human in appearance."[37] The scenes Bennett witnessed inside the cabins were, he wrote, such that "language utterly fails me," resembling "some hard and tyrannous delusion, rather than the features of sober reality." For Bennett, the inhabitants of Erris represented the degree-zero of human sociality, life stripped to its barest, functional necessities. The impression was confirmed for him by Alfred Bishop, a commissariat officer whom he met in Belmullet and who had traveled widely and "been among the native tribes of the most uncivilized countries." Asked by Bennett whether he had ever seen people living in so degraded a condition, Bishop replied, "No, not even the Ashantees and wild Indians."[38] Bennett's account, like Tuke's, is notable for its running together of an all-too-familiar primitivism with a staggered sense of disbelief that the conditions he describes should coexist in such proximity to England's centers of industry and commerce, as though bespeaking a covert synergy between these adjacent, but starkly contrasting, worlds.

In Bennett's opinion, Ireland could be viewed as divided in two by a line following the course of the River Shannon and extending northward to Lough Swilly and southward to Cork. To the east of this line was "distress and poverty enough," but to the west lived a people "in a state and condition low and degraded to a degree unheard of before in any civilized community."[39] Worse was to follow as Bennett traveled north through the Rosses in County Donegal, an area enclosed on one side by sea and on the other by mountains over which the roads were often impassable. There was no market town for 30 miles, and the coast itself was "foul, ragged and inaccessible," except in the calmest weather. According to a report by Valentine Griffith, the officiating Anglican minister of the parish, the land remained unplowed and the population was scattered among the mountains and thickly populated islands; there were no resident landlords in the area, with the result that "the mass of ignorance, poverty and destitution" remained unchecked.[40]

Bennett journeyed next by boat on March 24 to the island of Arranmore off the Donegal coast. Not being expected by the islanders, his party was able to land unobserved, but as soon as their presence became known, and Bennett began visiting cabins in the company of the medical superintendent, a crowd gathered, their numbers becoming such that Bennett and his companions were obliged to force their way in and out of each dwelling. The medical superintendent explained that the island's remoteness from the mainland had made the administration of relief difficult. There was only one soup kitchen on the island, and that "under the worst management." Bennett spent most of the day on Arranmore, traveling some 6 miles between villages and distributing tickets for Indian meal. He was struck by the similarity between each of the villages, the whole island appearing as "one deepsunk mass of poverty, disease and degradation."[41] Bennett soon came, however, to doubt this initial impression. He remarked that the houses were a "shade better" than the turf hovels of Erris. The islanders too retained a degree of vigor and animation, unlike the listless apathy he had observed in those close to starvation. They clutched eagerly at the meal tickets as he handed them out, in a manner suggesting, to Bennett's mind, "an older trade in beggary." These suspicions seemed confirmed by the reports of his son, who had observed the children of the island "up and running about" as soon as the visitors' backs were turned, having previously thrown themselves down on their sleeping-places as though sick. Bennett discerned in such gestures a tendency to exaggeration, if not outright pretense, as though the islanders were long accustomed to subsisting on the charity of outsiders, rather than supporting themselves by their own efforts: "The feature that struck me the most forcibly was, that among this whole population estimated at 1500, there was not a single particle of work of any description that we could see going forward, either inside the cottages or outside, upon the soil, except one old woman knitting."[42]

If the scenes Bennett observed in Erris had taken on a hallucinatory quality by virtue of their sheer physical intensity, the suspicion here is that the islanders of Arranmore are engaged in an elaborate pantomime, mimicking destitution for the benefit of gullible visitors. It is curious that Bennett should be assailed by doubts on this point at such a stage in his journey. Given the binary topography sketched out earlier in his account, this island off the Donegal coast ought to represent the culminating point of Irish destitution. Nonetheless, it is here, where the effects of famine might be expected to appear most starkly and obtrusively real, that the substance and solidity of the scenes described is called into question. The seeming unwillingness of the islanders (all but one of them) to engage in any form of productive work becomes further evidence of their mendacity. Estranged from the world of economic activity, they become instead purveyors of theatrical illusion. The islanders of Arranmore mark the point at which the logic of primitivism exceeds itself, with the result that its own informing classificatory distinctions (including racialized attributions of economic irrationalism) begin to unravel. The islanders are at once too real and not real enough, confounding the onlooker's ability to differentiate clearly between truth and falsehood. Yet it appears that this very capacity to elude ontological fixing depends precisely on their prior assignment to a preimagined niche of primitive destitution.

"Outrages" on the Public Works

In earlier decades, the anxieties of English commentators had found a focus in the agrarian secret societies known variously as the "Whiteboys," "Ribbonmen," and "Rockites" (followers of "Captain Rock") that had been a feature of rural life in Ireland since the eighteenth century. Secret societies were known for conducting sporadic (usually nocturnal) attacks against landlords, land agents, magistrates, military personnel, and large farmers, and for distributing anonymous letters and notices warning prospective victims of the consequences of offending against the "rules of the country." Many of these pronouncements invoked the prophecies of "Pastorini" (the English Catholic Charles Walmesley), whose commentaries on the book of Revelation, predicting an unleashing of divine anger against "heretics" during the 1820s, were widely circulated in Ireland in the form of tracts and handbills and were often taken to predict the impending overthrow of Protestantism.[43] Rockite attacks were most frequently reported along Ireland's west coast, including the counties of Mayo, Galway,

Limerick, and Clare, particularly during 1821, when the failure of that year's harvest brought the prospect of a regional or nationwide famine, along with intimations of impending apocalypse and matching forebodings in the minds of the clergy and middle classes.[44]

The later 1820s saw a seeming decline in the activities of secret societies, along with increasing support for Daniel O'Connell's Repeal Association (a development that did little to reassure many English commentators).[45] Police records, however, were to show a renewed rise in instances of agrarian violence for all districts in Ireland following the first failure of the potato crop in 1845. Andres Eiriksson's survey (from which the following examples are taken) of records relating to the province of Munster, focusing on the counties of Limerick and Clare, shows that the public works instituted by Peel's government provided both a focus for discontent and an organizational platform, bringing together otherwise geographically scattered farm laborers and smallholders and offering an opportunity to discuss tactics during working hours.[46] It was the latter aspect of the public works that was of most concern to local administrators and landed proprietors. Sir Gaspard Le Marchant, a public works inspector for Tulla, County Clare, wrote in November 1846:

I have found it to be the opinion of intelligent people in this neighborhood, that the Public Works, and their system of bringing together large bodies of men, who mutually inflame each other, and plot mischief to remedy the distress of themselves and their families, become daily pregnant with the greatest danger to the country. These man, by being brought together in masses, are taught to understand their own strength.[47]

Sir Gaspard's unease relates principally to the concentration of large numbers of paupers in a single place, risking their transformation into a potentially uncontainable insurrectionary mass. His anxieties seemed borne out by a series of incidents during the winter of 1846–1847 (as the cost of oatmeal and Indian meal doubled). These included strikes, threats against overseers, and attacks on farmers, merchants, and boatmen, aimed at lowering food prices by forcibly preventing the export of grain.[48]

Disturbances intensified during the spring of 1847, when it became known locally that the public works were to close. The bearer of the news to Newmarket-on-Fergus in County Clare, Captain Fishbourne, found himself surrounded by a large crowd, hurling stones and shouting that blood was better than starvation. Reports of the incident appeared in the *Clare Journal* on March 25 and the *Tipperary Constitution* on March 27, the local constabulary claiming that without their intervention, Captain Fishbourne would have been drowned in the River Fergus. During the months that followed, similarly large crowds assembled outside meetings of local relief committees and the residences of public works inspectors and superintendents.

From May onward, there were many reports of attacks against the soup kitchens set up to take the place of relief works. At Cloonlara, a crowd several hundred strong attacked the newly established soup kitchen, destroying the boiler and other utensils before proceeding on to Ardnacrusha, where a similar scene was prevented only by the intervention of police. Instead, the crowd assembled outside the home of a local justice of the peace, declaring that they wanted employment "and would not put up with and endure the use of soup and porridge." On May 14, following an attack on a soup kitchen in Kilfenora, County Clare, the *Limerick Reporter* told its readers that the people "abhor the idea of being beggars."[49]

Attacks on soup kitchens appear to have given way, gradually, to attempts to influence the management and running of the kitchens. On June 17, the *Clare Journal* reported that in the Union of Kilrush, later to become notorious as the scene of mass evictions during the winter of 1847–1848, many people objected to receiving cooked food, preferring instead to receive their rations in meal, which they could prepare themselves. A large crowd surrounded the residence of Captain Hill, the local poor law inspector, throwing stones and agreeing to disperse only when given his personal guarantee that meal would be given out instead of soup until the next meeting of the relief committee. Relief committees were, however, usually reluctant to distribute uncooked meal, claiming, variously, that inadequate cooking facilities and a lack of hygiene in people's homes might aggravate the spread of diarrhea and dysentery, and that the meal itself might be traded illicitly for alcohol, tobacco, or tea. If recipients of relief in certain districts succeeded in obtaining meal instead of soup, such victories were often short-lived. In mid-May, 1847, around five hundred people had surrounded the courthouse in Ennistymon, County Clare, demanding that the number of relief stations be increased and that meal be served in place of soup. A subsequent meeting of the Poor Law commissioners agreed to substitute meal for soup and to open a new relief station in the parish of Clooney. Ten days later, soup was reintroduced. In anticipation of riots, troops were sent into Ennistymon to assist the police. What followed, however, was not rioting but a series of peaceful protest marches, all of which failed to convince the commissioners to reconsider their decision.[50]

The transition from public works to soup kitchens appears to have brought an end to organized protest in Limerick and Clare (and elsewhere), as the rural populace were deprived of the organizational base that had so troubled Sir Gaspard and became cast instead as passive recipients of charity. In comparison with the events of the preceding year, a series of evictions in Kilrush, County Clare, in 1848 was reported as meeting with little or no collective resistance. Even so, the closing of public works did little to assuage the concerns of the British government and press concerning the possibility of further violent outbreaks. Indeed, it was precisely the closing of the works, unleashing a discontented populace to roam the countryside, that gave rise to renewed fears about large-scale unrest, finding expression in English press coverage of events in Ireland during the latter months of 1847.[51] Alongside accounts of disease, starvation, and mass mortality, there appeared a number of reports of agrarian violence and civil disturbance. The following are taken from the *Illustrated London News*:

September 11: a "frightful murder" carried out by two men and a woman in Sligo.[52]

September 18: a murder in Galway; the suspected murder of a child by its mother in Drumcondra, Dublin.[53]

October 16: a report from County Clare outlining "several cases possessing the usual features of agrarian uncivilization and disorder," including attacks on persons returning from Ennis market, raids on the property of Lord Fitzgerald, and the killing of a man engaged by Mr. Guinness, member of Parliament for Kinsale, County Cork, in the service of ejectment processes. The correspondent added that "A general hostility is manifest against the enforcement of all or any demands of rent by the landlords in whatever shape they may take proceedings to get them." The same edition featured a report of a meeting of the Limerick magistrates at Cashel, County Tipperary, to discuss the murder of Mr. Roe, a local landlord. Copious testimony was offered at the meeting as to the deceased's good character. Among those present, Lord Viscount Suirdale proposed a memorial to be adopted by the meeting to the earl of Clarendon (recently appointed lord lieutenant at Dublin Castle) "detailing the facts of the murder, the amiable character of Mr. Roe, his indulgence to the tenantry, and remission of rents on his lands, and proving that great insecurity to life and property arises from the indiscriminate possession and use of firearms by the very lowest classes of the population."[54]

The following edition (October 23) reported approvingly on the measures taken by Russell's government to suppress these outbreaks of violence in southern Limerick. These included reinforcements of cavalry sent to Charleville and Bruree along with an increased military presence throughout the county.[55] Even so, if both government and press acknowledged an increase in instances of agrarian violence in Ireland during the final months of 1847, they concurred in viewing these not as the result of an organized conspiracy, but as spontaneous and localized expressions of discontent. In January 1848, a commission of judges, dispatched to counties where murders had taken place, concluded that evictions and land clearances furnished the principal motives for the killings, which were to be classed as "the wild justice of revenge."[56]

Young Ireland and 1848

A similar disquiet regarding spontaneous outbreaks of collective violence can be found in the pages of the *Nation*, the journal of the Young Ireland party. Young Ireland, a group of militant nationalists, included Thomas Davis (who was to die of scarlet fever in September 1845), writer and balladeer, the son of an English army surgeon and an Irish Protestant mother; William Smith O'Brien, a Protestant landlord and member of Parliament from County Limerick; Thomas Francis Meager, a Catholic and the son of a former Mayor of Waterford; John Mitchel, the son of an Ulster Presbyterian minister; John Blake Dillon, a Catholic barrister from Mayo; and Charles Gavan Duffy (later to act as Carlyle's guide during his visit to Ireland), the son of a Catholic grocer from Monaghan. Given its editorship, its English-language format, and its price (6 pence, as against the 8–10 pence received by a worker on a government relief scheme), the *Nation*'s readership has often been assumed to have been predominantly middle class, although public readings of the journal were held in Repeal Association reading rooms, until a split occurred between Young Ireland and O'Connell's supporters in July 1846. While arguing for repeal of the Act of Union, editorials expressed hostility toward republicanism, Chartism, and socialism.[57]

After the first appearance of the potato blight in the summer of 1845, editions of the *Nation* reported O'Connell's speeches advocating practical measures to deal with the impending crisis: the halting of grain exports, the importation of Indian corn, the suspension of the domestic distilling industry, and the taxation of landlords, along with calls for an Irish Parliament with the legislative powers to address such matters directly. Meanwhile, editorials like the following (October 5, 1845) warned in lurid terms of the social unrest that might be expected to arise from food shortages and the absence of adequate relief measures: "agrarian outrage . . . will . . .

stalk, in blood and terror, over the land, leading to a general disorganiza-
tion of society and reign of terror which it is fearful to think of."[58]

As the blight returned in successive years, the threat to political sta-
bility came to be portrayed as more far-reaching. An editorial appearing on
April 17, 1847, warned that mass starvation, if not checked by further government intervention, would give rise to a generation of Irish permanently
hostile to England and English interests.[59] If these warnings were intended
to cajole Russell's government into augmenting its relief efforts, they testify also to a sense of profound unease on the part of the editors at the
prospect of a spontaneous mass rising, independent of any central authority. Such a possibility comes to be identified explicitly with the threat of
anarchy in much of the famine poetry published in the *Nation*, where the
projected collapse of political order is evoked in terms at once apocalyptic
and topical. "The Famished Land" by "C.S.," appearing on January 23,
1847, conjures the spectacle of "wild-eyed, hungry millions" demanding
bread and willing to go to any lengths to obtain it. The poem depicts
hunger as a force of nature: insatiable, unstoppable and impervious to law
or moral restraint:

> Wild hunger, stripped of hope and fear!
> It does not weigh, it will not hear
> It cannot wait.[60]

In "The Stricken Land," published in the same edition, Jane Elgee
(later to marry William Wilde) projects the reckoning for Ireland's present
sufferings onto the Last Judgment, when, at the trumpet's sound, a "ghastly
spectral army" will rise from the ground "in their charred uncoffined
masses" to accuse those who have robbed them of land and sustenance.[61]

If both writers envisage the possibility of violent redress for the
wrongs suffered by Ireland's population at the hands of a seemingly indifferent, Westminster-based government, the vengeance of the starving is
shown as partaking of desperation and despair rather than revolutionary
purpose and, in the case of Elgee's poem, is deferred to an unspecified
apocalyptic future. Significantly, the following week's edition (January 30,
1847) contained an attack on "ribbonism" (used as a generic term for agrarian protest), warning that a resurgence of violence in the present circumstances was likely to have consequences more deleterious than those of the
famine: "We speak of ribbonism. This, of course, is but a name, no matter
by what other lawless synonym it is known. Be it the north or in the south,
secret illegal societies, ruled by turbulent and intriguing and treacherous

spirits, were always a plague-spot on the social well being of Ireland. Now they would be immeasurable calamities, in comparison with which years of famine would be as nothing."[62]

The editorial goes on to reiterate previous warnings that the present situation should not be viewed as a pretext for lawlessness. Far from being a solution to Ireland's difficulties, the ad hoc retribution meted out by agrarian secret societies (and chronicled in the English press) is identified as one of their principal causes.

In July 1846, Young Ireland broke with O'Connell's Repeal Association, in part over the latter's refusal to countenance, under any circumstances, the use of physical force.[63] Members of Young Ireland set about establishing a new organization, the Irish Confederation, with the aim of creating a network of militant "clubs" at local and parish level, sufficiently numerous to force the British government to concede legislative independence for Ireland through repeal of the Act of Union.[64] In February 1848, Mitchel broke from the *Nation* to establish his own short-lived journal, the *United Irishman*, in which he openly advocated armed rebellion against British rule, arguing that such a course could succeed if Ireland's rural masses, presently employed on profitless relief schemes, were mobilized for the task.[65]

Duffy and others were, initially, more hesitant, but a series of successful popular risings across Europe during the early months of 1848—Vienna, Sicily, Piedmont, Venice, and, in particular, Paris on February 22—helped to convince them that a similar undertaking might succeed in Ireland. Editorials in the *Nation* proclaimed support for the insurgents and, in March, Meagher and Smith O'Brien undertook a mission to France, where they were received by the poet and revolutionary leader Lamartine, who had, however, been warned by Russell's government that any public show of support for the Young Ireland contingent would result in the severing of diplomatic ties.[66]

The revolutions of 1848 also alerted Russell's administration to the possibility of a large-scale rising. During the summer of 1848, the British military presence in Ireland was augmented with a further ten thousand troops, seventeen thousand stand of arms, and one and a half million rounds of ammunition. The Dublin Castle garrison was strengthened with two squadrons of light dragoons brought up from Newbridge, while the fleet, which had been stationed off Lisbon, was ordered to proceed to the Cove of Cork. On March 17, Meagher, Smith O'Brien and Mitchel were arrested and charged with making seditious speeches. Despite a packed jury, Meagher and Smith O'Brien were acquitted, but Mitchel, who was tried separately, was convicted and sentenced to fourteen years' transportation. On July 12, Duffy and Meagher (again) were arrested under a newly passed Treason Felony Act, which made it an offense punishable by transportation for life to recommend, in speaking or writing, the use of force for the purpose of effecting political change. Duffy was remanded in Newgate prison (where he was permitted to receive visitors and to edit the *Nation* from his cell), and Meagher was released on bail, pending his trial, scheduled for August 8. Ten days after Meagher's arrest, Dublin, Cork, Waterford, and Drogheda were "proclaimed" under a Crime and Outrage Act: persons not holding a police permit were required to surrender any weapons in their possession, under pain of one year's imprisonment. Detachments of troops were stationed outside major towns, with the Seventy-fifth Regiment bivouacked in Dublin's Phoenix Park. A further force, consisting of eight hundred infantry, two companies of rifles, a demibrigade of artillery, and two troops of cavalry, was dispatched to scour the countryside between Dublin and Thurles, County Tipperary. On July 22, a bill was rushed through the House of Commons, suspending habeas corpus in Ireland until March of the following year. Faced with the prospect of further arrests and of detention without trial for an indefinite period, the members of Young Ireland who remained at liberty resolved to fight, and Meagher and Smith O'Brien set about attempting to raise the countryside, focusing on the three adjacent counties of Kilkenny, Waterford, and Tipperary, an area of mostly higher ground, protected from the east by the river Barrow and to the west by the mountains of Kerry and west Cork. As leader, O'Brien's initial plan had been to seize the city of Kilkenny as the prelude to a national rising. As he and Meagher toured the south and southwest, however, it became clear that they had overestimated the level of support to be expected both from the confederate clubs and from a weakened and demoralized populace.[67]

Arriving in Carrick-on-Suir, County Tipperary, Meagher was gratified, at first, to find that the entire population had taken to the streets. Unfortunately, there were only three hundred rifles and muskets in the whole of the town, while nearby were stationed more than a thousand British troops, along with artillery: two howitzers and two field pieces. Faced with such odds, the local confederate clubs refused to undertake a rising, on the grounds that defeat would be certain. Further disappointments were to follow. In Cashel, supposedly a center of confederate support, the streets were deserted. In Mullinahone, a gathering of some six thousand people diminished to around five hundred when Smith O'Brien announced that those who chose to follow him would have to supply their own provisions. The same happened in Ballingary, where the majority of those assembled had been subsisting on government relief, consisting of one pound of meal per day. When local Catholic priests tried to dissuade their parishioners from what they saw as a suicidal course of action, Smith O'Brien's five hundred followers soon dwindled to a mere fifty. Despite the small numbers, adequate provisions proved difficult to obtain because Smith O'Brien, who had hoped to carry the support of the landlord class, refused to requisition supplies on the credit of a future revolutionary government. Meanwhile, rumors circulated in Dublin to the effect that a force of some twenty thousand insurgents was roaming the countryside, and arrests of Young Ireland supporters continued.[68]

On July 30, the insurgents received reports of a large body of police advancing on Ballingary. Smith O'Brien, who had been left in sole command (Meagher having gone to attempt to raise Templederry and the Slievemanon district) decided to make a stand. The rebels erected a barricade, behind which Smith O'Brien's remaining supporters, about a hundred in number, took position with some fifty firearms, supplemented by pikes, pitchforks, rocks, and stones. Around them assembled a much larger crowd of men, women, and children. The commander of the police detachment appears to have become convinced, on seeing the crowd from a distance, that he was facing a force of upwards of three thousand armed men. The police broke off their advance and took refuge in an adjacent farmhouse, situated in a cabbage garden belonging to a Widow McCormack, who was herself away from home, although her children (five or six of them, according to reports) were inside the house. An attempt was made by the rebels to fire the building, but this was abandoned when the widow returned and pleaded for the release of her children. Smith O'Brien approached the house to request that the police surrender their arms. As negotiations were proceeding, several of his supporters began to throw stones, prompting the police to open fire. The besiegers fled, sustaining a number of casualties, and the rising was, in effect, over. Smith O'Brien escaped on a captured police horse. He was later arrested on August 5 at Thurles station, attempting to return to his property in Cahirmoyle, County Limerick.[69]

"A New Race in Ireland"

Unlike the agrarian outbreaks castigated in the pages of the *Nation*, the Young Ireland rising has gone on to attain recognition in both popular and academic histories as a moment in Ireland's struggle toward independent nationhood.[70] Despite their lack of success, the participants' aims (political or legislative independence) were articulated in terms consonant with the idioms of secular politics and statehood, thus qualifying them, unlike the unnamed proponents of Ribbonism, as suitable protagonists in the retrospectively spun story of an independent Ireland. Even so, scrutiny of the abortive rising evokes a comic-absurd disproportion between expectations and outcomes, which threatens to undo any too clear-cut opposition either between official and unofficial histories or between the rebels themselves and the leaderless agrarian insurgents from whom they took such pains to distance themselves. Both the fears of the British government and the revolutionary aspirations of the Young Irelanders conjure a fantasy of armed revolt (sustained, in both cases, it appears, largely by force of imagination) that is finally plunged into bathos by events in the Widow McCormack's cabbage patch. Despite his experiences, Smith O'Brien refused to accept that the project had been doomed to failure from the outset. Rather than the debilitating effects of hunger and disease, he attributed the outcome to the apathy of the Irish populace: "the fact is recorded in our annals—that the people preferred to die of starvation at home, or to flee as voluntary exiles to other lands, rather than to fight for their lives and liberties."[71]

Duffy (the only one of the Young Ireland leadership to escape imprisonment or transportation) reached a different conclusion. Writing in the *Nation* on September 1, 1849, he recorded his impressions from a recent visit to the west of Ireland:

The famine and the landlords have actually created a new race in Ireland. I have seen on the streets of Galway crowds of creatures more debased that the yahoos of Swift—creatures having only a distant and hideous resemblance to human beings. Grey-haired old men, whose idiot faces had hardened into a settled leer of mendicancy, simeous and semi-human; and women filthier and more frightful than harpies . . . *shrieking* for their prey, like monstrous and unclean animals. . . . I have seen these accursed sights, and they are burned into my mind forever.[72]

For Duffy, the spectacle of hunger and destitution came finally to preclude ideological appropriation, the apportioning of political blame giving way, as the description progresses, to a stupefied inventory of the monstrous and the grotesque. If Smith O'Brien's disappointment at the failure of the rising stemmed from an abiding conviction that poverty and hunger might (given the collective will and the right circumstances) be harnessed to a project of national liberation, Duffy's reflections led him to question the possibility of such a movement from extremity to political praxis. The "new race" encountered on his travels—creatures of implacable and unreasoning appetite—may replicate earlier, English stereotypes of the rural Irish poor, yet in doing so they remain disturbingly and inassimilably other. Their condition is not one of liminality construed in relation to a fixed and stable center, but of an alterity that appears to have infiltrated and hollowed out the very ground of the social. Viewed in relation to the sense-making structures of political ideologies, whether revolutionary or conservative, nationalist or unionist, they are the gift made flesh, the shocking interimplication of death-in-life, which both undergirds and perennially threatens the classificatory ordering of the human world. The relationship between the cultural order and the starving body appears to have attained here to something more than the condition of radical undecidability that so troubled William Bennett in his dealings with the islanders of Arranmore. In Duffy's recounting, wild hunger discloses an irreducible and all too palpable excess troubling the borders of historical cognition, as though retrojected nature, in the guise of the famished body, had decisively ruptured the continuum of historical understanding, precipitating an abyssal collapse of meaning in which are implicated both the canons of academic and statist historiography and the reciprocal alignment of subjectivity and world.

In the Theater of Death

Descriptions of starvation- and disease-related deaths draw attention to another kind of excess—an unmanageable proliferation of corpses. In remembrances of the famine years, it is often the sheer number of the dead and dying that commands attention. Johnny Bat Sullivan, aged eighty, of Tuosist, County Kerry, interviewed by Seán Ó Súilleabháin of the Irish Folklore Commission in 1945, recalled being told as a child that, on one occasion, there were thirty dead bodies on the road to Kenmare at the edge of the town "between Dr Maybury's house and the Bell Height (a distance of a few hundred yards)."[1] Contemporary eyewitness accounts assert, more frequently, that deaths were too numerous for an exact figure to be given. The following, from the same locality, appeared first in the *Kerry Examiner* and was reprinted in the *Nation* on February 13, 1847. The potato crop had failed for a second successive year. Disease, in the form of typhus, dysentery, and relapsing fever, was rife, and as the winter progressed the death toll mounted:

The state of the people of this locality is horrifying. Fever, famine and dysentery are daily increasing, deaths from hunger daily occurring, averaging weekly twenty—men women and children thrown into the graves without a coffin— dead bodies found in all parts of the country, being several days dead before discovered—no inquests to inquire how they came by their death, as hunger has hardened the hearts of the people. Those who survive cannot long remain so—the naked wife and children staring them in the face—their bones penetrating through the skin—not a morsel of flesh to be seen on their bodies—and not a morsel of food can they procure to eat. From all points of the county they crowd into the town for relief, and not a pound of meal is to be had in the wretched town at any price.[2]

Although some attempt is made by the correspondent to specify the number of deaths in terms of a weekly average, the impression given is rather that of a tide of mortality that escapes quantification, the magnitude of which can be conveyed only through the piling up of imagistic snapshots. The seeming ubiquity of death and disease appears most starkly to the correspondent in the mixture of indifference and casual haste with which the bodies of the deceased are disposed of. "Hunger has hardened the hearts of the people," and death no longer wears an extraordinary but rather an everyday aspect, yet all the more harrowing for its very familiarity. What these accounts evoke, by way of the silent dramaturgy of the spectacle, is a theater of death in which mass mortality appears to have overrun the entirety of the social space. At stake in such descriptions, with their paratactic accumulation of instances and their eschewal of explication or commentary, is the primacy of the seen over what can be explained or quantified. The spectacle of death provokes simultaneous horror and fascination. Crucially, it is a spectacle that fractures or alters the spectator by impugning the physical separation of observer and observed. According to Julia Kristeva, the corpse and the decaying body inspire revulsion because they do not merely signify death in the manner of a flat encephalograph, but manifest in obtrusively physical form all that one thrusts aside in order to constitute oneself as a living being.[3] In presenting us as spectators with an image of ourselves (of the "I") reduced to base matter, the corpse impinges threateningly on the border we seek to maintain between death and life. We may be reminded of Carlyle's observation, made during his visit to Westport, County Mayo, in July 1849, that society in Ireland was collapsing in an orgy of autophagous self-annihilation: "Society *here* would have to eat itself, and end by cannibalism in a week, if it were not held up by the rest of our empire still standing afoot."[4] Carlyle's image of Irish society as a self-consuming artifact captures one of the salient characteristics of the theater of death: its homogenizing impetus, issuing in a tendency to efface distinctions between life and death, health and sickness. The following description of the workhouse at Ballinrobe, County Mayo, appeared in the *Illustrated London News* on April 3, 1847:

This building is nothing other than one horrible charnel house, the unfortunate paupers being nearly all the victims of a fearful fever—the dying and the dead, one might say, huddled together. The master has become the victim of this dread disease; the clerk has been added to the victims; the matron too is dead; and the respected, regretted and esteemed physician, has fallen before the ravages of pestilence, in his constant attendance upon the diseased inmates. The Roman Catholic chaplain is also dangerously ill of the same epidemic.[5]

Hierarchies no longer pertain, as death and disease, no respecters of persons or ranks, make patients and carers alike their victims. The descriptions suggest that death has managed to slip its socially assigned bounds—the hospital, the cemetery—to riot in the spaces of everyday human interaction. The result resembles a macabre saturnalia, in which all rules are to be broken, all limits transgressed. In this respect, the accounts prefigure one of the classics of twentieth-century experimental theater. It was just such a shattering of accepted boundaries between profane utility and sacred violence, between the everyday and the subterranean realms of dream and desire, that Antonin Artaud sought to achieve in his prescriptions for a "Theatre of Cruelty." In his "First Manifesto" (originally published in 1933), Artaud sought such a mode of expression in a language "halfway between gesture and thought," a language of action unfolding in space, reaching beyond conceptual content to furnish the spectator with "the truthful precipitates of dreams, in which his taste for crime, his erotic obsessions, his savagery, his chimeras, his utopian sense of life and matter, even his cannibalism pour out, on a level not counterfeit and illusory, but interior."[6] Above all, the Theatre of Cruelty was to offer a spatial and gestural showing forth of all that was habitually excluded from the sphere of mundane consciousness, a violent spasm through which humanity might be restored to its place in a wider universe.

It is here, in the avowed acceptance of what is "bloody and inhuman" as the substance and subject matter of theatrical performance, that Artaud's dramatic theory coincides with the extravagances of mortality recorded in descriptions of mid-nineteenth-century Ireland. In both cases, images of dissolution owe their power and efficacy to a forced rending of the socially sanctioned divide between life and death, the human and the nonhuman. Such a parallel between the modernist theatrical avant-garde and depictions of such "real-world" issues as hunger, death, and disease draws attention not only to the constitutive role of imagination and desire in shaping supposedly documentary accounts, but also to the ubiquity of performance, across genres and contexts, as embodying a range of possibilities for action and transformation, which, in Richard Schechner's words, are, in the last analysis, "amoral."[7] The protean energies unleashed by the dramaturgy of death, whether in the France of the 1930s (as the storm clouds of European fascism were gathering) or the Ireland of the 1840s, are capable of lending themselves, sometimes simultaneously, to the interests of power or resistance, dictatorship or revolution, political economy or the gift, while their affect and impact remain irreducible to and thus inexplicable in terms of interest, faction, or instrumentality. It is on these grounds that the image repertoire of death is to be situated within the domain of carnival, understood as a violent, temporary subversion of the everyday order, which may culminate either in the latter's overthrow or reestablishment, but which, while it lasts, is informed and energized by a collective sense of limits transgressed and excluded contents seeping back into view. As Kristeva reminds us, the carnivalesque needs to be understood here not in terms of parody, implying, ultimately, a strengthening of law and authority, but rather with reference to its ineffaceably dramatic aspects: "murderous, cynical and revolutionary in the sense of *dialectical transformation.*"[8] As such, carnival implies an opening to a life that sweeps away individuality in the same way that the theater of Artaud (whom Kristeva cites) aimed to blast asunder the spectator's everyday self through recourse to a language of bodily praxis that would exceed and subvert the symbolic function.

There will be more to say later about the carnivalesque, with reference to depictions of the physical depredations wrought by hunger and disease. For the present, however, I wish to focus on another widely disseminated motif in accounts of the famine: the perceived disruption of customs and rituals concerned with mourning and the burial of the dead. Famine burials, even when they took place in consecrated ground, are usually remembered as having been provisional and makeshift affairs. Among the difficulties, given the shortage of money in circulation, was raising the price of a coffin.[9] In some cases, reusable coffins were employed.[10] Alternatively, when no coffin was available, corpses might be wrapped in sheets or straw ropes.[11] Churchyard burials, however, even in attenuated form, are most frequently recalled as the exception rather than the norm. According to Martin O'Malley, aged eighty-five, of Mulranny, County Mayo, "People were often buried near where they died, there are plenty buried along by the seashore as you go down to the castle (Rosturk). There are several graves in Cnoc Rua on the S. side of the road to the west of the Post Office."[12] He adds that in the early years of the twentieth century, Stevens, the local landlord, wanted the graves in Cnoc Rua removed, but the workmen refused.[13] An account from County Tipperary suggests that many of those thus buried were itinerant or destitute people, making their way to the local workhouse, near Cashel.[14]

Dáithí Ó Ceantabhail, a sometime collector for the Irish Folklore Commission, describes the method employed in the vicinity of Croom (County Limerick) for burying such roadside corpses: "They were buried where they were found by opening the fence and shifting the poor corpse into the gap as formed. The ditch (raised fence) was then built over the body and some stones set into the breastwork of the fence to mark the grave."[15] Many of these bodies, however, were left unburied. Both contemporary newspaper and later folkloric accounts provide harrowing testimony to their fate: "Bodies actually lay unburied by hedges for rats soon devoured the flesh and only the skeleton remained. There is an instance of a family being found dead, with their skeletons only remaining and the efforts of the neighbors failed to frighten away the rats that were feeding on the flesh."[16]

Uncoffined burials, although by no means unknown in Ireland before the potato failure, were, for many observers, indicative of the ongoing disruption of social life and popular custom.[17] On February 6, 1847, the *Illustrated London News* reprinted an unsigned letter from a traveler in the west of Ireland (possibly William Forster, there with Joseph Crosfield on a fact-finding mission on behalf of the Society of Friends), in which it was asserted that the poorhouse and hospital at Carrick-on-Shannon, County Leitrim, were crowded with "half-naked, emaciated men, women and children," the majority of them prey to dysentery and fever.[18] The number of applicants far exceeded the available places in either institution, and many had to be turned away. The same source reported that, in Sligo town, in the neighboring county of Sligo, the poorhouse was becoming similarly overcrowded. Many of those seeking admission, according to the writer, did not expect to survive the winter, but were motivated by the belief that those who died there would be guaranteed a Christian burial. In the report submitted by Crosfield and Forster to the Central Relief Committee of the Society of Friends, the anxieties of such people were indicative of conditions throughout the west of Ireland and pointed to a wholesale breakdown of rural society: "One woman who had crawled the previous night into an out-house, had been found the next morning partly eaten by dogs. Another corpse had been carried up the street in a wheelbarrow. . . . Of burials without coffins we heard many instances, and to those who know the almost superstitious reverence of the Irish for funeral rites, they tell a fearful story."[19]

Beggars, they noted, often asked not for food, but for money to purchase a coffin. Richard Webb, of Dublin, undertaking a visit of inspection to Erris, County Mayo, in May of the same year (also on behalf of the Society of Friends), remarked, similarly, that many of those seeking admission to Ballina workhouse at the time did so in the hope of securing a coffin for their own funeral: "Before the present visitation, the poorer classes in this country were extremely tenacious of the credit and respectability attached to a good, large and well-attended funeral. Many who saved money for no other purpose were careful to preserve a hoard to defray their funeral expenses. Few of the popular customs appeared more firmly rooted than this; but it has been swept away like chaff before the wind."[20]

Like Crosfield and Forster, Webb interprets the neglect of funerary rites as pointing to a more general dereliction of proprieties and mutual obligations. Webb's claim is a far-reaching one, not least because it mimics the very concerns he himself takes to characterize prefamine rural society. Indeed, Webb and his associates appear no less anxious concerning the fate of the dead than are those of whom they write. Implicit in such a view perhaps is a sense that the uncoffined dead themselves represent a threat to the living. Because their passing has not been marked by the punctiliously observed funerary rites, which, in the eyes of these commentators, were previously such a defining feature of rural life, these dead seem destined to remain a potentially intrusive presence on society's margins.[21]

The Unquiet Dead

In his classic essay "The Collective Representation of Death" (originally published in the journal *Année Sociologique* in 1907), Robert Hertz argues that the period after a death is one in which energies are unleashed that threaten society as a whole. Mourning, funerary rites, and mortuary practices seek to remedy the incipient crisis by consigning the dead decisively to an afterlife, where they may be either forgotten, or where communion with them may be undertaken without risk. Hertz suggests, however, that there are certain categories of deaths (violent or accidental, deaths of women who die in childbirth, victims of drowning or lightning, suicides) for which these measures are deemed insufficient, and which are attended by special rites:

Their bodies inspire the most intense horror and are got rid of precipitately; furthermore, their bones are not laid with those of the deceased members of the group who have died a normal death. Their unquiet and spiteful souls roam the earth forever; or, if they emigrate to another world, they live in a separate village, sometimes even in a completely different area from that inhabited by other souls. It seems, in the most typical cases at least, that the transitory period extends indefinitely for these victims of a special malediction and that their death has no end.[22]

The out-of-the-ordinary character of such deaths means that the forces they unleash cannot be ritually contained or effaced, and society will maintain toward them the attitude of exclusion it has adopted from the first. Theirs will be a death without end, which will continue to impinge, menacingly, on the domain of the living. It is instructive to set Hertz's reflections alongside, on the one hand, the observations of Webb and his contemporaries, and on the other, the widespread social scientific characterization of modernity as instituted (at least in part) on the basis of a reconfigured relationship between living and dead. Historian Phillipe Ariès in his compendious study of western attitudes to death and dying makes the claim that the social presence of death has become progressively attenuated from the Middle Ages to the present, a trajectory culminating in the carceral spaces of the terminal ward, the crematorium, and the cemetery, where the dead are definitively sequestered from the living.[23] Ariès's account finds numerous echoes, from Schiller's and Weber's "disenchantment of the world" to Baudrillard's more recent notion of "the extradition of the dead."[24] Nonetheless, as Webb reminds us, Ireland has more frequently been seen as an exception to this tendency, characterized by an anachronistic attachment to death. Edmund Spenser, writing in 1596, remarked disparagingly that the Irish were prone to engage in excessive lamentation for their dead, "ymoderate waylinges" that he took to indicate both a lack of civility and a residual paganism.[25] Nor have such associations been confined to the colonial era. Practices of mourning, including the keen (*caoine*) or graveside lament performed by women, along with the games and amusements associated with wakes for the dead, have also furnished abundant material for twentieth-century folklorists concerned with uncovering the contemporary vestiges of a pre-Christian, Celtic past.[26] More recently, the supposed preoccupation of the Irish with death has resurfaced in a study by Nina Witoszek and Pat Sheeran, which castigates the "funereal culture" of Irish literature, past and present, as indicative of a morbid fixation on the past and a concomitant unwillingness to engage the present and future.[27] Leaving aside the merits (or otherwise) of such claims, it is striking to note that in each case, the persistence of practices and beliefs relating to death is taken as proof of Ireland's incomplete accession to modernity.[28] Given the no less widespread identification of Ireland in English imaginaries (up to and including the nineteenth century) as a place of savagery, incivility, and (latterly) economic backwardness, Irish funerary customs become both a further basis for the articulation of colonial differences and a disturbing reminder of death as a potentially uncontainable contemporary presence. Placed in this context, Webb's comments suggest that the abrogation of death ritual entails not the elimination of death as a collectively marked event, but rather its unleashing across the entirety of the social space. No longer ritually circumscribed or consigned to the status of an antiquarian curiosity, the anomalous character of death becomes instead generalized.

Linda-May Ballard, in a study of Ulster ghost traditions, notes that in Ireland (as elsewhere), supernatural manifestations are frequently associated with Hertz's segregated dead. Special burial sites may be set aside for such individuals—roadsides, crossroads, disused graveyards, the seashore—liminal places corresponding to the perceived status of those who lie there.[29] These too are among the characteristic locations remembered for famine burials:

There are several famine graves near Lír an Áir chapel. There is one or two in the sandpit just east of Rossgalive bridge, two or three hundred yards west of the chapel. There is one to the west of the bridge on the south side of the road, near a large rock. There are three graves in the chapel yard to the north of the chapel. There are a few near the road leading up to the old school in Rossgalive (the "soup" school once). There are others in Inis na Croise.[30]

Perhaps the most widely disseminated image associated with famine burials, however, is that of the mass grave, in which bodies were piled anonymously and indiscriminately. At Skibbereen, the principal burying ground was Abbeystrowry, on the banks of the river Ilen. Here, it is recalled, corpses were interred, several at a time, in a series of pits:

In these pits the dead were placed in "strata," a little clay being thrown over each "stratum," before the next was laid on. The pits were of various sizes, but I should think that in some instances one "stratum" would consist of ten or twelve bodies, ranged in double lines of five or six each, there being probably three or four strata in each pit; but I am of the opinion these regularities were not always observed and that the dead were thrown sometimes into the pits in a careless manner, and that the pits were covered in when they could hold no more.[31]

Again, the impression is of a surfeit of mortality triumphing over any attempt at the orderly disposal of bodies. Or perhaps what touches us here is the apparent intertwining of order and disorder—the proliferation of death simultaneously calling forth and subverting the officiousness of protocol and regulation, the digging of the pits, the layering of the bodies "in double lines of four or five each." One senses here the chaos lurking at the heart of the very attempt to contain chaos; the two locked in secret interdependence, breeding both further disorder and macabre invention. At the same time, the mass grave could double as a space of transformation and rebirth. Take the following account, also from the Skibbereen area:

But the most remarkable of all the famine victims in this district was Tom Gearins. Tom was a young lad at the time of the famine. With many others, he was taken and thrown into the famine hole at Skibbereen Abbey. He was not dead and somehow or other he was able to raise his hand. He was eventually rescued but it was found that his legs were broken and badly deformed from the weight that was on him. However, he lived, but his legs were all out of joint.[32]

Tom Gearins survives to become a well-known figure, traveling the roads of west Cork as an itinerant beggar and spending his winters at the newly built poorhouse at Skibbereen. The same account goes on to relate how on one occasion the Board of Guardians of the poorhouse was providing poor people with boots. Thinking that a pair would be a great relief to his misshapen legs, Tom applied. He was told that he would be given the boots only on condition that he composed a verse about himself. The following (known to many older people in the locality during the 1930s) was, allegedly, the result:

> I arose from the dead in the year '48
> Though a grave in the Abbey had near been my fate
>   And since for subsistence I've done all my best
> Though one leg points east and the other points west
>   And never a tax on the ratepayers I've been
> I've roamed the country enjoying each scene
>   I only appeal to you now for a pair
> Of boots and I'll vanish again into air.[33]

Tom Gearins's story, replete with echoes of mythological descents into the underworld, confirms that the designated realm of the dead can also give rise to new life, as the protagonist is reborn, permanently marked by his experience, but seemingly with his humor intact. As a living reminder of the events of the 1840s, he becomes both a subject of and (if the storyteller is to be believed) an active contributor to subsequent folklore. Yet the impression the story leaves (at least on this reader) is one of laughter intimately, perhaps indissolubly, tied to death, as though Tom Gearins's familiar but marginal status were more than the merely physiological result of his near interment.

Other reminders of the buried past were less obviously amenable to comedic reappropriation. Johnny Callaghan, aged 90, a retired baker, described an ingenious contrivance employed at the workhouse in Castlerea, County Roscommon:

When a person was near death, he or she was removed from the other parts of the workhouse to a large room at the gable end of the workhouse (the gable nearest the town of Castlerea) this room was called the "black room" and the gable the "black gable," for in this room the sick person was allowed to die. Sometimes there were up to seven persons in this room. From the window of this room there were a few boards slanting down to the earth and beneath was a huge grave or pit. When a death occurred the corpse was allowed to slide down the boards and into the pit beneath and "lime" was put over the corpse, along the boards and on the wall of the gable. This caused the wall to be black and gave the name to the "Black Gable." This black gable was to be seen up to a few years ago and had retained its black color.[34]

The workhouse itself, as an edifice intended to contain disease and mortality, becomes a monument to the impossibility of such a task, indelibly marked with the traces of death, which serves equally as a reminder to later generations. The black gable commemorates too the institution's complicity in the transforming and homogenizing work of death, converting dying inmates into so many nameless remains in its attendant lime pit. At the same time, we are reminded that this work of dissolution and metamorphosis does not—indeed, cannot—exist outside of particular histories, as the humanly defined contexts of its realization.

Underground

If the mass grave figured predominantly in popular imagining as a zone of transformation, ceaselessly disintegrating and recombining, it was also the place where the deceased themselves became assimilated to a preexisting corpus of beliefs and practices regarding death and the afterlife, where contemporary history fused with motifs from myth and folklore. The image of the underworld as relayed in Irish literature and mythology condenses multiple histories, comprising the pagan and pre-Celtic inhabitants of the land, the coming of Christianity, and, subsequently, the period of English conquest and settlement. According to the twelfth-century *Lebor Gabála Érenn* (Book of the Invasions of Ireland), the underworld was the adopted abode of the *Tuatha Dé Danaan* (People of the Goddess Danu), a semidivine, supernaturally gifted race who had once occupied Ireland and who had withdrawn beneath the earth's surface after the arrival of the Sons of Mil, the imputed forebears of Ireland's present-day inhabitants.[35] The story, as anthropologists from Tylor onward have noted, is a globally familiar one: a conquered or displaced race assume, in the eyes of their self-proclaimed overlords, the status of supernatural beings, a potential source of both malediction and supernatural benefits. For the Christian scribe responsible for the compilation of the *Lebor Gabála*, however, it was necessary to recast the pagan sources that form the likely basis of this origin myth in accordance with medieval Christian orthodoxy. Thus, the wanderings of the Sons of Mil (and successive waves of earlier invaders) are assimilated to biblical chronology via the Twelve Tribes of Israel and a host of details culled from such familiar medieval sources as the chronicles of Eusebius and Orosius and Isidore of Seville's *Etymologiae*. As a recent study of pagan and Christian elements in early Irish literature suggests, the aim appears to be the elaboration of a "native Christian" mythohistory, linking Ireland to the mainstream of medieval European Christianity.[36] As the folklore record testifies, however, the Christianizing interpretation did not entirely succeed in dispelling the underworld of pre-Christian belief. The *Tuatha Dé Danaan* lived on in altered guise as the fairies and spirits of popular belief (whose imminent passing Wilde was to remark in the aftermath of the famine).

The complex of stories and beliefs relating to fairies, or *sí* (pl. *síthe*), a race of beings existing alongside humans but largely invisible to them, has been attributed, variously, to folk memories of prehistoric races and to traditions relating to nature-spirits and the ancestral dead. Upon these was subsequently superimposed the medieval Christian interpretation of fairies as fallen angels, stranded between heaven and hell, pending their final liquidation at the Last Judgment.[37] Summarizing these various strands, folklorist Dáithí Ó hÓgáin points to the association between fairies and prehistoric burial sites and to their role as bestowers of magical gifts and agricultural benefits. The abode of the fairies is sometimes described as situated beneath the earth (in so-called fairy mounds or "raths," associated with prehistoric barrows and tumuli), or, less frequently, beneath the ocean or in idyllic overseas realms.[38] Whatever its location, fairyland, in contrast to the Christian hell, is usually identified as a place of luxury, magnificence, and fantastic abundance (although sometimes these qualities are dismissed as a magically induced illusion), a place at once seductive and potentially hazardous for those mortals who are permitted to visit it. Human visitors to fairyland may have difficulty, on returning, in readjusting to the everyday world. Sometimes, those who return discover that years or centuries have passed during their seemingly brief absence.[39]

The crucial point here is not the stubborn persistence of pagan belief in the face of an ascendant Christianity, but rather the way in which these stories themselves embody a complex and multifaceted history of religious conflict and cultural change. The folkloric iconography of the underworld is the repository of a history composed of diverse elements, the interpretation of which itself affords a shifting site of historical action and struggle. Accounts of famine burials too, insofar as they incorporate and refashion earlier elements, point to an intersection between contemporary events and a preexisting repertoire of meanings and associations that is reciprocally transformative, inflecting the present with reverberations of a vanished past and ushering that same past into a new and troubling proximity to the here and now.

In addition to crossroads, roadsides, and the seashore, former burial sites, or "killeens," often with medieval or early Christian origins, provided another favored location for the disposal of the segregated dead.[40] Many famine victims were buried in such sites or in the vicinity of the prehistoric forts (in some cases themselves burial chambers) that dot the Irish landscape.[41] The strong otherworldly associations already attaching to such locations, as places where ghosts or fairies might be encountered by night, may have prompted the assimilation of the famine dead to the existing pantheon of supernatural beings. In any case, as Dáithí Ó Ceantabhail discovered in the course of his researches, the location of burials in and around these forts continued to be noted and respected into the present century:

Some years ago I was visiting the archaeological monuments of the district immediately around Croom for the Kilmallock Archaeological Society. It meant that I had to visit every fort etc. in the place. In doing so I was warned by Paddy Macnamara of Drumloughan, Monaster parish, to be sure not to interfere with a small raised fort on his land as there were at least three famine victims buried there. I have heard of other forts also in which similar burials were made.[42]

The latter-day avoidance of famine graves was not confined to those associated with prehistoric sites. The son of a farmer from Kilcommon, County Mayo, had the following to say about the site of a supposed burial on his father's land: "The plough was always raised when approaching this 'famine grave' and it was left always green. I remember my father, R.I.P., cutting the grass over it every summer. . . . It was never given to stock or made use of in any way. The mound was consequently rising higher as years went by."[43]

Although many corpses from the 1840s were buried anonymously, it appears that those responsible for their interment did not always rely on oral transmission to ensure their remains were left undisturbed. Johnny Bat Sullivan recalled a grave near the "inch" owned by Eugene O'Sullivan Jr. in Drombohilly, near Lehud Bridge: "Behind this man's house in the haggard, is a grave-flag, inscribed '1847 LET NONE MEDDLE HERE.'"[44]

"Let None Meddle Here"

The accounts collected by the Irish Folklore Commission attest not only that the locations of famine burials were widely remembered into the early decades of the twentieth century, but also that they were frequently identified as a potential source of supernatural danger:

The memory in later years of famine burials having been made at a certain point produced a superstitious fear in the minds of the people, a fear which had its origin, I think, in the horrible dread of contagion which filled the survivors in an area where death mowed a wide swath.[45]

There is a place near my house . . . near the road going through the townland of Knock-a-taggil at the end of a small hill. This spot is still avoided at night because of ghosts, which by the way were never seen to my knowledge haunting the spot. It is popularly supposed to be the burying place of many people during the famine days.[46]

The lingering presence of the famine dead in later years, in the form of stories relating to ghosts and other apparitions, appears to confirm Hertz's insight concerning the ineffaceable character of violent or anomalous deaths. Although long buried, these dead have continued to haunt the imagination of the living, eliciting both fear and deference. They endure too, in more palpable guise, through visible traces left on the landscape, most frequently the stone cairns, or *leachtaí* (sing. *leacht*), that marked the sites of numerous wayside burials in Ireland: "There are numerous and nameless stone heaps or 'lachta' [*sic*] on the mountains in the vicinity of Glenamoy, believed to be the spots where dead bodies were found—victims of hunger—and it is believed that many of the victims were merely on their journey to Rossport when they collapsed from exhaustion and died there."[47]

Leachtaí are more generally associated in Ireland with out of the ordinary deaths. In addition to famine victims, stone heaps cover the bodies of murder victims (Galway), drowned sailors ("Sailor's Cairn" or *Leacht a' Mháirnéalaigh* on the Mullet peninsula, County Mayo), or army deserters (Mayo, Galway, Cork, Kilkenny).[48] Passersby, on encountering a wayside cairn, were expected to add a stone, failure to do so resulting in bad luck (Donegal). Sometimes, this was thought to involve suffering the same fate as the person whose death was commemorated by the heap (Donegal, Galway, Cork, Kerry, Cavan). Although the orthodox Catholic interpretation of this custom (for example, as recorded in Leitrim) stressed that the stones were raised as a reminder to pray for the dead, it was sometimes suggested that the practice was intended rather to hold the dead down more securely and prevent them from rising. Adding a stone thus constituted a form of protection against the vengeance of the deceased: "Níl conntabhairt ar bith go dtiocfaidh taidhbhse nó spiorad an té a d'imithigh ar an té a chuirfeas cloch ar an leachta" (There is no danger that the person who is gone will come upon the person who puts a stone on the cairn).[49] Wayside cairns were associated too with apparitions of the dead (usually in malign or vengeful guise) and with a variety of other supernatural manifestations: unexplained wailing and clamor (Doine Beag, County Donegal), leprechauns (Killasnet, County Leitrim), banshees, phantom pipers and harpers (Erris, County Mayo), and mysterious black dogs (Ennis, County Clare).

As sites of supernatural power and ritual prophylaxis, wayside cairns marked not only burial places, but also places of death, where the body of the deceased first touched the ground before being transported elsewhere for interment.[50] In such cases, the perceived danger was seen to emanate not from the physical presence of the deceased, but from a force, intangible except in its effects, drawing on the exceptional or wayward character of the death there enacted, a force imparted and transmitted by means of physical contact and contiguity. In County Galway, according to folklorist Máire MacNeill's researches, the malign power attendant upon a death place was referred to by the Irish term *tir* (*teir*, meaning "evil omen" or "portent of ill luck"): "Whenever a person is killed it is said there is *tir*. There is *tir* in the first puppy of the litter. What is understood by *tir* is a permanent fatal power for evil existing from the beginning in certain things, places and animals, Whoever is born on Whit Sunday, for instance, is fated to kill, and from that *tir* there is no escape."[51]

As a primordial malign energy existing "from the beginning," *tir* was associated not only with actual sites of death, but with any place a corpse or coffin had touched. In Erris, County Mayo, stone heaps marked the spot where a coffin was laid down so that a mother could see her son who had died and been waked away from home. The same source noted a more general aversion to letting a coffin touch the ground: "I have seen a coffin resting on men's shoulders for almost an hour while waiting for a 'currach' [boat] to carry it across the bay to the burial ground. Of course the bearers were regularly relieved by relays of men while waiting for the boat."[52] Another account from County Clare and pertaining to the time of the famine related how four people carrying a corpse were so weak with hunger that they let it fall. Rather than being moved, it was buried where it fell, and a *leacht* was raised to mark the spot.[53]

Stories relating to burial cairns recall Frazer's magical principle of contagion, by which "things which have once been in contact with each other continue to act on each other at a distance after the physical contact has been severed."[54] More specifically, one is prompted to consider the implications of Frazer's formulation for an understanding of memory as embodied in material objects and features of landscape. Burial cairns serve not only as a visible reminder of past events (or a prompt to more sustained recollection), but also as a physical conduit through which the past is able to irrupt into the present. Sites allocated for the disposal of the anomalous dead are characterized both by spatial segregation and by the imputation of a dangerous permeability between the spheres of the living and the dead. It is in such settings that the dead are uniquely, threateningly able to breach the divide between these realms. Burial sites associated with those who have died violent or anomalous deaths are thus places where the past appears to press upon the present in a manner defying symbolic containment. More is at stake here than the now-familiar nervousness inhabiting classificatory boundaries.[55] Segregated burials reveal the relation between the living and the dead to be marked by an irreducible ambivalence between repetition and forgetting, evoking a past that is at once repudiated and yet continuously, even obsessively, alluded to.

Hungry Grass

Also associated with death places, according to MacNeill, and implicated in a similar logic of contagion and contact transmissibility was "hungry grass" (*féar gortach*). If a person were to step on it, he or she, it was claimed, would be assailed by a terrible hunger, which would cause death if not sated immediately. Death cairns were often associated with this danger, especially for those who forgot to add a stone—for instance, the so-called Hungry Rock on the highest point of the main Ballina-Sligo road to Coolaney in Sligo, where a priest was said to have been killed, and, in the adjoining county of Leitrim, a prehistoric cairn on Benbo mountain. Specifically, hungry grass was said to appear in spots where a corpse had fallen mouth downward: "Anywhere a person was killed or died and fell mouth downward, they say Hungry Grass is in that place. If you step on the spot the mouth touched, even if it were a thousand years before, you will be stricken by Hungry Grass."[56]

In addition to confirming the power attributed to prior contact with the deceased, the account given here of the origins of hungry grass recalls also a recurrent image in remembrances of the famine years: that of corpses whose mouths have been stained green from eating grass and nettles. Surely the horror and poignancy of this image derive, to a large degree, from its compounding of vision and tactility, the stain being the visible residue of a now otherwise severed physical connection. As in all cases of magical contagion, there is here an implied blurring of boundaries between persons and material objects. It was just such a sense of the interconnectedness of persons and things that Mauss had deemed necessary to the functioning of gift exchange, prior to the ascendancy of private property and a correspondingly privatized subjectivity.[57] Hungry grass, with its potentially fatal effects on the unwary trespasser, like the force of *tir* associated with wayside death cairns, belongs by definition to a time before the present, a time whose continuing claim upon the present it nonetheless continues to urge. Such a claim might be likened to that of the gift, as the simultaneous negation and precondition of all forms of "balanced" exchange. Its informing logic of tactile transmission recalls too Bataille's lost, but ritually restored, order of "intimacy," of being in the world as like among like, associated variously with the animal condition, with sacrificial violence, and with states of religious ecstasy and frenzy, involving the temporary liquidation of the protagonist's everyday social self.[58] The principle of contagion operates here as a mode of embodied memory activating the contemporary return of the repressed through the lingering traces of prior contact adhering to the surfaces of things long since separated, investing landscape with an unsettling mnemonic supplement as the medium through which both the dead and the retrospectively imagined past of pre-subjectival undifferentiation are able to maintain a contemporary presence.

It is striking that hungry grass should be further associated with failure to observe certain protocols regarding the consumption and distribution of food. Susceptibility to hungry grass was sometimes attributed, for instance, to eating in the open without letting a crumb fall, or without saying grace to offer thanks for the food about to be consumed.[59] Supernaturally induced hunger could thus be regarded as a form of punishment for a misguided retentiveness, a desire to hold onto more than one's share. It may be tempting to characterize such observations as an anonymous, folkloric critique of an emergent possessive individualism, a critique fueled by the collective remembrance of a now-vanished world of peasant cultivators and drawing its urgency from the social transformations perceived to be taking place in Ireland in the wake of the famine. I wish, however, to resist such a reading for two reasons. First, it seems insufficiently mindful of the extent to which memory is articulated from the standpoint of the present: the image of the past thus invoked owes its power and poignancy to the contemporary experience of estrangement and loss. Second, the moralizing interpretations sometimes appended to stories of hungry grass can be accounted secondary to the visceral apprehension of chronological slippage, allowing the reciprocal interpenetration of pasts and presents through the material medium of landscape. More is at stake here than the symbolic encoding of place and physical geography (including the perceived duty of the living to remember the dead), albeit that this forms a central component of the cultural logic through which such encounters with the past are rendered meaningful. Stories appended to death places can be seen rather as secondary elaborations, narratives that secrete their own antecedents in the guise of a mode of knowing predicated on physical contiguity and tactile appropriation, a mode that is not reducible to a logic of symbolization, understood as the representation of a (by definition) absent content, much as it grounds and enables the articulation of such a logic. It is through the rupturing of linear time thus effected, along with the implied bypassing of human agency and intentionality, that a retroactively configured image of the past is able to take on a contemporary subversive charge.

Haunted

"What is the time and what is the history of a specter?" inquires Jacques Derrida, invoking both the specter of a communism yet to come that Marx and Engels (at the opening of *The Communist Manifesto*) perceived haunting nineteenth-century Europe and its latter-day, postsoviet counterpart, that apologists for the new world (dis)order have sought wishfully to relegate to a receding past. What, Derrida asks, is the mode of being of a specter? Can the irruption into the present of the nonpresent past (or future) be accommodated to linear chronology and dreams of history as progress? Doesn't spectrality, affirming as it does the simultaneous absence and presence of the dead, impel us, rather, to question the assembled binarisms on which the authority and self-identity of the present are founded?[1]

Like Hertz, Derrida prompts us to consider what happens if the dead refuse to stay dead, but maintain a wayward and more or less obtrusive presence within the world of the living. In Ireland (at least until the late 1930s), the practice of adding to wayside death cairns owed much to the expectation of and desire to forestall such an eventuality. The dead, particularly those who had died accidental or violent deaths, could not be relied on to lie quietly. Victims of starvation from the famine years were, it seems, similarly prone to rise and wander, whether in the guise of the white-clad apparitions seen haunting the site of a former fever hospital near Kiltartan, County Galway, or, in County Leitrim, encountered (by night) in the company of the fairies.[2]

The dead might also manifest themselves in more tangible form. Because many famine victims were buried in shallow or unmarked graves, their remains were easily disturbed. Near Cashel, County Tipperary, bones were unearthed during the digging of the foundations for a new house.[3] The son of a farmer in Sneem, County Kerry, recalled that his father, while fencing near the ruins of a house where a family had died from starvation, came upon the bones of an old man and a child—"the arm of the old man was around the child."[4] Human (or animal) intervention was not always necessary to bring these buried traces of the past to light. The same result might be achieved by the slower, more implacable rhythms of wind, tide, and seasonal change. During the 1930s, on Oileán Úna, a small island off the Mayo coast near Mulranny, decades of erosion by the sea exposed a series of burials:

There were several bodies, big and small, buried in Oileán Úna, on the shore opposite Mulranny Pier. This island is being washed away from year to year. Years ago a coffin was exposed and had to be buried elsewhere. From time to time bones became visible and were reburied. Finally, a good many bones were exposed a year or two ago, and all the remains were taken up and reburied in the New Cemetery at Béal an Gheata in Murrevaugh.[5]

Like the bog bodies later apostrophized by Heaney, historical presences whose latter-day significance seems predicated, uncannily, on their prior sojourn in the earth's occluded depths, the human remains jettisoned on Oileán Úna's dwindling shores are disconcerting because they suggest the possibility of a random slippage between pasts and presents that the logic of historical explanation can never adequately master. If the dead (or at least the bones constituting their physical residue) can manifest themselves in so seemingly spontaneous a fashion, then the possibility of maintaining any consistent separation between life and death is thrown disturbingly into question.

Not only did the dead rise unbidden from the grave, they also threatened to lay claim to the living. As the death toll in Skibbereen mounted and hospitals and workhouses became full to capacity, living and dead were forced into uncomfortable proximity. I quote again from Dr. Donovan's medical diaries:

On my return home, I remembered that I had yet a visit to pay; having in the morning received a ticket to see six members of one family, named Barrett, who had been turned out of the cabin in which they lodged, in the neighbourhood of

Old Chapelyard; and who had struggled to this burying ground, and literally entombed themselves in a small watch-house that was built for the shelter of those
who were engaged in guarding against exhumation by doctors, when more respect
was paid to the dead than is at present the case.[6]

The shed, as Donovan describes it, was exactly seven feet long by
about six in breadth. To the side of the western wall was a long, newly dug
grave. By either gable were two smaller graves, both recently filled, and
near the hole that served as an entrance, two or three children were interred. The hut was in effect surrounded by a "rampart of human bones,"
which had accumulated to such an extent that the threshold, which had
originally been level with the ground, was now two feet below it. In this
makeshift shelter, six individuals, men and women, all of them suffering
from fever, had, as Donovan put it, "entombed themselves." Donovan had
visited the scene at eleven o'clock at night, amidst roaring wind and driving rain, accompanied by his assistant, Crowley. They took with them
bread, tea, and sugar. Thrusting his head through the entrance, Donovan
had to withdraw because of the stench. Although long familiar with death
and disease, he confessed to being "unnerved" by the scene that greeted his
eyes: "six fellow creatures were almost buried alive in this filthy sepulcher."
On hearing his voice, one of the inmates cried out, "Is that the priest?" and
another, "Is that the doctor?" The mother of the family begged him to have
them removed, "or else they would rot together." Crowley produced the
tea and sugar, but they said it was of no use to them, as they had nowhere
to light a fire. What they wanted, they said, was water: they had placed a
jug to catch the droppings from the roof but would not have enough even
for that night. The next day Donovan obtained the consent of the Poor
Law guardians to have his patients removed to the nearby fever hospital,
where their condition later improved.[7]

The good doctor's concern seems prompted, in equal measure, by the
physical condition of these unfortunate people and by the fact that they
have, quite literally, sought refuge in the abode of the dead. Their gesture
is at once a shocking category mistake and grimly prophetic of a more general encroachment of the dead upon the domain of the living. The cemetery is no longer a zone of seclusion, where the deceased slumber peacefully
beneath the solicitous eye of the night watchman, as in the days "when
more respect was paid to the dead than is at present the case." Instead, the
living and the dead now find themselves thrown together, as the accumulation of corpses overflows society's capacity for their orderly disposal, and

as survivors ejected from the company of the living are driven by desperation to seek lodging amid the decomposing remains of their less fortunate fellows.

Mahony too had remarked on the frequency with which the dead were left to lie alongside the living, often for several days at a stretch before the bodies were removed for burial. On first arriving in Bridgetown, Skibbereen, he wrote, "I saw the dying, the living and the dead, lying indiscriminately upon the same floor, without anything between them and the cold earth, save a few miserable rags upon them."[8] This tardiness in the disposal of bodies seemed to point to something more than the overstretching of hospital and burial facilities. It was as though, given the apparent ubiquity of death, it had ceased to be worth distinguishing too clearly between the living, the dead, and those hastening toward death.

Even more disturbing was the tendency of those still living to assume the appearance of the dead. Visiting Skibbereen on December 15, 1846, the Cork magistrate, Nicholas Cummins, found himself surrounded by some two hundred "phantoms," famished people clamoring for assistance, whose "demoniac yells" reverberated in his ears and whose appearance was that of "frightful specters."[9] The transformations effected by hunger here are both physical and ontological. The starving body, even as its fleshly substance dwindles, becomes an object charged with a disconcerting otherness. Victims of hunger resemble not the peacefully slumbering dead, but the unquiet souls referred to by Hertz. Hesitating between two counterpoised worlds, these walking dead acquire the maledictory force of matter out of place. Yet it is matter charged, at the same time, with an uncanny supplement of intangible and unformulable presences, like the elusive force of *tir* associated with burial sites and death places. The spectral victims of hunger who crowd about Cummins as he distributes bread display in their persons every symptom of physical decline and imminent dissolution, but they continue to cling to life with a tenacity bordering on unearthly frenzy. Their "demoniac yells" disturb the onlooker not only because they appear to represent the irruption of death into life, but also because they call into question the very possibility of maintaining such a distinction. If the dead are at liberty to walk the earth, then perhaps the living themselves are no more than specters, already dead or consigned to a lingering death in life.

"With Death Looking Out of Their Eyes"

Such a possibility seems greatly to have troubled Alexander Somerville, as he traveled Ireland's west coast during the winter and spring of 1847, on behalf of the *Manchester Examiner*. Held up in Limerick by a snowstorm, Somerville took stock of what he had seen to date on his journey:

the ghastly faces, hollow and shrunken, which I have seen, with death looking out of their eyes . . . the masses of population amongst whom I have travelled through Tipperary and part of this county, sinking from health to sickness, from life to death—not yet dead, but even more terrible to look upon than if they were dead . . . living, but with death and his attendants in possession of the tenement, and keeping possession until the indwelling spirit of the clay is ejected, thrown out, out at the windows where it has already been struggling to stay within, and glaring horribly upon the passer-by.[10]

Physically transformed by extreme hunger, the people described here seem to have been already claimed by death, their countenances assuming an other-than-human appearance, as though possessed by a malign spirit that has displaced the victim's everyday self. Traveling north, Somerville continued to encounter a population of animated corpses. Arriving in Strokestown, County Roscommon (the setting for the present-day Famine Museum), on February 26, he reported that "The people are going about, those who can go about, with hollow cheeks and glazed eyes, as if they had risen from their coffins to stare at one another." In the course of his wanderings, he was accosted by a starving woman, begging for food, not for herself but for her child, "for it is dying, and it does not die." Of the woman and her child, he remarked "They were literally skin and bone, with very little life in either of them, and no food. And they were but fractions of a population wandering to and from a fertile land which they are not allowed to cultivate."[11] Here, the otherness imparted to the body of the famine victim becomes an index of material dispossession, specifically of the landlordly indifference, which, as Somerville never tired of pointing out, allowed people to go hungry in the midst of what might otherwise have been richly productive agricultural land. The inhabitants of Strokestown, it is suggested, have been rendered strangers in the landscape of their birth.

Traveling onward to Newcastle West, County Limerick, at the end of March, Somerville was confronted by another such spectacle as he toured the smallholdings on an adjacent hillside:

A man called Thomas Killaheel and two small children, boy and girl, were digging out stubble. He held two cows' grass [a measure of land, its extent varying according to quality, on which the rent was £3, 10s per annum] under Mr. Lake. He had only two pecks of oats for seed. This man was tall: his children were tall for their age; all three looked like specters with spades in their hands. I have seen other such sights, but none worse. Their purpose was to dig for life, but they looked as if they were breaking ground for their own burial, as if a very shallow grave would serve them, they were so thin.[12]

From Thomas Killaheel's farm, Somerville proceeded to the top of a nearby hill, to get a view of the turf bogs of the plain of Limerick, traversed by the river Shannon below. After some minutes, he noticed that the "phantom farmer" had followed him—"He said nothing, but looked—oh! such looks and such thin jaws!" Somerville's attention was drawn by his guide, Michael Hearn (the son of another local farming family), to the iron and coal deposits located a mile away, popularly supposed to stretch for some 50 miles through the hilly country. Turning to survey these "mountains of treasure," Somerville again caught sight of the "lean hungry man," who seemed to catch at his words when he observed that a mountain of iron was worth more than a mountain of gold. Surely, the man objected, gold would buy more bread than an equivalent quantity of iron would. Somerville replied that the iron would make better spades and plows to till the ground and make corn grow, "and corn must grow and bread be made from it before it can be purchased with gold." Thomas Killaheel made no reply, but his facial expression etched itself upon Somerville's memory:

The lean man looked as if his spirit, starved in his own thin flesh, would leave him and take up its abode with me—I even felt it going through me as if looking into the innermost parts of my body for food to eat and for seed oats. It moved through the veins with the blood, and finding no seed oats there, nor food, searched through every pocket to the bottom, and returned again and searched the flesh and blood to the very heart; the poor man all the while gazing upon me to see what the lean spirit might find; and it searched the more keenly that he spoke not a word.[13]

The gaze of the starving man assails his interlocutor, traversing the distance between them and probing the innermost recesses of the latter's being in search of nourishment. Why should the sight of another's suffering produce such an effect? Is it (as Slavoj Žižek has suggested in another context) because the possibility of viewing hunger as a spectacle, to be regarded from a safe distance, is here called into question?[14] The invasive, interrogatory gaze of the hungry person threatens to implicate the observer in the scene observed to the point where the boundaries of subject and object, self and other, are effaced. The hungry gaze threatens evisceration, annihilation, death. There is surely much to be learned here concerning the emotive impact of hunger as a spectacle, both in mid-nineteenth-century Ireland and in a contemporary context where audiences in Europe and North America have become accustomed to encountering media images of starvation and sickness in what was once called the third world. The gift (of money, food, or medical supplies) might be seen to take on, at least in part, a defensive function, being called forth by a perceived threat to the integrity of the self, yet carrying with it always the risk of an expenditure defying containment.

For contemporary observers in the employ of the British government, scenes of mass starvation presented their own dangers. On December 23, 1846, Captain Wynne, an inspecting officer for the commissariat, visited Clare Abbey. The following evening, he sat down to write two letters, substantially the same, one to Colonel Jones of the Board of Works, and one to Trevelyan, urging that the public works in the district (which had previously been closed on his own order, after an attack on one of his overseers) be reopened, as they were on December 28:

I ventured into the parish this day to ascertain the condition of the inhabitants, and altho' a man not easily moved, I confess myself unmanned by the intensity and extent of the suffering I witnessed more especially among the women and little children, crowds of whom were to be seen scattered over the turnip fields like a flock of vanishing crows, devouring the raw turnips, the mothers half naked, shivering in the snow and sleet, uttering exclamations of despair while their children were screaming with hunger. I am a match for anything else I may meet with here, but this I cannot stand. When may we resume the works? Nothing but dire necessity would make me advocate this step, feeling as I do that I thereby throw away the only armour we possess against the bullet of the assassin, but it cannot be helped.[15]

Captain Wynne's plea for the reopening of the works associates the spectacle of hunger both with the problematic of gender and with the need of governmental agencies to maintain social control (or at least the illusion of control). Although, as he tells us, habitually impervious to scenes of human suffering, the captain finds himself "unmanned" by the sight of these starving, half-naked women, and thus prey to emotions deemed incompatible with his public role. He acknowledges that the rationing or withholding of relief is a measure necessary to guard against the threat of insurrectionary violence, yet the immediacy of the scene by which he is confronted makes it necessary, he writes, to set aside such considerations. More might be said about the contrast implied in Wynne's account between the imperative to accede at once to the entreaties of the starving, and the forward-looking parsimony decreed by official relief policy. For the present, however, I wish to inquire further into the poetics and politics of eyewitnessing, as these were implicated both in the shaping and implementation of relief policy, and in the arguments of its critics.

It was the perceived likelihood of excessive or inappropriate subjective involvement by those entrusted with the administration of relief at the local level that made their judgment suspect, in the view of the *Thirteenth Annual Report of the Poor Law Commissioners*, published in 1847. The increasing pressure on workhouses during the final months of 1846 had led Cork and some other unions to resort to "outdoor relief," dispensing food on the premises to people not admitted as inmates. The commissioners criticized this practice on the grounds that the resources available to the unions were not sufficient to support such a program, and, in the case of Cashel, County Tipperary, an order was issued forbidding its continuance. In other cases, "remonstrances" were considered sufficient. The commissioners also regretted that local boards of guardians were, in their view, too ready to admit new inmates, thus contributing to overcrowding and the consequent spread of fever and dysentery and making it impossible to separate the sick from the healthy—"every person admitted is a patient":

That which we believe to be the right course, under such trying circumstances, is the course least in accordance with the feelings of the parties locally conducting the administration of relief;—eye-witnesses of the distress endured, they find it difficult, almost impossible, to resist the immediate impulse of the desire to relieve the individual cases brought before them; thus applicant after applicant is admitted to the workhouse by the Guardians, long after the limit of sanitary safety has been reached.[16]

The message to those concerned with the implementation of relief is clear: governmental directives are to be adhered to by the letter as the only alternative to administrative chaos. According to the authors of the report, it is the policy makers in Westminster and Whitehall who, armed with the principles of economic reason, are best able to determine the correct course of action. In the view of the editors of the *Nation*, it was precisely the "objectivity" called for by the commissioners that was the problem. In response to the queen's speech at the opening of Parliament, which had invited the House of Commons to take just such a "dispassionate" view of Ireland, there appeared the following in the edition of January 23, 1847: "Yes; from that distance they take a dispassionate survey;—there are no verdicts of Death from Starvation ringing in their ears there; no wasted corpses searing their eyeballs, and grinning frightfully through their dreams there. Before Heaven, they disbelieve all this, and have taken care not to admit the horrid tale."[17]

The neat formulations of civil servants and parliamentarians, it is argued, are possible only for those ensconced at a comfortable distance from events in Ireland. Their detachment is seen to constitute a form of self-deception, shielding them from the actuality of mass starvation. If such accounts are examined carefully, however, it becomes apparent that more is at stake than a debate over the merits and efficacy of political economy as a solution to Ireland's problems. Both the commissioners' report and the *Nation* editorial share a sense of the uncanny power exerted upon the viewer by the spectacle of hunger: in the one case, a power to disarm the imperatives of economic prudence, eliciting displays of feckless and ill-advised generosity, and in the other to dispel the observer's sense of distance from the scene he or she beholds. It is as though the sight of a starving person is felt to preclude a merely spectatorial response—as though the viewer is, inexorably, drawn out of his or her assumed detachment and impelled, willingly or otherwise, to become a part of or an actor in the scene that unfolds. Like Artaud's ritualized Theatre of Cruelty, with its violence and stylized physicality, this is a spectacle that refuses to allow the spectator the luxury of merely looking. Terror, compassion, loss of self, and the compulsion to give are here strikingly interwoven. The figure of the starving other, encountered face to face, challenges the observer's own sense of self by appearing to demand an impossible gift, requiring the disbursement not only of one's money or goods, but of one's very being.

It is significant too that such a demand should emanate from figures so often identified as specters or the walking dead. The specter's wordless reproach is addressed from a past that is not fully past (or a future in the process of becoming), which the presumed immediacy of the present can never entirely foreclose. It is necessary to distinguish two distinct but interdependent temporalities at work here. The echoic reverberation of the before-time of the specter bespeaks an encounter not only with the past understood in chronological terms (that is, with bygone events and persons), but also with that which resists assimilation to such a scheme of sequentially ordered presents. The specter can thus be seen to give fleeting substance to an unnameable, unsymbolizable residue, the inexpressible content of a founding repression that both fractures and enables the constitution of the human subject as a historical being, an actor in linear time. The ground from which the specter emerges is that both of the collective past and of prehistory.

For Benjamin, *prehistory* referred to the fantasy of primordial undifferentiation, by turns threatening and potentially emancipatory, that he perceived haunting the commodity culture of nineteenth- and twentieth-century Europe. Behind the provisional fixity of social forms lurked a vision of originary formlessness, recalling in equal measure Bachofen's "swamp world" of primitive promiscuity and Horkheimer and Adorno's "prehistory of subjectivity," a notion invoking both the earliest stages of childhood, prior to the emergence of a stable and fully differentiated ego, and the world of "primitive" magic, in which the magician-performer's mimetic entanglements with animate nature were understood as refracting subjectivity into multiple projections and identifications.[18]

Such a hypothetical Ur-stage in the constitution both of the social world and of the human subject (at least in its modern western configuration) should not be considered a simple chronological beginning. Rather (as Kafka's stories, according to Benjamin's reading, affirm), it is to be thought of as belonging, simultaneously, to the orders of synchrony and diachrony, present and origin, insofar as it perpetually founds and implicates the subjectivity formed in relation to it.[19] The prehistoric realm can be thought of as marking the human subject with an insuperable alterity, insofar as subjectivity is understood to emerge out of that which precedes or exceeds its own determinations. Such an opening to a notional outside is, however, one that modern regimes of subjectivity and modern philosophies of the subject have often sought to relegate to a supposedly superseded "premodern" past. In the case of nineteenth-century Ireland, the discipline of political economy played a central role in the project of creating such a new class of "modernized" Irish subjects, schooled in habits of moderation and the disciplined pursuit of rational self-interest. The ethos of thrift, hard work, and economic prudence, proclaimed and disseminated through bodies such as the Dublin Statistical and Social Inquiry Society, was persistently invoked in contradistinction to a receding past of superstition and irrationalism, destined to be displaced by the inexorable momentum of progress. Nonetheless, as contemporary descriptions of Ireland demonstrate, the new ethos of economic reason remained conceptually and practically entangled with its own posited antecedents. The present of industrial progress and capitalist development was haunted by an image of the past that remained stubbornly contemporaneous, whether in the guise of the seemingly uncontainable (and potentially insurrectionary) masses of the Irish poor, or, no less disturbingly, as the descriptions of Cummins, Somerville, and others attest, through the publicly disseminated iconography of the famished body.

If the specter or revenant provides an apt figure for the modern subject's failure to foreclose alterity and for the anxieties arising out of that failure, it should be emphasized that the threat of loss and self-evisceration that stirs so many contemporary descriptions of famine victims is more than an allegory of the travails of modern thought. The body of the famine victim is able to mobilize contradictory impulses of horror and fascination, as an other who threatens to invade and take possession of the observer's self, in part by virtue of its ineffaceable physicality. One should be wary, however, of attributing the power of these stories and images to the simple fact of embodiment, as though the affective sting were sufficiently explained by the fleshly vehicle. Indeed, the nature and meaning of the physical are very much at issue here. Famine bodies evince a materiality at once grossly substantial and elusively phantasmal, evoking a materialism that, far from offering a refuge of certitude, threatens instead to dissolve the familiar boundaries between self and world.

"So Changed as Not to Be Recognized"

The palpable enigma posed by the starving body is perhaps most disturbingly manifested in the imagery of physical transfiguration that recurs in contemporary descriptions of the starving. A report from the *Freeman's Journal* from the closing months of 1846 describes the fate of the destitute in Mayo during the winter of that year: "Some are so changed by want as not to be recognised by their friends—their looks wolfish and glaring as madmen, without clothes or food of any kind, they roam about in search of food until death seals their misery."[20]

For the writer, these naked wanderers, soon, presumably, to join the ranks of roadside corpses, are barely recognizable as human, bereft of clothing and other trappings, their appearance altered to the point where they resemble nothing so much as ravenous animals. These motifs, so widespread in contemporary descriptions, were to become part of an established iconography of hunger. The same imagery would later be deployed more self-consciously in William Carleton's story "Fair Gurtha: or the Hungry Grass: A Legend of the Dumb Hill" (published in the *Dublin University Magazine* in April 1856). Carleton tells the story of a miser's proposed marriage to a generous young girl, which is prevented by his falling victim to hungry grass.[21] The following passage describes the miser, or "Man of Hunger" in his first encounter with the character of Mat Magennis:

He was above the middle size, but so emaciated, whether by great age or protracted hunger it was difficult to say, that Magennis would scarcely believe him to be possessed of fleshly substance. It is true he was clothed in grey garments, but were it not for that circumstance, honest Mat would have looked upon him as something not far removed from the very shadow of a skeleton. As it was, the dress that enveloped him displayed the fearful anatomical structure of his limbs and ribs as clearly as if it had been transparent. His skin was drawn so close to the bones of his face, the structure of the cheekbones was so completely revealed, and rose so attenuated, that Mat, after he had surveyed him, looked upon the country and the objects around him, and paused to listen to the various sounds we have described, before he could feel that he was not in a dream. If there was any one feature, however, about him more startling than another, it was the vague and extraordinary expression of his eyes. His lips, if they could be called so, were a little drawn back, as if by suffering, and displayed a set of white, charnel-like teeth, that were long and sharp; but the strange light which emanated from his eyes seemed to proceed from a wolfish fire within, such as is said to appear in the eyes of an animal when in a state of mild but debilitating famine.[22]

Himself the product of a (relatively prosperous) farming background and the author of a novel, *The Black Prophet*, published in 1846 (in eight parts, also in the *Dublin University Magazine*), dealing with earlier crop failures in 1817 and 1822, Carleton draws on many commonplaces to be found in reports of the famine years.[23] The acutely observed physicality of the starving man—the tautness of the skin, the bone structure visible even through his clothes—rather than giving substance to the description, has the effect of calling into question the reality of the figure described. The man is so starkly a creature of skin and bone that his presence becomes uncertain and ghostlike—"the very shadow of a skeleton." What remains is the "wolfish fire" within, a half-concealed animal presence glaring from the eyes and animating the shrunken human frame.

Bodies Swollen to Twice Their Natural Size

Wraithlike emaciation was not the only, or even the most disconcerting, characteristic of famine bodies. In contemporary sources, it is often described as accompanied by the condition known popularly as *famine dropsy* (and to medical science as *hunger edema*), in which the limbs and body swelled, often to several times their normal size.[24] Elihu Burritt, an American philanthropist and amateur scholar, visiting Skibbereen in February 1847, recalled seeing men employed on the public works, their bodies swollen to twice their natural size; a boy of twelve, his body three times its normal size, bursting his garments; and the body of a baby of two, swollen (allegedly) to the size of that of an adult, although the arms remained "like pipe stems." In nearby Schull, according to a report compiled in the same month, although three-quarters of the population were reduced to "skeletons," swelling of the limbs was "universal."[25]

The starving body becomes the paradoxical locus of simultaneous diminution and expansion, as though flaunting the prodigality of its physical being even as the life of the victim ebbs and dwindles. The flesh assumes a monstrous autonomy, seemingly indifferent to the imminent threat of personal extinction. In the very moment of dissolution it appears capable of disgorging itself in a defiant assertion of becoming. Similar descriptions are to be found among the accounts collected in the 1940s by the Irish Folklore Commission: an itinerant beggar woman, having asked permission to boil a turnip and a handful of meal in a house, proceeds to vomit what she has eaten before she expires; a worker on a relief scheme, arriving with his own breakfast of yellow meal, "drank it, swelled up and died."[26] Such images recall Bakhtin's celebrated account of the grotesque image of the body, as propagated in medieval and Renaissance art and literature. Associated with periods of social upheaval and uncertainty, grotesque imagery evokes a body "in the act of becoming," never finished or completed, "it is continually built, created and builds another body."[27] The grotesque bespeaks an interest in protuberances and cavities, points where the body breaks its confines and conjoins itself with other bodies and the outside world, and with the activities of feasting and devouring, followed by shitting and vomiting, correspondingly prodigious regurgitations of what has been consumed. Bakhtin suggests that the grotesque body can be regarded as immortal, partaking of a primordial life force antecedent to personhood and enduring beyond the death of the individual.

The logic of the specter, as outlined by Derrida, also pertains here. Famine bodies puncture linear time in a manner analogous to the returning dead, evoking the irruption into the present of all that the present seeks to exclude, converting privation and scarcity into excess by conjuring the ebb and flow of a life anterior and indifferent to personal mortality. The temporality of famine bodies, like that of the grotesque in Bakhtin's recounting, is recursive rather than linear-historical, challenging the irreversibility of cause and effect through the fleeting and shocking reemergence of forgotten or repressed contents.

This recursiveness finds one of its most unsettling expressions in descriptions of starving children. Visiting Belmullet, County Mayo, on March 16, 1847, William Bennett declared himself most moved by the plight of the children he encountered there, many of them too weak to stand, their limbs attenuated, except where "frightful swellings" had taken the place of emaciation. Along with these familiar symptoms of extreme hunger, the children exhibited an alarming loss of childlike characteristics: "Every infantile expression had entirely departed; and in some, reason and intelligence had evidently flown."[28]

On November 30, 1846, William Forster, James Hack Tuke, and Joseph Crosfield of the Society of Friends carried out an investigation of the workhouse at Carrick-on-Shannon, County Leitrim. More than a hundred people, they reported, were waiting outside for thirty vacancies. Among them were mothers begging that two or three of their six or seven children be taken in, as it was impossible to feed them on 8 or 10 pence a day. The children, Forster recalled, were "like skeletons," their limbs emaciated, their features sharpened by hunger to the degree that expression of infancy were replaced by "the anxious look of premature old age."[29] The appearance of premature ageing, combined with skeletal attenuation of the limbs and body, points to a disturbance of chronology, conjoining death with life, infancy with senescence. The faces and bodies of these children seem to mark them out as already belonging to the realm of the dead.

Equally disturbing was the growth of hair on the faces of starving children, while the hair on their heads in many cases fell out. According to a report from County Clare (1847), hair was to be found on the children's heads only in patches, but over their foreheads and temples, "a thick sort of downy hair grows."[30] This caused them, it was often remarked, to take on the appearance of wizened chimpanzees. According to Richard Webb, starving children looked "like monkeys"—presumably as a result of hair on their faces.[31] Such a demotion to a prehuman rung on the evolutionary ladder accords both with the widespread portrayal of famine victims as creatures reduced to pure appetite, bereft of conscience or reason, and with the equally familiar "simianizing" of the Irish Celt in British cartoons and caricatures.[32] More generally, it points to the famished body's radical estrangement from the everyday social world, such that its burgeoning alterity can no longer be adequately subsumed either within derogatory stereotypes or within the lexicon of medical science, with its proffered etiologies of death and disease. Instead, what is evoked in these images is at once topical and primordial, suggesting the mapping of specific, historically constituted differentiations (including class, gender, and racial hierarchies) onto a retroactively configured scene of originary bipartitioning, the traces of which continue to mark and compromise the domain of independent subjecthood. Famine bodies fracture the spectator's experiential present by gesturing backward and downward to the dark interiority of personal and collective prehistories.

Bakhtin reminds us that the grotesque body, with its cavities and protuberances, its protean transmutations and endless self-regenerations, has been linked in popular imagination to the depths of the earth, which perform a similar work of ingestion and regurgitation, converting death and decay into new life. These chthonian recesses have found their literary and pictorial analogue in the figure of the underworld. Accessed through caves and other apertures in the earth's surface, corresponding to the body's external orifices (to which they are often likened in literature and folklore), the underworld serves too as a repository for images of the historical past. During the Christian Middle Ages, the popular iconography of hell came to subsume elements of bygone paganism, with pre-Christian deities reassigned to the role of devils and tormentors of damned souls.[33] In the process, however, these interdicted images of defeated evil came to be invested with significances unintended by proponents of religious orthodoxy. Christian eschatology was modified by the folkloric vision of the "gay underworld," combining elements of popular belief and superseded paganism, in which the earth's depths were recast as a source of newness and fecundity, the terror inspired by the pagan dead giving way to humor and ribaldry.[34] The duality evidenced in portrayals of the underworld corresponds to the comic-transgressive potentialities of the grotesque body, linking together life and death, dissolution and the promise of rebirth. It testifies to the covert dependence of the dominant order on that which it seeks to exclude. The subterranean realm functions as society's antiself, a spectral double, granted periodic release in the form festivals and popular celebrations (the topos of "the world upside down"), but threatening always to overrun the bounds assigned to it. Taussig has suggested that the underworld occupies a privileged place among cultural articulations of the "space of death," a zone of radical otherness on the far side of sociality and signification, identified variously with the supernatural, with death, putrefaction, regeneration, transformation, and vision.[35] If all of these terms must be understood as so many placeholders, standing in for a content that eludes discursive formulation, they nonetheless represent in their sequential unfolding an unacknowledged history of what has been called the "western tradition" in its successive engagements with the problematic of alterity: European Christianity's protracted struggles against paganism and popular heterodoxy; the travails of conquest and colonization (in Europe and beyond), and the still-unfolding global drama of modernization, in which industrialism, capitalist production, and the ethos of economic and scientific reason attempt to subsume pockets of seeming backwardness in the name of freedom and progress. As the assigned receptacle for all that has been superseded or discarded, the space of death, with its shifting, historically contingent valences, nurtures the shadowy counterpart to these triumphalist narratives, the intransigencies and stubborn singularities on which their pretensions to irreversibility and universality trip and stumble.

In the image repertoire of the famine years, this fecund underground is figured both as the earth, from which the spectral victims of hunger appear to have risen (and to which their bodies will eventually be consigned), and, more particularly, as the burial pit or mass grave, into which bodies were piled indiscriminately, the living alongside the dead and dying, their cries and writhings stifled beneath shovel loads of soil and quicklime. For a few fortunate individuals, however, this place of premature interment could also be one of rebirth—individuals like Tom Gearins, who traversed the realm of death and returned, physically marked by their experiences, a reminder to the living. To grasp the duality here imputed to the death-space of the mass grave, it must be appreciated that the underworld into which Tom Gearins descended was already densely populated with images of the superseded past, including both the Tuatha Dé Danaan and their latter-day counterparts, the fairies (*sí*), themselves frequently identified with the dead of past generations. To these can be added the pervasive rhetoric of primitivism and animality that has informed so many English depictions of the Irish, from the twelfth-century account of Gerald of Wales, in which the native Irish are described as a *gens silvestris*—a people of the woods, lacking civility and stable institutions—to the Quaker James Tuke, in equal measure shocked and bemused by the troglodytic inhabitants of northwest Erris, with their makeshift dwellings cut into the side of the bog.[36] The earth into which the bodies of famine victims were cast had already absorbed numerous histories of dispossession and displacement. We are confronted here not with an instance of the tenacity of "tradition," but with an image of the collective past that is fluid, metamorphic, constantly shifting. The phantasmagoria of death enacted in and around the mass grave belongs as much to the mythology of modernity as to the world of peasant belief that William Wilde and others thought was being expunged before their eyes.

Beyond these imputed historical significances, what remains most troubling about the figure of the specter is its insurmountable yet unquantifiable materiality.[37] Like the underworld with which it is popularly associated, the disruptive force of the specter appears to depend on the bringing together of specific historical contents with a vision of insurrectionary somaticity at seeming odds with canonical formations of historical knowledge. It is from this juxtaposition that much of the specter's power to disconcert can be seen to derive. A materialism of the specter, if one were to entertain such a notion, would be bound to acknowledge that the subject-agent of historical cognition, as propounded in modern philosophies of knowledge and experience, is founded on the attempted sublation of a material-organic substratum that resists or exceeds its own operations. Like the Freudian *Unheimlich*, the specter might then appear as a secret familiar, the transfigured remnant of a founding repression, affording a glimpse of the protean matter (formless, shifting, conjoining life and death, dissolution and rebirth) from which both historical agency and the possibility of historical understanding are distilled.

Hungry Ghosts and Hungry Women

On December 15, 1849, the *Illustrated London News* published a description of the present state of the village of Moveen, in the Union of Kilrush, County Clare. The article forms part of a series describing the consequences of the Poor Law Extension Act of 1847, which had sought to secure local, rather than national, funding for relief through a poor rate levied on landed property. The result, predictably in the view of the correspondent, had been an increase in the number of evictions as landlords hastened to rid themselves of responsibility for destitute tenants. In the Kilrush Union, a series of evictions during the preceding year had made more than sixteen thousand people homeless in the district. The correspondent describes the now-abandoned village, its houses standing roofless, empty shells exposed to wind and rain, resembling "the tombs of a departed race, rather than the abodes of yet living people." The remaining population are described as eking out a ghostlike existence amid the ruins of their former dwellings—"one beholds only sunken frames covered with flesh—crawling skeletons who appear to have risen from their graves, and are ready to return, frightened to that abode." As for their clothing, "they have little other covering than that nature has bestowed upon the human being."[1] The report does not particularize these wraithlike wanderers, but it goes on to relate the story of one Bridget O'Donnell, evicted from her home the previous November because her husband owed rent. She was, by her own account, seven months pregnant and in a fever when the bailiffs arrived to tumble her house. Ignoring her protests, they had proceeded to demolish the house around her, until she was rescued by two neighbors and carried out to a nearby cabin, where a priest and doctor attended her. Eight days later, her child was born dead. Another of her children, a thirteen-year-old boy, had died from hunger during the weeks that she lay sick. She had nothing for her remaining children to eat, a supply of corn and oats having been taken away and sold by the landlord's men. The accompanying illustration shows a young woman, probably aged between twenty and thirty, framed by her two children, both girls, their emaciated forms clad only in an assortment of filthy rags.[2]

The juxtaposition of text and image is notable given the preceding description of Moveen as a land of the dead, of ruined buildings now inhabited only by a population of specters. Against this backdrop, the survivors who continue to haunt this denuded landscape appear suddenly out of place amid the remains of their former habitations. According to the correspondent, their appearance suggests that they belong, properly, among the dead, but like other similarly described victims of the famine, they linger disquietingly into a present that seems unwilling or unable to accommodate them.

It is significant that a female image, specifically an image of motherhood, should have been chosen to exemplify this condition. Bridget O'Donnell, along with her children, appears both as a contemporary personification of hunger and destitution, and as an image of the past caught in the moment of its eclipse—in this case, one of the many west of Ireland rural communities for which the 1840s were to sound a death knell. As such, she embodies not only historical loss but also the spectral persistence of the vanished past, its continuing capacity to trouble the present in the guise of an untimely revenant.

Ireland as Woman

The story of Bridget O'Donnell anticipates the interfolding of national past and political present that also defines the work of the Irish Folklore Commission and its archive. Like the archive, it evokes a scene dense with the echoes of other, earlier times and places, in this case a host of literary and mythological female figures, spanning the intervening centuries from the period of earliest settlement to the present. The cooptation of feminine images as political icons of nationhood is, of course, a phenomenon extending far beyond the Irish context.[3] Anne McClintock has written of the way in which such images function as intermediaries between the political present in which national claims are staked and the immemorial collective past to which formulations of nationhood and national community are obliged to appeal. Feminized images of nationhood are the point at which nation-state ideologies intersect with those of gender. They point to a powerful link between gender categories and the multiple temporalities of the modern nation-state, constituted as it is at the interface between the homogeneous, empty time of linearity and progress and archaic time of origin that it persistently reinvokes as a source of contemporary legitimacy.[4] In Ireland, antecedents of the gendered iconography of latter-day nationalisms are to be found in the earliest written sources. The earliest recorded identification of Ireland as a woman is afforded by the figure whom scholars have labeled the "sovereignty goddess" and who appears in early Irish myths and sagas as a personification of the land and the sometime supernatural consort of its male rulers. In the twelfth-century *Lebor Gabála Érenn* (Book of the Invasions of Ireland), the Sons of Mil, legendary forebears of the Irish, are met, following their arrival, by three female figures, identified as divine eponyms of the country—Banba, Fodla, and Erin. The poet-priest Amhairghin assures them that the country will take its name—*Éire*—from them, and they, in turn, prophesy that Ireland will belong to the Sons of Mil for all time. It is the role of the tripartite goddess not only to welcome a further wave of settlers (the Sons of Mil having been preceded by a succession of earlier invaders), but also to act as an intermediary both between the human and supernatural worlds, and between the nascent civilization of the Celts, shortly to enter upon the world-historical stage, and the unchronicled before-time of the land itself.[5]

Coexistent with the land, the sovereignty goddess appears as a figure through whom the transition from unreclaimed nature to culture is accomplished and narrated, a collectively construed symbol gesturing toward a past figured as antecedent to symbolization. Early Irish literature abounds in female figures with similarly strong supernatural associations, who become the partners or spouses of local rulers. These women are associated both with domestic prosperity and the successful cultivation of crops, and with the untamed fecundity of forest and wilderness. Marriage to the king often appears to be a means of harnessing the latter to the benefit of the former. In the story of "Mor of Munster" (Mor Muman, daughter of Aed Bennan, an early seventh-century king of Luachair in the province of Munster), the eponymous protagonist, identified with the province as the divine spouse of its kings, becomes deranged and wanders far from human habitations, until given hospitality by Fingen, son of Aed, the rightful king of Cashel. When he sleeps with her, she regains her senses and becomes his queen. Sometimes the transition from wilderness to domestic hearth is seen to involve also the woman's physical transformation from aged crone to youthful virgin, as in the story of "Niall and the Nine Hostages," where a hideous hag, guarding a well, offers water to the hero and his brothers in exchange for a kiss. Niall alone accepts, and both kisses and sleeps with her, whereupon she is transformed into a beautiful young woman, who identifies herself as the sovereignty of Ireland, and prophesies that his descendants will rule the land.[6]

At the same time, female figures could appear as harbingers of death, a role perpetuated by the banshee (or supernatural death messenger) of latter-day folk tradition.[7] Scholars have speculated that the "sovereignty goddess" may have been the recipient of blood sacrifices, specifically of a young man whose blood was allowed to sink into the ground and that, if not thus propitiated, as protectress of the land and its fertility, she was capable of causing barrenness or famine. She was credited too with bringing about the downfall of rulers who had misused their power, or failed to observe the ritual taboos (*gessa*) incumbent on the office of kingship, as in the story *Tógáil Brúidne Da Derga* (Taking of Da Derga's Hostel), dating from around 1100 in its earliest written version, where the death from supernaturally induced thirst of King Conaire is linked to the appearance at nightfall of two hags, who are subsequently admitted to the hostel in contravention of Conaire's *gessa*.[8]

In the centuries following the Anglo-Norman invasion of Ireland and the subsequent waves of English settlement during the sixteenth and seventeenth centuries, the association of female figures with death and sacrifice was to undergo a nativist transformation, as the revival of Ireland's fortunes was proclaimed to be dependent on the self-sacrifice of "her" native sons.[9] Personifications of Ireland in Irish-language writing of the seventeenth and eighteenth centuries, after the collapse of the medieval Gaelic order and the system of literary patronage that it sustained, recapitulate much of the imagery associated with the archaic figure of sovereignty.[10] Ireland might be depicted either as a vulnerable virgin (the *spéirbhean* or "sky woman"), ravished by the English invader, or as a lascivious hag (*meirdreach*), offering herself for the invader's pleasure. It was the former figure who provided the staple of the eighteenth-century poetic genre known as the *aisling* (vision), where Ireland, portrayed as a woman, was addressed under a variety of names—Erin, Fodla, Banba, Caitlín Ní Houlihan, Róisín Dubh. As developed by poets such as Aogán Ó Rathaille (c. 1675–1729), perhaps the best-known exponent of the genre, the *aisling* characteristically took the form of a vision in which the poet encountered a beautiful woman, subsequently revealed as a supernatural emissary, embodying the land and its misfortunes.[11] In Ó Rathaille's poem "*Mac an cheannaí*" (The Redeemer's Son) the woman is described as an *ainnir sheibh*, or "mild maiden," with green eyes and curled, thick hair. She appears initially as an erotic figure, her supernatural aspect being made manifest only when she reveals her name: "Éire." Ó Rathaille's "Gile na Gile" (Brightness Most Bright) underscores the association between such figures and the pre-Christian past, as the apparition, who remains nameless, takes flight when the poet invokes Christ and seeks refuge in a "rath," or fairy fort. In the same poem, the narrator voices his disgust at finding the fairy woman in the clutches of an ugly goblin, identified with the English invader, and announces that "'*s gan leigheas 'na goire go bhfillid na leoin tar toinn*" (and no remedy near till our lions come over the sea).[12]

The women who feature in these vision poems are both fleshly objects of male desire and emissaries of the supernatural, charged with connoting a nebulous ancestral past. Their role is invariably that of passive victims, exemplifications of the national plight, needing to be rescued through the rallying of Ireland's native sons. In this respect, it is, arguably, the poet who here usurps the role of active intermediary between the human and supernatural worlds, because it is he who experiences the vision and passes on its content in the form of verses. The limited autonomy accorded to female figures of sovereignty in early Irish literature is thus eclipsed by a wholly masculine ethos of poetic divination and heroic action. Nonetheless, the darker ambivalence of the sovereignty goddess is not altogether dispelled by this altered guise. The charms of the fairy woman can appear not only as a spur to action in Ireland's behalf, but also as a potential distraction from such a task. The poem "*Úr-chill an Chreagáin*" (The Churchyard of Creggan) by Ó Rathaille's younger contemporary Art Mac Cumhaigh, describes an encounter between the poet and an unnamed woman who attempts to lure him away to a paradise in the west: "go tír dheas na meala nach bhfuair Gallaibh ann cead réim go fóill, mar' bhfaigair aoibhneas ar halláibh do do mhealladh le siansa ceoil" (to that honey-sweet land untouched by alien rule, to find pleasure in halls there, wooed by strains of music). He declines, however, citing his responsibilities to his family and friends.[13] The temptation offered—that of abandoning the struggle against the invader and reverting to a state of passivity and idleness—highlights the contradictory associations condensed by the image of Ireland as woman. On the one hand, such an image appeals to a collective origin that founds and legitimates the national struggle; on the other, it suggests the potential collapse of historical agency back into vegetative torpor. Such a collapse is predicated precisely on the sexual allure of the female body as the mythified site of intersection both between "nature" and "culture," and between a nostalgically invoked image of the collective past and the prosaic reality of a disenchanted present.

In English-language nationalist poetry of the famine years, Ireland is most often personified as a mother, mourning her dead sons. The part of the invader is taken, variously, by famine itself, portrayed as an alien presence "stalking" the land (as in Ellen Fitzsimon's "Sonnet: 1849"), or by the cholera that often followed in its wake, which John Keegan, in his "To the Cholera" of 1848, likens to a malevolent spirit ("Sprite, goblin, demon, whatso'er thou art"), recalling the unsightly ravisher of Ó Rathaille's "Gile na Gile."[14] In Jeremiah O'Ryan's "Ireland's Lament," famine and disease are identified explicitly with English rule ("Such woes were never seen since Cromwell's horde/Spread famine o'er this isle"), continuing the work of spoilage and desecration carried out by earlier invaders.[15] The land itself, characteristically, remains passive in the face of this onslaught, which, in the anonymous "Thanatos, 1849," is attributed to an abnegation of responsibility on the part of her sons—"God sent a curse upon the land because her sons were slaves."[16]

Motherhood is also one of the characteristic guises under which women appear as victims in much famine poetry. Matthew Magrath's "One of Many" (first published in the *Irishman* in June 1849) describes a destitute woman in search of food, clutching her child. Having been evicted from her own home, she presents herself at "the rich man's house": "She stood at the door like a statue tall . . . Motionless; waiting, not asking for food." She is turned away empty-handed, and the poem ends by recounting her inevitable fate:

> On yonder pathway last nigh she died!
> Her infant lay close to her clay-cold breast;
> In a world to come they are both at rest.[17]

The mother described in Magrath's poem appears concerned primarily with procuring food for her child. Literary critic Margaret Kelleher has suggested, however, that the exemplary status assigned to female figures in such accounts is often fraught with ambivalence: "female images are chosen to represent famine's worst consequences, in characterizations ranging from heroic self-sacrifice to 'monstrous' perversions of 'Nature.'"[18] On the one hand, women are defined by their role as mothers, desperately solicitous for the plight of their children; on the other, they appear as beings of pure appetite, driven by hunger to perpetrate the most horrifying excesses. These two visions are shockingly conjoined in the anonymous "Thanatos, 1849." In an apocalyptic vision, replete with references to the Book of Revelation, the poet describes a mother driven by hunger to perpetrate the unthinkable:

> A mother's heart was marble-clad, her eye was fierce and wild—
> A hungry demon lurked therein, while gazing on her child.
> The mother-love was warm and true; the Want was long withstood—
> Strength failed at last: she gorged the flesh—the offspring of her blood.[19]

Instead of sacrificing herself for her child, this mother devours on its flesh to sustain her own life. Hunger, portrayed as a possessing demon, is shown effecting a monstrous inversion of the maternal relation. The body of the famished woman becomes the abode of an indwelling otherness, an asocial rapacity, bereft of conscience or reason. Nonetheless, the woman's recourse to endocannibalism is portrayed as the outcome of a protracted struggle between the physiological imperatives of hunger and a real and acknowledged sense of maternal affection. Her action is thus rendered as the calamitous collapse of the social into the biological. Moreover, it is precisely as a mother that she is subject to the temptation to which she finally succumbs.

A similar ambivalence is discernible both in contemporary journalism and the Irish Folklore Commission accounts, many of which describe the efforts made by bereaved mothers to secure a Christian burial for their deceased children.[20] At the same time, it is often women who personify the most extreme and dehumanizing effects of famine.[21] The consumption of unusual or inappropriate foods is a recurrent motif. An account from Killarney, County Kerry, describes a girl on the seashore, her hands worn from scraping the stones of the strand for shellfish. Having picked the strand bare, she is found lying dead.²² In Tullaghan, County Leitrim, an elderly man, one "J. McGrath," recalled that, as a boy, he saw a "little woman" brought into his family's house from the dunghill, where she had been found searching out and eating the juices of potato peel thrown out there. It was, he recalled, impossible to tell the woman's age, because her face, which had lost all its natural color, was "wrinkled and puckered and covered with white downy hair."²³ In the same district, a woman of similar age, Bessy Clarke, recounted a story concerning a "little stray girl" found eating the hen's share of pounded potatoes and meal. The narrator's mother offered her bread, but had difficulty getting her to accept, "as she thought the hen's share was very good, not having eaten any food for a week."²⁴

The identification of women with hunger in its starkest and most so-cially disruptive aspects is reiterated in official texts of the period. Historian Dympna McLoughlin has shown that able-bodied women represented the largest category of workhouse inmates in mid-nineteenth-century Ireland and formed one of the principal subject matters of workhouse minutes. Each of the thirty-two Poor Law Unions kept a minute book in which were recorded the number, age, and sex of the inmates, together with details of food distribution, punishments, and proposed emigration schemes, aimed at easing Ireland's supposed overpopulation. These accounts included fre-quent reference to the absence of a rooted domestic existence, the prepon-derance of foundlings, the practice of infanticide, and the abandonment of children. The minute books indicate that penalties for the latter offense were for the most part imposed against single mothers, many female work-house inmates having been deserted by their partners, or presenting them-selves as such to the board of guardians in order to gain admission. The women who appear in workhouse minutes are thus portrayed both as symptoms of social pathology, specifically the presumed impact of the po-tato failure on settled family life, and as themselves a potentially disruptive force in need of supervision, management, and regulation, a role in which, again, their status as mothers features preeminently.²⁵

A number of charitable initiatives were directed specifically at women. Roman Catholic religious orders, predominantly female religious, in addition to tending the sick in their homes, in hospitals, and in work-houses, instituted a variety of schemes aimed at the relief of female pau-pers, such as the lace-making industry set up by Presentation nuns in Youghal, County Cork, intended to provide employment for girls rendered destitute by the famine. Projects of this kind aimed to furnish women both with a means of livelihood and with a religious and moral education. A similar intention informed numerous schemes established by Protestant middle-class women, with a view to assisting (and where possible converting) the female Catholic poor. Among these was the Belfast Ladies Relief Association for Connaught, established in 1847 under the direction of the prominent temperance advocate the Reverend John Edgar, which had as its declared aim "to improve, by industry, the temporal condition of the poor females of Connaught and their spiritual [condition] by the truth of the Bible."[26] The association raised funds that it used to establish schools where skills such as knitting and needlework could be taught, alongside religious instruction, a combination intended to effect "a reformation of habits and character." Other such bodies included an association established in 1847 under the patronage of the Duchess of Leinster aimed at the encouragement of "habits of patient and persevering industry" among the "female peasantry" of Ireland by organizing sales of their embroidery, lacework, and knitting.[27] In each case, the social reformist aims of the project (whether Catholic or Protestant) were to be realized by subjecting poor women to a coordinated program of work and religious and moral instruction, with a view to inculcating in them the habits of thrift and industry deemed necessary for economic self-reliance, the implied hope being that henceforward these women might labor to produce commercially salable goods, rather than (as Malthus and others had feared) surplus children as a further drain on Ireland's overstretched subsistence base.

The disciplinary and reformist efforts of workhouses and charitable organizations furnish an illuminating counterpart to the folkloric and journalistic depiction of women as personifying the worst depredations of famine. The women described in these latter accounts seem to enact the effacement of human personhood by extreme hunger. Driven to desperation, they become animal-like, creatures of instinct and appetite. As the poem "Thanatos, 1849" makes clear, however, such descriptions cannot be readily dissociated from the iconography of virtuous and suffering motherhood deployed elsewhere, as though gender (and reproductive sexuality) were somehow the key to this physiologically induced shedding of the social self. This conflation of seemingly incongruous attributes parallels the association of women in nineteenth-century and earlier literature with images of Ireland's past. If, however, in both early Irish literature and later nationalist writings, the identification of women with the archaic presence of the land serves both to anchor the claims of collective belonging and to construct and authorize a contrastively defined (male) realm of historical agency and national struggle, portrayals of women in accounts of the famine suggest a more precarious relationship between the present and the recollected past. Conflating literary and mythological associations with the obtrusively physical presence of hunger, disease, and death, the women described in these accounts evoke an origin scene that is here credited with the disturbing capacity to return and disrupt the historical world to which it has given rise. The bodies of famished women here provide the material medium through which this interdicted past is enabled to manifest itself in a contemporary setting.

Figures of Distorted Life

According to Benjamin, "distortion" (*Entstellung*) was the form that persons and things assumed in oblivion. Benjamin's usage of the term accords with Freud's account of psychic disturbances and their physical manifestations insofar as repressed contents are understood to find expression in altered or transfigured guise, whether it be in the form of the dream, the symptom or, in the case of Benjamin, of the dialectical image, through which an as yet unredeemed mankind is afforded an intimation of its own forgotten past.[28] For Benjamin, it was the body as "first matter" that provided the principal medium of forgetting and distortion. In the essay "Franz Kafka" (1934), it is asserted that "the most forgotten alien land is one's own body." Benjamin describes Kafka's literary work as a "codex of gestures" in which physical forms appear distorted and self-alienated— Gregor Samsa, Odradek, the little hunchback. These misshapen creatures appear at once estranged from their origin, yet preserve within themselves the traces of the forgotten, albeit in a form that is no longer readily decipherable. In Benjamin's reading of Kafka, it is the body in distorted guise that occupies the site of intersection between the realm of the forgotten and the contemporary social world. Kafka's creations no longer belong, strictly speaking, to prehistory: they function rather as intermediaries, who have emerged into the domain of present consciousness, but who remain obscurely marked by what they have left behind.[29]

Prominent among these intermediary figures in Kafka's work discussed by Benjamin are the "whorelike women," like the barmaid whom K. encounters in *The Castle* and in whose embrace he experiences the feeling that "he had wandered farther than anyone had ever wandered before, to a place where even the air had nothing in common with his native air, where all this strangeness might choke one, yet a place so insanely enchanting that one could not help but go on and lose oneself further."[30] These women serve to mediate the passage between the present and an alluring, but usually inaccessible elsewhere. Sigrid Weigel sees them as evidence of Benjamin's abiding concern with female images.[31] The early essay "Conversation" (written in 1913, at the age of twenty-one) speculates on the relation between women and language. Benjamin asks, "How did Sappho and her friends speak?" and concludes that language could not have provided a suitable vehicle for their conversation: "The language of women was left uncreated. Speaking women are possessed by a language that is mad."[32] Instead (in a move that anticipates Julia Kristeva's positing of the semiotic and the symbolic as distinct but interrelated components of the signifying process), Benjamin situates women on the far side of discourse and verbal communication: "But the women are silent. In whatever direction they listen, the words are unspoken. They draw their bodies closer and caress one another. Their conversation has liberated itself from subject-matter and from language. . . . Silence and sexual pleasure—eternally divided in conversation—have become one."[33]

If, however, for Kristeva the subject's accession to language is contingent on the supercession of a preexisting relationship to the maternal body, the sapphic women in Benjamin's essay manifest an eroticism detached from the exigencies of reproduction: "The love of their bodies is without procreation, but their love is beautiful to behold."[34] Their closest counterparts in this respect are to be found not in the "whorelike women" of Kafka's fiction (who are identified with Bachofen's "hetaeric" stage, at which the roles of whore and mother have not yet become socially distinct), but with the figures of the prostitute (*Dirne*) and whore (*Hure*) who appear as "allegories of modernity" both in Benjamin's early essays and in his writings of the 1930s. "Berlin Chronicle" (1932) identifies the whores both as "guardians of the past" and as threshold dwellers, existing on the margins of the present and pointing the way to obscure and dimly remembered depths: "the places are countless in big cities where one stands on the threshold to nothingness, and the whores are as it were the *lares* of this cult of nothingness and stand in the doorways of the tenement blocks and on the more softly resounding asphalt of the railway platforms."[35]

Like the figures of distorted life who populate Kafka's literary works, the whores are cast as intermediaries between the prehistoric and the modern. Dwellers on the threshold, occupying the ambiguous, in-between spaces of doorways and railway platforms, they belong strictly speaking neither to the present nor to the realm of the forgotten. Benjamin's account is notable for assigning a specifically gendered character to this in-between status. Like other female figures discussed in his work, the whores are associated preeminently with the liminal and interstitial zones of the modern landscape. Themselves products of modernity, with its pervasive commodification of objects and bodies, their persons reveal at the same time the enigmatic traces of a past that is at once repressed and obscurely contemporaneous.

Guardians of the Threshold

The role of women as guardians of the past is vividly attested in one of the most widely read literary treatments of the famine years, Liam O'Flaherty's novel *Famine*, first published in 1937. O'Flaherty's recreation of the famine, set in a fictional rural community in the west of Ireland, is greatly concerned with the experiences of women as they are forced into theft, prostitution, and, in one instance, infanticide. At the same time, O'Flaherty's female characters are closely identified with those aspects of Ireland's past that the potato blight and its aftermath had, in the opinion of commentators like Wilde, swept away. Here, for instance, is the initial description of Kate Hernon, the "wise women of the valley":

Her kind was common enough in those days, a relic of old pagan times, when under Druidic law medicine had reached a high degree of perfection among us. Through centuries of degeneration, the ancient art had become a species of black magic among the people. And so this old woman cast spells, to lend importance to the herbal cures she concocted. Even so, she had talent and she was marvellously efficient as a midwife.[36]

The old woman, with her wrinkled countenance, her contorted features, and her fragments of half-forgotten lore, is an apt figure of distortion. It is through her person that the premodern and pre-Christian past is shown to manifest itself in altered and transfigured guise. O'Flaherty portrays her as a figure at once central and marginal to the life of the community. She lives alone, in a broken-down, single-roomed cabin on the edge of the village and she is feared by her neighbors as a witch, yet her expertise as a physician and midwife is regularly called upon. Her role is con-

cerned in particular with birth and death, with mediating the passage between counterpoised states. After the death from tuberculosis of Michael
Kilmartin, it is she who presides over the mourning:

Kate sprinkled ashes on the women's heads and began to recite the death chant.
She bent forward until she was almost prone, with her hands stretched towards the
fire. Her body, forward from the hips, then broke into movement, miming the tor-
tures of the human soul as it struggles to break free from its prison in the human
body. Her back twisted slowly, like an animal with a broken hip dragging itself
along the ground. Her hands and arms also twisted, as if she were kneading bread
in the air. She raised her shoulders as her hands reached outwards, urging forth the
spirit, miming the act of birth.

Her chant was mostly an inarticulate cadence, while the other women, rock-
ing themselves, now and again uttered prayers to God, begging him to accept the
departing soul. At times, the old woman's voice imitated the death rattle. At times
it rose to a wild shriek of triumph, during which she plunged forward, seized ashes
in her hands, and scattered them towards the open door, as was customary, to ex-
orcise evil spirits that barred the soul's flight to Paradise. At last she stood up
straight from her knees, paused for a moment as if listening and then thrust her
arms above her head, crying with great fervor:

"God of Glory! Have mercy now and open your gates."

"Amen!" said the other women.

Thereupon they all lay prone on the ground for some time with their heads
covered, until Kate Hernon rose and said in a normal tone:

"We'll go now and lay out the corpse."[37]

The passage is notable for the gendered division of labor that it depicts with regard to the social management of death: the women are responsible for keening and laying out the corpse, the men for organizing the
wake, including the laying in of a supply of *pocheen*, despite the likely misgivings of the parish priest: "He's God's messenger, but he has no right to
interfere with the customs of the people."[38] In contrast to the men's public
and organizational role, the women mourners present, behind closed
doors, a dramatic enactment of the soul's passage from the body, miming
its struggles to break free and its traumatic birth to a new life. Until the final prayer, the language throughout is one of gesture, rhythm, and cadence, of bodily innervations and wordless vocalizing that aspire to mimic
rather than describe these realities.[39] Allusions to the act of giving birth are
of paramount importance here, serving both to conjoin physical dissolution with the promise of new life and to confirm the quintessentially gendered character of the scene enacted. The women's role in consigning the

dead to an afterlife is shown to parallel their role in giving birth to future generations. Both experiences evoke the possibility of a preverbal idiom of physical enactment, an idiom that is associated specifically with moments of transition and transformation, where the boundary between worlds (past, present, or future) is crossed.

There is a remarkable convergence between O'Flaherty's fictional account and Commander Caffin's description (in a letter to the *Times*, Saturday, February 20, 1847) of conditions in Schull, County Cork, where, as master of Her Majesty's steam sloop *Scourge*, he had lately been engaged in discharging a cargo of meal. Caffin, who was accompanied on his tour of the locality by the Anglican rector of Schull, the Reverend Robert Traill, professed to be familiar with newspaper accounts of starvation and destitution in west Cork but admitted that he had assumed them to be "highly colored to attract sympathy." What he saw, however, defied exaggeration: "famine exists to a fearful degree, with all its horrors!"[40] Caffin found starvation and disease, along with diarrhea and swellings of the limbs and body, to be ubiquitous. In one cabin, he and Traill found a mother and daughter, the former emaciated, lying against the wall, the latter naked on some straw on the ground, "a most distressing object of misery." The daughter, marginally the stronger of the two, "writhed about and bared her limbs to show us her state of exhaustion . . . she cannot have survived until this time." In another cabin, its door stopped with dung, was an elderly woman, along with the corpse of another woman, who had been passing by and asked permission to stop and rest. She had died from exhaustion within the hour, and the body had remained for four days because there was no one to remove it. The surviving woman had blocked up the door in order that she too might die without being disturbed. Although she had some little money ("a trifle") by her, she had been unable to obtain food, because the village was 4 or 5 miles distant and she had not strength to stand. She had asked her neighbors' children to buy food for her, but they were too taken up with themselves: "She had nothing to eat in her miserable hole and I fear she must be dead ere this."[41]

Not the least disconcerting aspect of Caffin's account is his prophetic appeal to the future anterior. In each case, he professes himself convinced that those he describes must undoubtedly be dead by the time of writing, not to say of publication. The effect of the pronouncement is an uncanny one, consigning these figures to an intermediate zone between life and death. Caffin's description seeks to bring them before us in all their misery and degradation, yet we are told confidently that they must already have passed beyond the reach of these tribulations. The commander's certainty on this matter confers on the women the status of ghostly emanations, flickering emissaries from a beyond that language can no longer adequately describe. As ghosts, however, they show themselves at the same time to be indubitably creatures of flesh, blood, and bone. Indeed, as Caffin describes them, they appear at times to flaunt the physical depredations wrought by hunger, the daughter in the first cabin visited writhing and bearing her limbs as though miming her own condition for the benefit of himself and his companion.

Comparable scenes were witnessed by William Bennett, arriving in Belmullet, County Mayo, on March 16, 1847. On entering a cabin, he discerned, stretched in a dark corner, and scarcely visible because of the smoke and the rags covering them, the forms of three children, too weak to rise, their limbs emaciated and their voices gone, evidently in the final stages of starvation. Crouched over the embers of the fire was another figure "wild and all but naked, scarcely human in appearance," who likewise appeared not to notice the visitors. However, their attention was attracted by another occupant of the cabin, "a shrivelled old woman," lying on some straw, who proceeded to bare her limbs partially, to show how the skin hung loose from the bones. Above her, on "something like a ledge," lay a younger woman (perhaps the children's mother?) with sunken cheeks "who scarcely raised her eyes in answer to our inquiries, but pressed her hand upon her forehead with a look of unutterable anguish and despair."[42]

Like the mother and daughter encountered by Caffin and Traill and the ill-fated protagonist of Magrath's poem "One of Many," the two women eschew verbal communication, relying instead on performance and gesture to evoke their plight. The starving body becomes its own dramatic medium, the vehicle for an expression founded not on words but on corporeal display. Like Sappho and her friends in Benjamin's essay, the women appear dispossessed by language, relegated to an outside. It appears, however, that it is this very marginal status that confers a certain power to stir the imagination of the beholder, combining stark physicality with intimations of an elusive and ungraspable otherness.

As in the scenes of domestic privation witnessed at Schull by Caffin and Traill, it is by way of performance and mimicry that these seeming contraries are conjoined. Writing in 1933, Benjamin identified mimesis as an archaic compulsion, apparent in "former times," to "become and behave like something else," a capability seen as manifesting itself both in nature and in such forms of human practice as dance, ritual, music, and, more covertly, language. Significantly, Benjamin's discussion points both to the attenuated status of the mimetic faculty under the conditions of modernity (as compared to earlier ages when, he claims, humans were more fully aware of living in a mimetically charged universe) and to the possibility of its reemergence as a powerful, if frequently unrecognized presence in contemporary life.[43] It is here that female bodies and ideologies of gender can be seen once again to play a decisive role, linking what is understood as a primordial capacity spanning the human and natural worlds to specific sites and idioms of cultural memory. O'Flaherty's novel, like the descriptions of Caffin and Bennett, points to close association between women and the mimetic capability. The women who attend upon Michael Kilmartin's deathbed appear not only as custodians of tradition, but also as cultural analogues for a form of communication that eschews symbolization and the articulation of the linguistic sign as the absence of an object, the latter being, for psychoanalytic theorists like Kristeva, the precondition for the speaking subject's accession to the symbolic order. As such, the women's cries and gestures suggest the possibility that the past might cease to appear as an object of detached historical scrutiny and become instead a force to be viscerally reexperienced in the present.

Charitable Woman

If women feature widely as exemplifications of hunger and destitution in journalistic and literary sources, in much of the material recorded by the Irish Folklore Commission, they are just as likely to appear as figures of charity, bestowing food and sustenance on the starving. Often, such generosity is seen to bring magical recompense:

There is a story told of a charitable lady who lived in Killala who had a large plot of cabbage. People came from far and near for leaves and at last there came two poor old women and the charitable lady found that all the cabbage was gone. She was very disappointed and told the women to come again next day. On looking out her window the following morning, she was amazed to see a full plot of cabbage, with heads as plentiful as possible and each "as large as a two stone plot."[44]

Stories of this kind were recorded throughout rural Ireland.[45] They vary according to the identity of the "charitable woman" (frequently described as an ancestor of the speaker or of persons still living in the locality) and the nature of the food given. The protagonist, however, is always female. In some versions, the woman's seemingly unlimited generosity provokes the anger of her husband, who is pacified only through supernatural intervention:

I often heard that Mrs. Cremin the grandmother of Father John Cremin, Lissyconnor, Rathmore, was very good and full of charity to the poor and hungry in the famine days, she used always to boil a lot of potatoes for the meals and she never used the ones left over after dinner for either pig or cows or poultry but collected the best of them and put them near the fire in order to have a few of them for any hungry poor person who might chance to call to the house and the owners of it. . . . One day her husband, seeing so much cabbage being carried away went into the house to blame her for giving away all the cabbage and asked her did she want to leave themselves with nothing at all? She denied giving away so much of it and said she only gave a few heads to a few poor women who were starving. Come out now, said the man of the house, and show me what cabbage is left for ourselves. She went out fearing the worst and hoping he would not blame her too much for helping God's poor. When they reached the cabbage field great was her surprise to find that there was not a single head missing out of the whole field. There it was the whole field of cabbage without the loss of a single head but what was used for their own household. She was greatly surprised and fell on her knees to give thanks to God for thus miraculously saving her from her husband's censure and for acknowledging her kindness to the poor. Her husband was speechless with surprise as he knew well that she had been giving away the cabbage and refusing none for it. He was so impressed by this miracle that he told her to continue on the way she was doing and that he'd never again object to her helping God's poor.[46]

Such stories articulate gender distinctions with reference to a greater or lesser willingness to give. In each case, it is the husband who makes the case for economic prudence, seeking to ensure that the household has sufficient supplies of food for the months ahead. In contrast, the generosity of the charitable spouse shows a flagrant disregard for futurity. The charitable woman is, seemingly, prepared to give everything away at once to meet the demands of her impoverished neighbors. From the husband's standpoint, such a disposition appears dangerous or excessive, putting the survival of one's own family at risk. The fact that the woman is, invariably, spared her husband's anger through supernatural intervention does little to mitigate this picture. Indeed, it is only the woman's willingness to give away everything she has that makes such unexpected recompense possible. In this respect, the differing perspectives of husband and wife can be seen as exemplifying a tension between, on the one hand, the claims of accumulation and forward planning, and on the other, the impetus to expend without hope of return. The gendered attribution of these antagonistic viewpoints is indicative not only of the socially differentiated involvement of men and women in the sphere of production (it is significant that the woman usually engages in her charitable dispensations while her husband is away working in the fields), but also of a view of women's charity as posing a potential threat to the male-identified world of economic calculation.

The stories also provide a suggestive counterpoint to the well-documented involvement of upper- and middle-class women in charitable work in nineteenth-century Ireland. Maria Luddy has noted that the nature and degree of such involvement was clearly demarcated along religious and sectarian lines, being, among Catholics, largely the preserve of independently wealthy female religious, such as Catherine McAuley (1778–1841), founder of the Sisters of Mercy, whose image until recently adorned the £5 notes issued by the Bank of Ireland.[47] The nuns acted under the direction and close supervision of male clergy. It was invariably the latter who made final decisions in matters of administration and financial expenditure, always informed by a prevailing sense that the involvement of women in business dealings and commercial enterprises (even of a purely philanthropic character) should be tightly restricted.[48]

In contrast, Protestant women engaged in charitable work appear to have enjoyed a higher degree of autonomy, being for the most part organized into groups that functioned as auxiliaries to the male-run bible societies. Groups like the Dublin Female Association (auxiliary to both the Irish Evangelical Society and the London Missionary Society) established homes for destitute women and children where the acquisition of practical skills like needlework was combined with religious instruction, the intention being both to instill in the female poor the habits of thrift and industry deemed necessary to equip them for economic independence and, wherever possible, to win converts from Catholicism. It is the latter aim and the (sometimes) conditional character of the relief offered that is most frequently remembered in later accounts. The women's proselytizing efforts, however, like those of some landlords and Protestant clergy, are usually remembered as being unsuccessful. Take, for example, the following account from Seaghan MacCartha (b. 1893) of Newmarket, County Cork:

In famine days some of the Protestant ladies tried to buy the babies in the district with gifts of food and blankets, but were refused.

Lady, here are your blankets clean
Take back your meat and gold
I would not part with my heart's blood
I could not see them sold

But souperism [the offer of soup made conditional on the recipient's religious conversion] fared better in Newmarket district. Here Lady Mary Allworth, a famous proselytizer, tempted many starving victims with the soup kitchens. There was no proselytism in my home district as there were no Protestants. They never settled down in a poor district.[49]

It is evident from such descriptions that these Protestant ladies, with their offerings of food made conditional on the recipient's willingness (or apparent willingness) to change religion, have become a focal point for latter-day narratives of resistance, affirming, albeit belatedly, the local community's refusal of assimilation to the values of the then-dominant religious group.[50] As such, they afford no less powerful a contrast to the folkloric figure of the charitable woman (a figure equally shaped by the prism of hindsight) than do the Catholic nuns, whose charitable expenditures remained subject to the parsimonious scrutiny of their male clerical overseers. In both cases, the incipient dangers of an expenditure without constraint are annulled in favor of a transaction whereby the circuit of exchange remains firmly closed, whether by the male-imposed dictates of economic prudence or by the conditions appended to the gift itself, founded on the pious hope that financial outgoings will be matched and recompensed by the winning of souls. In contrast, the figure of the charitable woman, whose memory has been transmitted alongside those of proselytizers and charitably inclined female religious, appears to maintain a view of expenditure as irreducibly fraught with ambivalence and risk. If her largesse is finally requited through a form of supernatural cost accounting, the unexpectedness of such an intervention, combined with the threatened domestic clash that furnishes its pretext, suggests a perennial willingness to go too far, to exceed the bounds of fiscal prudence and forward calculation.

Such a desire, embodied in the persona of the female protagonist, lingers uncannily within subsequently configured narratives of modernization and progress, for which the accumulated archives of the Irish Folklore Commission (where these stories are now housed as evidential tokens of the national past) have themselves provided an indispensable resource. Derrida, let us remember, describes the gift as that which simultaneously founds and breaks the circuit of economic exchange.[51] In this case, both the gift and the explicitly feminized giver serve to inflect the present with the reverberation of a foreclosed but stubbornly recurrent origin, the meddlesome ghost in political economy's slickly conceived machine.

Equally significant, given subsequent construals of the famine as a moment of cultural loss, is the appeal to supernatural intervention. Not only does the gift threaten to subvert the dictates of economic reason, in doing so, it establishes a palpable link to a world in which human praxis is permeated by forces and agencies that escape determination by a sovereign and centered human subject. The charitable woman, like Benjamin's figures of distorted life and the iconic images of land and nationhood promulgated in medieval and later Irish literature, stands at a point of interface between a modernized historical process and the past in the moment of its supposed eclipse.

Keeping in mind Benjamin's emphasis on the body as both object of forgetting and repository of memory, one can begin to approach the articulation of epochal social change around the gendered and acculturated female body. If women appear repeatedly as liminal or intermediary figures, guardians both of the historical past and of the retroactively figured prehistory of modernity, this is surely the result of their perceived implication in a seismic shift marking the inception not only of institutionalized forms of male power, but of the cultural order itself, as that which makes possible the differential fashioning of gendered subjectivities. Benjamin's own abiding concern was with images of women as cultural articulations of the buried or discarded past. As the essay "Conversation" makes clear, women are identified too with an originary, presymbolic language of bodily praxis, which is taken to antedate humanity's "fall" into symbolization. Like Kristeva's theory of the semiotic as a modality linked to the submerged but ineradicable presence of the maternal body, Benjamin's formulation suggests a view of women as situated simultaneously inside and outside the order of discourse. On the one hand, women appear as historical presences whose fate has been shaped by specific practices of marginalization and subjugation. On the other, they are invoked as an ontological absence, the objects of a founding gesture of exclusion, whereby effects of cultural signification and historical agency are produced. The distinction is one that feminist theory has sometimes elaborated as a contrast between "women" as historical subjects and the "feminine," understood as that which is banished by regimes of patriarchal power precisely to the degree that it eludes and therefore threatens their informing logic of identity and the binary oppositions by which it is shored up.[52] The ambivalence discernible in the female protagonists of these famine stories may therefore be read as the product both of women's assigned liminality within the social and cultural order (as documented in academic histories and official texts) and of their resultant capacity to trouble its discourses of power with subversive intimations of a suppressed scene of origin.

The mimetic faculty, as switching point between "culture" and retrojected "nature," is a key operator here, affirming the interimplication of pasts and presents as well as the potentially transformative character of remembrance itself. It is this transformative capability that imbues these images with their power as repositories of the has-been, evoking at the same time the threatened return of the primordially repressed. Comparisons can be drawn with Luce Irigaray's advocacy of mimesis as a strategy of subversion by which women might inhabit and iteratively transform the masculinist structures of signification from which, she claims, they are debarred as a constitutive absence.[53] Such a displacement from within, dependent as it is on a certain ontological instability, a capacity to be both the same and yet not the same, inside and outside, might instruct also a practice of critical historiography seeking to rethink the modern by way of its posited antitypes, its founding exclusions and repudiations, thus linking an archaeology of the forgotten to projects of political and cultural intervention in the present. These might involve opening up the subject of cognition elaborated by modern philosophies of experience and knowledge to other ways of experiencing and knowing, as much embodied as mindful, seeking the displacement of reflection in sensuousness, not simply as an alternative to the pursuit of knowledge as the project of a self-enclosed subjectivity, but as the latter's unformulated precondition, its own "prehistory."

A final word should be said about the folklore archive that supplies the contemporary setting in which these stories are encountered. It is here that the "feminization of famine" referred to by Margaret Kelleher coincides most visibly with the gendered iconography of Irish nationhood. If the folklore archive represents the attempt of the post-Independence Irish state to coopt a national-cultural past distilled from the heterogeneous fragments of site-specific stories and idioms, then gender affords a privileged point of intersection between this project, the history of earlier national self-representations and the temporal logics informing ideologies of modernization. In furnishing both a resource and a contrapuntal foil for the composition of colonial and postcolonial national histories, the female protagonists of these accounts testify simultaneously to the eclipse of the premodern past and to its persistence, whether overtly, as a reference point of nation-state discourses, or, more obscurely, as an unacknowledged remainder troubling the signifying surface of contemporary and later accounts. The female figures who feature in famine narratives as, variously, embodiments of charity and of the worst ravages of hunger can be viewed as imagistic and narrative distillations, not only of humanity's "fall" into a mode of communication where mimeticity and bodily praxis are repressed or denied, but also of the specific (and frequently contested) cultural forms through which such an imagined trajectory has been articulated both in the self-designated epoch of capitalist modernity and in the more narrowly defined context of mid-nineteenth-century Ireland. Situated on the threshold between modernity's constitutive break with the past and its attendant prehistory, the accounts hold out the possibility of deciphering the historical mechanisms that have generated so powerful a set of cultural associations between women and the superseded past, against which the modern has so persistently been defined. As such, they offer a still forceful reminder that modernity, even in the moment of its self-proclaimed triumph, remains haunted by other possibilities of being-in-the-world, informed by a symbiosis of self and other, past and present, substance and phantasm scarcely dreamed of in its various philosophies.

9 ![decorative header]

The Coming Event (Before and After)

Constructing a Present

Histories, as Greg Denning reminds us, both refer to a past and construct a present.[1] The present to which commemorations of the famine's hundred fiftieth anniversary (1995–1997) contributed was, not least, that of Ireland's much-vaunted economic boom of the past decade. The so-called Celtic Tiger economy of the 1990s, fueled by foreign investment, information technology, and tourism and accompanied by an unprecedented wave of return migration, provided the setting for a variety of commemorative events far outstripping the more quietly marked hundredth anniversary. To conduct research in Ireland between 1994 and 1998 was to be confronted by a bewildering proliferation of famine-related materials, adding constantly to the range of available sources. A series of new academic and popular works on the history, politics, and folklore of the famine appeared on the shelves of Dublin bookstores, several of which created specially designated "famine studies" sections to accommodate the succession of new arrivals. A number of these new publications sought to engage once more with the question of British governmental culpability and with the famine's enduring consequences both for Ireland itself and for the Irish diaspora that the famine helped to create.[2] Others reprinted the testimonies of contemporary observers, in some instances making them available for the first time to a late twentieth-century readership.[3] Also, between 1995 and 1997, the *Irish Times* reprinted a succession of contemporary newspaper accounts under the heading "Famine Diary," these being reissued later in book form.[4] In addition to this expanded textual presence, information about the famine and its various legacies was conveyed to a wider audience, both within Ireland and beyond, by radio and television broadcasts. These included a public lecture series broadcast by RTE Radio and a four-part television drama recounting the famine's impact upon a small rural community in County Donegal (1846–1847).[5]

New publications (and new editions of old ones) were joined by a proliferation of famine-related Web sites and a variety of other commemorative events, exhibitions, and conferences, many of which sought explicitly to link the Irish experience to latter-day instances of famine.[6] The year 1994 had already seen the opening of a Famine Museum at Strokestown Park, Strokestown, County Roscommon. Occupying the stable yards of a former manorial house, which was also the scene of a much-publicized murder of a landlord during the famine years, the museum includes documents from the estate office recording pleas from impoverished tenants and the responses they received, alongside displays highlighting the persistence of famine in the contemporary world.[7]

Similar connections between the Irish famine and contemporary famines were made by an international conference on hunger held in New York in 1995 and addressed by the then president of Ireland, Mary Robinson. Robinson's address, like a speech delivered on February 2 of the same year to the Oireachteas (the two chambers of the Irish Parliament), voiced a recurrent theme both of her own presidency and of many commemorative events: that of the perceived need to engage the Irish diaspora.[8] As a geographically scattered community of Irish descent, the diaspora were appealed to both as a possible constituency within which the contemporary significance of the famine might be debated, and as themselves products, in many cases, of the large-scale emigration that characterized the famine years and extended into the twentieth century.[9] The one hundred fiftieth anniversary thus assumed an increasingly deterritorialized scope in comparison to its predecessor. In the process, the famine came to be recast not only as an event of national significance, but also as an episode in an emergent narrative of globalization, in which Ireland, by virtue of the worldwide dispersal of its emigrant population, was assigned a distinctive place.[10]

Motifs of emigration (and, in some cases, return) were a feature of many commemorative events. In July 1997, at the foot of Croagh Patrick, County Mayo, was unveiled a bronze replica (sculpted by John Behan) of a "coffin ship," like the ones on which numerous famine-era emigrants departed Ireland, many of them to die as a result of disease and unsanitary conditions before arriving at their destinations.[11] Across the Atlantic, meanwhile, in New York, the port of entry for many emigrants who survived the crossing, lower Manhattan's Battery Park City provided the setting for an "Irish Hunger Memorial," opened to the public on July 16, 2002. Designed by Brian Tolle, the memorial comprises a representation of a west of Ireland rural landscape, elevated on a limestone plinth and including stone walls, fallow potato fields, and an abandoned stone cottage, shipped from the townland of Carradoogan in County Mayo and reassembled on the site. Audio installations and accompanying texts, arranged in illuminated bands around the base of the memorial, reproduce nineteenth-century and later sources (letters, parliamentary reports, oral traditions) with materials relating to contemporary hunger crises.[12]

More controversial were a "homecoming" concert ("The Gathering") held at Millstreet, Cork, during the June Bank Holiday weekend, 1997, featuring artists from Ireland and the United States and a famine memorial on Dublin's Custom House Quay (the point of embarkation for many famine-era emigrants), designed by sculptor Rowan Gillespie and showing an assortment of gaunt figures (men, women, and children) cast in bronze. Despite its fund-raising aims (divided between domestic and international charities), the Millstreet concert drew criticism from Action from Ireland (AfrI), an Irish-based overseas aid organization, for its celebratory and thus (allegedly) apolitical character. AfrI objected too to the support given to the event by the US government, whose foreign policies were blamed for the spread of hunger and human rights violations in contemporary Africa, Asia, and Latin America. The concert featured a live satellite linkup with US President Bill Clinton, speaking from the White House, in which he recalled Ireland's sufferings during the 1840s, pointed to the prominent role played by Irish emigrants in the United States, and referred to Ireland's contributions to contemporary famine relief.[13] The Custom House Quay memorial elicited the disapproval of AfrI and other groups less for its content than for its use of private and corporate sponsorship, whereby individuals and companies could have their names engraved on accompanying plaques for a cost of between IR£750 and IR£5,000. In an exchange chronicled in the pages of the *Irish Times*, AfrI representatives decried as "grotesque and offensive" the use of the famine dead to sell advertising space, while the organizers (the Irish Famine Commemoration Fund) drew attention to the project's aim of raising IR£10 million for charities concerned with homelessness and disadvantage among Irish youth. To date, only the names of individual donors have appeared on the memorial, many of them politicians or figures from the entertainment industry.[14]

The tendency of contemporary debates concerning the famine to escape national boundaries (while retaining the Irish nation-state as a point of reference) was further illustrated by the activities of the New York–based Irish Famine Genocide Committee, formed in 1995 and dedicated to the position that the Irish experience during 1845–1852 "was marked by acts and omissions on the part of the imperial British government that today would be termed genocide as that term is defined in modern international conventions." The Committee sought to publicize its views by promoting the teaching of famine history in New York public schools as part of the state's human rights curriculum and through a series of symposia ("Breaking the Silences: Legacies of the Irish Starvation") held at Cooper Union and the Irish American Club of Hunter College, involving historians, artists, and educators, along with activists from both the nationalist and unionist communities in Northern Ireland.

The Trouble with Trauma (A Digression)

The interpretation of the famine as an act of genocide, with reverberations extending to the present, was given still wider currency by the Dublin-born singer-songwriter Sinead O'Connor with her song "Famine," released in 1994, which described both the sufferings of starving people while meat, fish, and vegetables were shipped under armed guard to England, and the concomitant experience of cultural loss resulting from the widespread decline of the Irish language, concluding that the memory of these events continues to cause pain into the present ("this is what I think is still hurting me").[15] Aligning themselves (like the arguments of the Irish Famine Genocide Committee) with an analysis of the famine dating back to the writings of Mitchel and his contemporaries, the song's lyrics appeal to a trope that has circulated widely in contemporary discussions of the famine and its legacy: that of the "trauma" of the Irish past, of the pain engendered by the interlinked violences of colonization, governmental negligence, and mass starvation, which must, so the argument goes, be recognized and named in the present in order to be healed. Examples from the time of the famine's hundred fiftieth anniversary are numerous. The following is taken from a 1997 essay ("Confronting the Ghosts of Our Past") by John Waters, a columnist for the *Irish Times*. Waters writes of a reluctance on the part of the Irish people to face the "trauma" of their own history, a reluctance accounting, as he sees it, for Ireland's current desire to see itself as an "advanced Western society," despite the enduring legacy of the colonial past in the form of unemployment, emigration, and the continuing incidence of alcoholism and mental illness:[16]

Because we refuse to remember, we are doomed to repeat. The famine, the most extreme expression of the violence inflicted on the Irish nation by the tyranny of the colonizer, is the door by which that colonial experience can be assessed. Viewed in its proper perspective, it reveals itself as the most powerful metaphor of life in modern Ireland. It is present as a hidden motif on much of our literature and music, for all that the creators of these works may deny it legitimacy. It casts a dark shadow over the way we live our lives both in private and public.[17]

Although the effort to puncture official self-definitions should not be dismissed, there are, it seems to me, a number of difficulties with recent appeals to the notion of trauma in the Irish context. These concern not only the too-easy transposition of such a notion onto a reified "national psyche" (a phrase used by Waters and others), a move tending to obscure the no less significant divergences between the various protagonists involved in these acts of commemoration—states, academic institutions, individuals, groups—but also, as Mikkel Borch-Jakobsen has astutely noted, in the underlying assumption that "memory liberates, narration heals, history redeems," and that retrieval of the past is thus necessarily an emancipatory gesture.[18] Such a gesture, however, especially as articulated in terms of nationhood, might equally be thought of as one of containment, involving the substitution of a knowable, narratable origin for one that potentially escapes or exceeds figuration. If the missed encounter with the past that is at the imputed origin of trauma carries repetition of that same past as its inevitable price, then narratives of national healing and reconciliation with the past of the kind circulating in sections of the Irish media might be seen as prey to a different kind of compulsion to repeat—in this case to repeat the gesture of foreclosure whereby the heterogeneous reality of the famine and its storied afterlife become reconstituted as moments in an institutionalized national history, which can now, it seems, be safely affirmed as such from a distance of a hundred fifty years. Notions of trauma thus applied, whatever the oppositional claims made on their behalf (and Waters's intention is certainly to critique the national self-representations current in contemporary Ireland), are all too easily elided with the imputed uniqueness of such a national history. To write of an unproblematically given, albeit repressed, national past is to overlook the ways in which such a past, construed in precisely those terms, has itself served and continues to serve as a resource for the self-legitimation of the modernizing state.

It is instructive also to consider Waters's by no means atypical account alongside the current upsurge of interest in the subject of trauma in both psychotherapy and cultural theory. Trauma, as theorized by, for example, physician Bessel van der Kolk and literary critic Cathy Caruth has been defined in terms of "unclaimed experience," of sudden, catastrophic, or overwhelming events that, to the extent that they have never become fully conscious, are destined to manifest themselves in the guise of uncontrolled repetitions.[19] Trauma thus comes to be seen as a form of visceral or embodied memory, which eludes conscious articulation and which, particularly for literary theorists such as Caruth and Shoshana Felman, finds linguistic expression only in those moments where the referential function appears to break down and where the nonsignifying materiality of language is made manifest.[20] If traumatic experience is thus defined as incommunicable on a verbal level, trauma is nonetheless understood as "contagious" and thus capable of being transmitted from patient to therapist in a clinical setting, or, as Caruth writes of "historical" trauma (of which the Holocaust furnishes the preeminent modern example), from survivor to interlocutor, or from one generation to another.[21]

If the work of Caruth and others provides an often suggestive discussion of the ways in which both subjectivities and histories are formed in relation to that which eludes their conscious determinations, there remains the danger that the theoretical framework proposed serves to inhibit recognition both of the geographical and historical specificities of the traumatic event and of the possibility of its critical or transformative reverberation within the present. Most obviously, the analytic lexicon invoked, which tends to recognize manifestations of trauma in a variety of settings, runs the risk of denying the particularity of such manifestations by treating them as so many instances of a more generally occurring phenomenon. A further difficulty concerns the ambiguities inherent in the notion of trauma itself. Ruth Leys has argued that successive theorizations of trauma, from the early writings of Freud to contemporary psychology and neurophysiology, have turned on an unresolved tension between, on the one hand, an insistence on the literal and unmediated repetition of the traumatic experience in the form of symptoms and anxiety dreams (a view reiterated in the writings of both Caruth and van der Kolk), and on the other, a view of the traumatized subject as existing in a state of passivity and heightened suggestibility, raising the possibility that traumatic memories may be modified or even implanted in the course of therapy, particularly through the use of hypnosis or drug therapy. Leys suggests that these ambiguities raise profound questions regarding both the status of traumatic memories (particularly those "recovered" in the course of therapy) and the nature of the intellectual object constructed by trauma theory, which is shown to oscillate between different and potentially incommensurable understandings of memory and subjectivity.[22]

It is on these grounds that I have avoided reference to trauma in the preceding pages, much as I share the interest of Caruth, Felman, and others in the ways in which the ostensibly forgotten past continues to impinge, to disturbing effect, on the present and in the consequences of that impingement for contemporary theorizations of historical memory. If my discussion has been concerned in part with questions of memory and repetition, as these pertain not only to national histories, but also to the limits of professionalized historical knowledges, then my desire to explore the past not simply as past, but as an abiding, if unacknowledged, contemporary presence has led me to seek a different theoretical vocabulary through which to address these questions.

Resituating National Histories

Belated recognition of the shortcomings of governmental relief efforts was afforded by British Prime Minister Tony Blair in a statement read out at the Millstreet concert by Irish actor Gabriel Byrne, in the presence of the British ambassador to Ireland, Veronica Sutherland. Stopping short of a full apology (as the *Irish Times* noted the following day), Blair acknowledged the insufficiency of the measures implemented by Peel's and Russell's administrations and praised Ireland's subsequent ascent from adversity to prosperity: "Those who governed in London at the time failed their people through standing by while a crop failure turned into a massive human tragedy. We must not forget such a dreadful event. It is also right that we should pay tribute to the ways in which the Irish people have triumphed in the face of this catastrophe."[23]

Like Clinton's satellite message, Blair's statement implicitly links the current upsurge of commemorative activity to Ireland's repositioning of itself and its own history in the light of its more recent prosperity. We are reminded that the Ireland of the late twentieth and early twenty-first centuries, with its much publicized economic growth, its increasing cosmopolitanism, and the declining social influence of the Roman Catholic Church, appears very different both from the Ireland of the 1840s and from that of the 1940s, in which the Irish Folklore Commission survey and the commemorative volume *The Great Famine* were first conceived.[24] If both of the latter mark crucial moments in the inscription of the famine as an episode in a specifically national history, the significance of such a gesture must surely be reassessed in the now all too familiar light of globalization, neoliberalism, and transnational flows of capital, people, and information. Nonetheless, as politicians and the media affirm Ireland's definitive (if belated) achievement of first world status and as images of Ireland, past and present, circulate through a variety of media among national and international audiences, the remembrances of the famine preserved in the folklore record and in contemporary accounts (many of which have been made newly available to a present-day readership) continue to sit awkwardly beside these resurgent grand narratives of progress and emancipation, just as many of the rural localities referred to in the Irish Folklore Commission accounts have manifestly failed to share in the much-publicized economic growth of urban centers like Dublin.[25]

Subaltern Pasts/Prehistory

I began this book by suggesting some of the ways in which the modern discipline of history might be thought of as complicit in the ideological project of modernization, insofar as the framing of historical knowledge appears, at least in theory, to necessitate the overcoming and supercession of other possible modes of engagement with the past. I have attempted not to compile an alternative history of the famine years, but rather to extricate the famine from the proprietary claims of historians, which have tended to dominate famine-related scholarship up to the present. To this end, it must be appreciated that the linked ascendancies of industrialization, capital, and their attendant ethos of human progress and emancipation (of which modern historiography affords but one possible expression), far from being accomplished without residue, have often presupposed the reiterated summoning of their own disavowed antecedents. These are what Chakrabarty terms "subaltern pasts," those "other" histories, disregardful of the protocols of academic explanation, in which human actors are apt to rub shoulders with a variety of nonhuman or supernatural agencies. For Chakrabarty, these alternative visions of the past serve, by virtue of their irreducible contemporeity, to "interrupt" official and academic histories. So-called "histories of belonging" are thus the ineradicable counterpart to the developmental logic informing histories of capital, showing the latter to be synergetically linked to the very local specificities they promise to eradicate. It is at this point, however, that Chakrabarty is perhaps too cautious in his engagement with the protocols of academic historiography. Subaltern pasts, he argues, serve as a "supplement" to historical understanding, simultaneously enabling the claims made on behalf of historical knowledge and calling attention to its constitutive limits. By paying closer attention to such limits, he suggests, historians can better resist the "imperious instincts" of their own discipline and thus produce less totalizing, more pluralistic histories. Such an approach has the obvious advantage that it does not seek simply to dismiss nonhistoricizing visions of the past or to explain them away with reference to an overarching social context that is itself presented as unproblematically transparent to the historian's gaze. Even so, the notion of "interruption" itself is not without its difficulties. People who seek to account for human events in terms of supernatural or other nonhuman factors do not, it can be assumed, do so primarily in order to keep academic historians on their toes. Chakrabarty's claims regarding subaltern pasts thus involve a process of translation, whereby the significance of those pasts comes to be rendered in terms other than those proposed by their adherents. If such a translation seems both less patronizing and less reductive than many of the alternatives discussed by Chakrabarty, it nonetheless runs the risk of being appropriated as an argument for business as usual on the part of historians, despite Chakrabarty's own, manifestly critical intentions with regard to the historical profession. If subaltern pasts are understood as offering a challenge to institutionalized forms of historical knowledge and understanding, the proposed response to that challenge appears to consist, finally, in the revision from within of the historiographical canon through an ongoing process of critical self-scrutiny rather than, say, the cultivation of alternative knowledges and historiographical idioms that might be directly informed by these subaltern visions. This begs the question of how one is to arrive at such alternative formulations. As a starting point, however, one might insist more forcefully on Chakrabarty's own claims regarding the "out of joint" present that historians (like everyone else) inhabit, a present constantly displaced from within by the indelible persistence of a proliferation of present-pasts and present-futures and that, if redescribed in such terms, might yield a range of novel social, political, and historiographical possibilities.[26]

With regard to my own sources, I have suggested that remembrances and eyewitness accounts of the famine have been both an indispensable resource for the Irish postcolonial state's attempts to align itself within an emergent global order and profoundly subversive of that project and its informing teleology. This point is perhaps most readily made with regard to the genealogy of the folklore archive itself, which is at once implicated in the project of nation-state building, both through state funding and through the invocation of a national culture and national past, and yet which, in grounding itself on a multiplicity of locally embedded voices, stories, and idioms, testifies to a necessary incommensurability between the synthesizing ambitions of nation-state discourses and the recalcitrant specificities of their constituent elements. A corresponding ambivalence invests the identification of the famine as a historical watershed, a view challenged in some recent famine historiography but reiterated in folklore scholarship from the nineteenth century to the present. If the famine is indeed to be construed as a moment of cultural loss, or, in E. Estyn Evans' words, as "the end of prehistoric times in Ireland," then the proclamation of that loss itself comes to furnish a charter for the recuperation of the ostensibly vanished past as a contemporary presence, a gesture given palpable form in the folklore archive and in the successive publications associated with it.[27]

I have argued too that the interimplication of pasts, presents, and futures manifested by the folklore archive pertains not only to the contemporary resurfacing of representations of the past (that is, of stories and images relating to the famine) but also to the forcible irruption of other knowledges and other temporal idioms as a direct result of the same societal and epistemic transformations that have secured the institutional ascendancy of contemporary variants of historicism. It is here that I have recourse to Benjamin's dizzying vistas of prehistory, of the unforeseen resurfacing of the archaic past within the present, and its concomitant fantasia of primordial undifferentiation, bespeaking the threatened dissolution of temporal and subjectival boundaries and serving as potential prelude to transformative remaking of the world, as past, present, and future are loosed from their assigned subservience to one another. Working, as Benjamin suggested, through the conjunction thus posited between the present, the archaic, and the more recent past, the time of prehistory presses most urgently upon the here and now in settings such as death places, the informing logic of which is one of contagion and mimetic interconnectedness, or, as in the case of *féar gortach* (hungry grass), of tactile transmission predicated upon the physical contiguity established between the experiential present, the famine years, and the immemorial, maledictory force of *tír*. It emerges too in the iconography of the famished body as a site of both privation and excess, the latter figured most strikingly in the guise of an uncontainable materialism, removed equally from notions of corporeal symbolism and more recent anthropological discussions of embodiment.[28] In this rendering, the body appears not as a source of symbols to be reinvoked in other contexts, nor yet as the imputed existential ground of culture, selfhood, or social power, but as the recalcitrant matter that both enables and perennially thwarts cultural and historical understanding. Equally important is the privileged place occupied by gender and sexual difference in the image repertoire of the famished body. Gendered imagery pertains both to English characterizations of Ireland and the Irish before, during, and after the famine and to the complex and layered genealogy of discourses on Irish nationhood as these have been deployed in a colonial, oppositional setting, no less than in a postcolonial official one. As such it engages both the historical fate of the women described in famine narratives and objectified in nationalist iconography and a more elusive set of linkages between prehistory and the feminine, understood not simply as the product of socially assigned systems of sex-gender differences (the shifting contours of which remain themselves susceptible to historical tracing), but rather as that which appears excluded from philosophical, political, and linguistic economies as the assumed precondition of their functioning. The idiom of prehistory therefore opens the way to a potentially subversive reimagining of the spatial and temporal logics informing the project of modernization and of the knowledges, subjectivities, and gender categories produced in its wake. Such a task, as Chakrabarty rightly suggests, must involve the acknowledgment that the other worlds allegedly displaced by the trajectories of a modernized historical process are inassimilable to the latter's teleological and universalizing imperatives and as such remain ineradicable contemporary presences. The transformative impetus of prehistory entails the recognition that subaltern pasts are not really past at all, but that gods, spirits, ghosts, magic, metamorphosis, along with the interlinked iconographies of death and the feminine, remain irreducibly part of the heterogeneous present we all of us inhabit, a present that includes both oral tradition and the Internet, both the still-haunted death spaces of Ireland's western seaboard and the famine memorial adorning Dublin's Custom House Quay. These juxtapositions, needless to say, disturb any too straightforwardly assumed chronology of historical progress, evoking the coexistence and overlap of multiple time frames, rather than their ordered succession. To adapt Bruno Latour's phrase, neither the Irish nor anyone else has ever been modern.[29]

I began this study by invoking the historian's "bizarre relation" to death as one partaking of both professed distance and unacknowledged intimacy. I end by posing the question of how the present might be redescribed in terms that make explicit the secret familiarities that I have sought to delineate between the modern and its assembled others: the feminine, the archaic, the primitive, the traditional, the premodern—a lexicon of contrastive terms that has played a central role too in articulating Ireland's colonial past and its postcolonial present and future. The question concerns not least the possibility of rendering justice to the famine dead by affording them a contemporary presence, neither as statistics nor as casualties of economic progress, nor yet as anonymously exemplary minor characters in a national narrative scripted by politicians and academics, but rather in order that their stories might resound to potentially disruptive effect alongside scholarly histories and state-sponsored acts of commemoration. The historical vision invoked here professes to be a redemptive one, not in the sense of therapeutic narratives of national healing, but rather in that of Benjamin's "messianic" revision of historical materialism. The possibility of historical action and transformation becomes available in the moment that the relationship between past, present, and future ceases to be perceived as fixed and determinate. The messianic moment, understood as a decisive break in the continuum of homogeneous empty time, affords a conduit both for the returning dead and for the reawakening of a hitherto disenfranchised material nature.[30] It is precisely in its dissolution of historical certainties, its refusal to furnish an ontological ground, and its affirmation of matter, not least that of the famished body, as endlessly (and disturbingly) productive rather than passive, that such a materialism aims to facilitate the fashioning of possible futures, enabling a rearticulation of commonalities and differences beyond the axiomatics of historical progress, race, nation, or culture.

If a sense of Irish "difference," including the singular cultural forms generated by Ireland's often contradictory interaction with histories of capital and modernity, is not to be recuperated by a logic of identity (as yet one more "national culture" in the contemporary global marketplace) then it needs to be understood, not in exclusively national terms but, as David Lloyd has suggested, with reference to a more encompassing sense of modernity's own difference from itself.[31] It is the attempt to think this internal difference, as it is refracted through particular sites and histories, that has occupied me in the present study. It has taken me, in some cases, far from the established canons of historical inquiry to consider the alternative modes of presenting the past evoked by aspects of postcolonial theory, by Walter Benjamin's dissident historiography, and, most tellingly, I hope, by the stories, anecdotes, and remembrances of eyewitnesses, survivors, and their descendants. If I choose to end with a question—how to describe the transfigured present revealed by the lifting of modernity's definitional spell?—it is because this inquiry has never aimed at closure. My aim, rather, has been to effect an opening, however provisional, to a prospective space of encounter, in which modernity and the subject of historical knowledge might be rendered truly porous to an alterity issuing as much from within as from without, a space in which to attend to the coming event and all its terrors.

Notes

1. Wilde, *Irish Popular Superstitions*, 9. Historian Emmett Larkin refers to the "devotional revolution" of late nineteenth-century Irish Catholicism, facilitated by a greatly increased ratio of priests to people in the wake of the famine, and comprising a campaign against "superstition," the encouragement of regular attendance at mass by all sections of the population, and the adoption of a variety of devotional practices imported from continental Europe, with a view to increasing the control of the clergy over the religious lives of their flocks. The results have been further characterized by anthropologist Lawrence Taylor as akin to a Reformation in miniature, entailing a Weberian shift from "magical" to "ethical" forms of religious belief and practice. Larkin, "Devotional Revolution"; Taylor, *Occasions of Faith*, 64, 135–37.

2. The potato was first introduced into Ireland in the late sixteenth or early seventeenth century. Initially grown as a garden crop (especially in the provinces of Leinster and Munster), it made the transition to field cultivation when rising cereal prices made it more attractive to farmers and smallholders. The method of cultivation involved the digging of ridges (called "lazy beds"), in which the sprouting tubers were placed. By the early nineteenth century, more than 2 million acres were under cultivation, with an average yield of 6 to 8 tons per acre. By this point, the potato had become a staple food, rather than simply a dietary supplement. With the initial appearance of the blight in 1845, one-third of the total crop was lost. The following year, the proportion had risen to three-quarters. The year 1847 brought average yields, but little had been sown, as seed potatoes were scarce. The following year's yields were only two-thirds of what would previously have been expected. By 1847, the number of acres under potatoes had been reduced to a quarter of a million. Salaman, *History and Social Influence*, 188–221, 273–316.

3. A temporary relief commission was set up in November 1845 to provide relief supplementary to that provided by the Poor Law (Ireland) Act of 1838 (see Chapter 4). The commission's remit was to advise the government as to the extent of the potato loss and the scale of distress in Ireland, to oversee the storage and distribution of $100,000 worth of Indian meal, purchased from the United States as an emergency measure, and to direct, assist, and coordinate the activities of the lo-

cal relief committees established on its instruction in February 1846. These were voluntary bodies, made up of local dignitaries, county officials, Poor Law commissioners, and clergymen. Their principal duties were to encourage local employment, to raise subscriptions, and to purchase and distribute Indian corn from the depots established by the relief commission. They were also instructed to maintain lists of residents in each locality and to issue tickets for employment on the public works to those perceived to be in need. After allegations of mismanagement, the latter function passed directly to the Board of Works (a body established fifteen years previously). By August 1846, some 650 local committees were in existence, the majority being in the south and west of Ireland, with far fewer in the midlands and east, and none in the counties of Armagh, Fermanagh, Derry, and Tyrone. The replacement of Peel's Conservative government with the Liberal administration of Russell saw public works and the Poor Law system assume greater importance in the provision of relief, while the role of the commission became more limited. Burke, *People*, 101–24; Daly, "Operations"; Donnelly, "Famine and Government Response"; Kinealy, *This Great Calamity*, 31–70, 175–231, 232–64, and *Death-Dealing Famine*, 59–65; Ó Gráda, *Ireland Before and After the Famine*, 48–137, and *Ireland: A New Economic History*, 187–99.

4. Economic historian Joel Mokyr suggests a higher figure of 1,498,000 if "averted births" are taken into account. Mokyr, *Why Ireland Starved*, 34, 266.

5. *Census of Ireland* (1851), 242; repr. Killen, *Famine Decade*, 246–47.

6. The Church of Ireland, the largest Protestant church in Ireland, was established under the Act of Supremacy of 1537 and functioned as the established state church, with the English monarch as its head, until its disestablishment in 1870, since which time it has been an independent, self-governing church and a member of the Anglican communion. See Ford, McGuire, and Milne, *As by Law Established*.

7. Wilde, *Irish Popular Superstitions*, 11.

8. Stocking, *Victorian Anthropology*, 208. See also Abrams, *Natural Supernaturalism*; and Butler, *Romantics, Rebels and Reactionaries*.

9. Polanyi, *Great Transformation*; Laslett, *World We Have Lost*; Schneider, "Spirits and the Spirit of Capitalism"; Weber, "Science as a Vocation" and *Protestant Ethic*.

10. De Vries argues that the idioms of secular politics have, from the outset, been involved in a reciprocally constituting exchange with religion that renders any clear-cut separation between the two spheres untenable. De Vries, "In Media Res," 3–5. On the relationship between religion and the contemporary mass media, see de Vries and Weber, *Religion and Media*; and Weber, *Mass Mediauras*.

11. Comaroff and Comaroff, *Modernity and Its Malcontents*; Geschiere, *Modernity of Witchcraft*.

12. Lash, *Another Modernity*; Latour, *We Have Never Been Modern*; Rofel, *Other Modernities*.

13. Connections between colonial power, ideas of progress, and forms of his-

torical knowledge are explored by Chakrabarty, *Provincializing Europe*; and Prakash, introduction to *After Colonialism*. On the legacies of imperialist historiography in contemporary development administration, see Ferguson, *Anti-Politics Machine*; and Escobar, *Encountering Development*.

14. See Hayles, *Chaos Bound*; and Stengers and Prigogine, "Reenchantment." Recent uses of chaos theory to forge links between the natural and social sciences include Benitez-Rojo, *Repeating Island*; and de Landa, *Thousand Years*.

15. Evans, *Irish Folk Ways*, 282, 295–306; Bourke, "The Baby and the Bathwater," 79, 90–91.

16. De Certeau writes that "Modern Western history essentially begins with the differentiation between the *present* and the *past*." De Certeau, *Writing of History*, 2.

17. Trevelyan, "The Irish Crisis" (published anonymously and reprinted under Trevelyan's own name, London, 1848); Mitchel, *Last Conquest*, 219.

18. The preface to the published volume thanks Séamus Ó Duilearga (James Hamilton Delargy), director of the Irish Folklore Commission (see Chapter 2), for first suggesting the project, possibly at the prompting of the Taoiseach (prime minister) Eamonn de Valera, who maintained an interest in the volume up to and after publication. Ó Gráda, "Making History in Ireland," 269–73.

19. Edwards and Williams, *Great Famine*. A document submitted by the Irish Committee of Historical Sciences, which supported the project, to the Taoiseach's department in 1950 included outlines for a projected nine "sections," together with an epilogue ("The Irish Famine in History"). In the event, only seven were included in the published volume. Ó Gráda, "Making History in Ireland," 273–77.

20. For example, Daly, *Famine in Ireland*; and Foster, *Modern Ireland*. At the time of publication, the volume's avowedly nonpartisan stance was praised by Tarlach Ó Raifeartaigh, deputy secretary of the Department of Education and himself a historian, who wrote of a draft of the proposed book that "there was nothing which could be termed biased history or which might cause political controversy." De Valera (by this time in opposition), who received a complimentary copy of the book at the time of publication, appears to have been less impressed. In thanking the authors, he reminded them in his reply of the conditions endured by ordinary people in Bruree, the Limerick village where he spent his childhood. He later expressed his dissatisfaction with the book and his preference for Cecil Woodham-Smith's *Great Hunger* (see below). Ó Gráda, "Making History in Ireland," 276, 280, 286.

21. Bradshaw, "Nationalism and Historical Scholarship." A striking contrast to the reception history of *Great Famine* is afforded by Cecil Woodham-Smith's *Great Hunger*, originally published in 1962, a work that, although criticized by many professional historians for the quality of its scholarship, its populist style, and its unashamedly partisan stance, remains probably the best-selling book on Irish history. See Foster, "We Are All Revisionists Now"; and Lyons, review of Woodham-Smith, *Great Hunger*.

22. On the question of governmental culpability, see Kinealy, *This Great Calamity* and *Death Dealing-Famine*; Scally, *End of Hidden Ireland*; and Gray, *Famine, Land and Politics.* The famine's long-term consequences are discussed by Ó Gráda in a study of Irish-language famine folklore, *An Drochshaol*, and, more recently, in *Black '47 and Beyond.*

23. See below (Chapter 9).

24. For a more comprehensive review of nineteenth- and twentieth-century famine historiography, see Daly, "Revisionism and Irish History"; and Lee, "Famine as History." For a range of perspectives on the so-called revisionist controversy in contemporary historical scholarship on Ireland, see Brady, *Interpreting Irish History.*

25. Two notable examples of literary scholarship are Morash, *Writing the Irish Famine*; and Kelleher, *Feminization of Famine.* Worth noting too is the preponderance of historians among the contributors to two recent anthologies of famine studies: Morash and Hayes, *Fearful Realities*; and Póirtéir, *Great Irish Famine*, based on RTE's commemorative lecture series.

26. Bury, *Idea of Progress.* On notions of rational predictability, see Hacking, *Emergence of Probability* and *Taming of Chance.*

27. Benjamin, "Theses on the Philosophy of History," 261–62; Anderson, *Imagined Communities*, 24.

28. Hegel, *Reason in History*, 75–77.

29. Goux, *Oedipus Philosopher*, 121.

30. Ibid., 159–81.

31. See Leach, "Two Essays Concerning the Symbolic Representation of Time"; Piña-Cabral, "Paved Roads and Enchanted Mooresses"; and Zonabend, *Memoire Longue.*

32. Asad, *Genealogies*, 1–24; Dirks, "History as Sign." A classic statement of this position is provided by R. G. Collingwood, writing in 1946, who offers a four-part definition of history: "*(a)* that it is scientific, or begins by asking questions, whereas the writer of legends begins by knowing something and telling what he knows; *(b)* that it is humanistic, or asks questions about things done by men at determinate times in the past; *(c)* that it is rational, or bases the answers which it gives to its questions on grounds; namely appeal to evidence; *(d)* that it is self-revelatory, or exists in order to tell man what man is by telling him what man has done." Such a conception is seen as emerging over four thousand years in Europe and Western Asia and as displacing both "myth," concerned with the actions of gods, and "theocratic history," in which divinities and other supernatural beings are credited with the capacity to intervene directly in human affairs. Collingwood, *Idea of History*, 18.

33. Chakrabarty, *Provincializing Europe*, 97–113.

34. Lloyd, *Ireland After History*, 44–45.

35. For example, Curtin and Wilson, *Ireland from Below*; Silverman and Gulliver, *Approaching the Past*; Curtin and Cohen, *Reclaiming Gender.*

36. Chakrabarty, *Provincializing Europe*, 98–99.

37. Guha, "Prose of Counter-Insurgency," 80; see also below (Chapter 5).

38. Guha, "Prose of Counter-Insurgency," 78.

39. Comaroff and Comaroff, "Occult Economies."

40. See Gramsci, "Notes on Italian History."

41. De Certeau, *Writing of History*, 56.

42. Chakrabarty, *Provincializing Europe*, 63. On the "prepolitical" character of peasant movements, see Hobsbawm, *Primitive Rebels*. On agrarian movements in nineteenth-century Ireland, see below (Chapter 5).

43. On notions of an "origin time," see Caillois, *Man and the Sacred*; and Lévy-Bruhl, *Primitive Mythology*. On Victorian folklore scholarship, see Dorson, *British Folklorists*; Gomme, *Ethnology in Folklore*; Silver, *Strange and Secret Peoples*.

44. De Certeau, *Writing of History*, 5–6.

45. Nietzsche, *Use and Abuse*, 40.

46. Bataille, *Accursed Share*, 197–212.

47. Derrida, *Given Time*, 34–70.

48. Blanchot, *Writing of the Disaster*, 5.

49. Lyotard, *Inhuman*, 75.

50. James Clarence Mangan (b. Dublin, 1803, d. 1849). Mangan's famine poetry is discussed at greater length by Morash (*Writing the Irish Famine*) and his work as a whole by David Lloyd in *Nationalism and Minor Literature*.

51. Mangan, *Collected Works*, 37–38.

52. Morash, *Writing the Irish Famine*. The phrase "A Very Victorian Apocalypse" appears as a chapter title.

53. See Benjamin, *Origin of German Tragic Drama*, 166.

54. Adorno, in setting out his own account of "Natural History" (*Naturgeschichte*), would later applaud Benjamin's discussion of allegory for exposing the "originary contingence" on which the history of meaning, and thus the discipline of hermeneutics, was founded. Beatrice Hanssen points out that such a reading tends, however, to privilege the work's interest in ruins, fragments, etc., over its avowedly redemptive and messianic implications. Adorno, "Idea of Natural History"; Hanssen, *Walter Benjamin's Other History*, 13–23, 102.

55. Benjamin, *Origin of German Tragic Drama*, 224–25.

56. Benjamin, "Storyteller," 94.

57. Benjamin, "On the Mimetic Faculty."

58. Benjamin, *Origin of German Tragic Drama*, 227.

59. Benjamin himself was to invoke such a possibility in his essay (written between 1919 and 1922) on "Goethe's *Elective Affinities*." Here it is proposed that human beings become subject to the implacability of "mythic nature" precisely to the degree that they consider themselves to have escaped its clutches: "Human beings must themselves manifest the violence of nature, for at no point have they outgrown it." "Goethe's *Elective Affinities*," 303–4.

60. Beatrice Hanssen traces the connections between Benjamin's early engage-

ment with the problematic of natural history in the *Trauerspiel* study and the concern with interrogating philosophical conceptions of the human subject developed in his writings of the 1930s (notably the essays on Kraus, Leskov, and Kafka). In these later writings, she suggests, the attempt to dislodge the category of the "human" as a privileged reference point involves a renewed attention to the "infrahuman," as represented, variously, by animals, minerals, angels, the figure of the *Unmensch,* and the "unfinished" hybrid beings who populate many of Kafka's literary works. Hanssen, *Walter Benjamin's Other History,* 103–50.

61. Benjamin's eighteenth thesis seeks to place human history in relation to the larger timescale of organic life on earth, citing the claim of a modern biologist that "the paltry fifty millennia of *homo sapiens* constitute something like two seconds at the close of a twenty-four-hour day." Benjamin, "Theses on the Philosophy of History," 263.

62. Lyotard, *Inhuman,* 59.

63. See, for example, Biersack, *Clio in Oceania;* Borofsky, *Making History;* Dening, *Performances;* Neumann, *Not the Way It Really Was;* Sahlins, *Historical Metaphors and Mythic Realities* and *Islands of History.*

CHAPTER 2

1. See, for example, Herzfeld, *Ours Once More;* Hosking and Schopflin, *Myth and Nationhood;* Stephens, *Giants in Those Days;* Wilson, *Folklore and Nationalism in Modern Finland.*

2. See Anderson, *Imagined Communities,* 5.

3. Burke, *Popular Culture;* Cocchiara, *History of Folklore;* Dorson, *British Folklorists.*

4. Ó Giolláin, *Locating Irish Folklore,* 94–141.

5. Hutchinson, *Dynamics of Irish Cultural Nationalism,* 151–95, 250–303; Ó Tuama, *Gaelic League Idea.*

6. Garvin, *Evolution of Irish Nationalist Politics,* 102.

7. Ó Giolláin, *Locating Irish Folklore,* 114–19.

8. Curran, *Birth of the Irish Free State.*

9. Almqvist, "Irish Folklore Commission"; Ó Muimhneacháin, "An Cumann le Béaloideas Éireann."

10. Ó Duilearga later visited folklore institutes in Scandinavian countries, while Seán O'Súilleabháin, later to serve as the commission's archivist, spent a period of training at the Dialect and Folklore Archive of Uppsala University. Ó Giolláin, *Locating Irish Folklore,* 132.

11. Ó Duilearga, "Editorial Address," 5.

12. Ó Giolláin, *Locating Irish Folklore,* 128–41; Almqvist, "Irish Folklore Commission," 9–22; Ó Danachair, "Progress of Irish Ethnology," 8–10.

13. Ó Giolláin, *Locating Irish Folklore,* 133; Almqvist, "Irish Folklore Commission," 10.

14. Almqvist, "Irish Folklore Commission," 13.

15. Ó Súilleabháin, *Handbook of Irish Folklore,* 534–35.

16. Irish Folklore Commission, *Irish Folklore and Tradition,* 17.

17. Ibid.

18. Almqvist, "Irish Folklore Commission," 12–13. The decision to collect materials relating to the famine (and possibly the content of the questionnaire) was prompted by the planned commemorative volume edited by Edwards and Williams, for which Ó Duilearga's suggestion had provided the initial impetus (see Chapter 1, note 18). Topics covered by the famine questionnaire included the initial appearance of the blight in 1845 and subsequent years; stories and traditions relating to death and burial; accounts of the dissolution of local families by death or emigration; evictions; alternative foodstuffs resorted to in the absence of potatoes; and funding and administration of relief schemes at local level.

19. McHugh, "Famine in Irish Oral Tradition."

20. Póirtéir, *Famine Echoes* and *Glórtha ón Ghorta.*

21. Ó Gráda, *Black '47 and Beyond,* 199.

22. On de Valera's cultural politics, see Ó Crualaoich, "Primacy of Form."

23. Ó Duilearga, "Volkskundliche Arbeit in Irland"; Ó Giolláin, *Locating Irish Folklore,* 136–41.

24. Ó Duilearga, "Editorial Address," 3–6.

25. Irish Folklore Commission, *Irish Folklore and Tradition,* 3.

26. Ibid., 4.

27. See, for example, Wilde, *Irish Popular Superstitions*; Evans, *Irish Folk Ways*; Bourke, "The Baby and the Bathwater."

28. Benjamin, "Storyteller," 84.

29. See Giddens, *Nation State and Violence,* 41–49; Goody, *Domestication of the Savage Mind* and *Interface Between the Written and the Oral*; Ong, *Orality and Literacy.*

30. See Tyler, "On Being Out of Words."

31. See Taussig, "Construction of America," 349–50.

32. Compare Joseph Falaky Nagy's account of the relationship between orality and textuality in medieval Irish literature. Nagy's study is concerned in particular with the staging of oral performances within written texts, a motif he sees as linked to efforts by an imported text-based Christian culture (responsible for the earliest written texts in Irish) to assimilate and recast preexisting (and hitherto orally transmitted) stories and traditions. Nagy, *Conversing,* 1–22.

33. Derrida has characterized the archive as partaking simultaneously of both "commencement" and "command," as seeking, on the one hand, to fix and record a moment of origin and, on the other, as implicated in questions of power and authority, of who controls access to the archive and who has the right to interpret it. Derrida, *Archive Fever,* 1–5.

34. On Anderson's seeming neglect of this aspect, see Silverstein, "Whorfianism and the Linguistic Imagination of Nationality." Silverstein notes that Anderson, in locating the preconditions for national consciousness in print capitalism

and linguistic standardization, appears taken in by the trope of "we-ness" that serves to construct such a discursive space and thus fails to recognize that such a regime of language does not correspond to an objective reality, but is rather produced and promulgated in a context of linguistic, cultural, and political-economic contestation. For a discussion of the Irish language in relation to projects of nation-state building in twentieth-century Ireland (and in particular to emergent conflicts between state bureaucracies and contemporary speakers of Irish regarding definitions of linguistic community), see Coleman, *Return from the West*. On the more general question of tensions and discrepancies between "official" and "unofficial" representations of national culture, see Herzfeld, *Cultural Intimacy*.

35. Bhabha, "DissemiNation," 294–95.

36. Michael Corduff, Rossport, County Mayo, IFC 1072, 44.

37. Phantasm refers here to the relationship between the historical erasures supposedly brought about by the birth of (in this case) the modern Irish nation-state and the reinscription of those imputed losses as part of an ongoing discourse on national identity. The event of originary loss is thus graspable only via a structure of *Nachträglichkeit* (Freud's term for the way in which subjects invest past events with significance by retroactively revising them at a later date). On this point, see Ivy, *Discourses of the Vanishing*, 22; Laplanche and Pontalis, *Language of Psychoanalysis*, 112.

38. Offa West, County Tipperary, IFC 1068, 32–33.

39. Kilcubbin, the Ards, County Down, IFC 1069, 11–12.

40. Benjamin, *Origin of German Tragic Drama*, 179, 235; Pandolfo, *Impasse of the Angels*, 218.

41. Ned Buckley, Knocknagree, County Cork, IFC 1071, 109.

42. The term *vanishing* is borrowed from Ivy and refers to the ways in which both national imaginaries and teleologies of modernization are imbued with a phantasmal logic of repetition and temporal deferral. As in Ivy's discussion of the beginnings of "nativist ethnology" in early twentieth-century Japan, the centrality assumed by otherwise peripheral cultural forms in discourses of national identity and belonging illustrates the nation-state's ideological appropriation of "folk tradition" even in the moment of its supposed effacement. Ivy, *Discourses of the Vanishing*, 20, 66–97.

43. For a discussion of linkages between romanticism, aesthetic theory, and nationalism in the European context, see Kaiser, *Romanticism, Aesthetics and Nationalism*; Eade, *Romantic Nationalism*.

44. De Man, *Allegories of Reading* and *Rhetoric of Romanticism*. On the relationship between allegory and repetition, see Ronell, *Stupidity*, 97–161.

45. See Taussig, *Magic of the State*, 3, 99–108.

46. See Laclau and Mouffe, *Hegemony and Socialist Strategy*, 93–148; and Žižek, *Sublime Object of Ideology*, 11–53.

47. Irish Folklore Commission, *Irish Folklore and Tradition*, 3.

48. One of Ó Cadhain's most bitter polemics against academic folklorists was

delivered in a speech to the Writers' Club (Cumann na Scribhneorí) in Dublin in 1950, in which he described such institutions as the National Museum, the Royal Irish Academy, and the Irish Folklore Commission as comprising the "chief cemetery of Ireland," containing the "dead clay" (*an chré mharbh*) of fossilized tradition in contrast to the "living clay" (*an chré bheo*), represented by contemporary speakers of Irish, who appeared to hold much less interest for many folklorists. Ó Giolláin, *Locating Irish Folklore*, 149–53. For a more extended discussion of Ó Cadhain's work and influence, see Coleman, *Return from the West* and "A Cat and a Mouse."

49. Žižek, "Enjoy Your Nation as Yourself," 201.

50. Chatterjee's phrase "the nation and its fragments" describes the relationship between capital and community that he takes to be constitutive of the history of modernity. "Community" refers here not to the historically superseded past (as in Durkheimian sociology and its variants) but remains irreducibly contemporaneous with the history of capital and its concomitant transformations: "Community, which ideally should have been banished from the kingdom of capital, continues to lead a subterranean, potentially subversive life within it because it refuses to go away." Chakrabarty makes an analogous point with reference to the coexistence of histories of capital and "histories of belonging." Chatterjee, *Nation and Its Fragments*, 234–39; Chakrabarty, *Provincializing Europe*, 47–71.

51. Ó Conaill's volume can be compared to a number of other works from the same period featuring the repertoires of individual storytellers, notably a series of autobiographical writings produced by residents of the now uninhabited Blasket Islands, off the coast of County Kerry. These included Tomás Ó Criomthain (1855?–1937), Muiris Ó Súilleabháin (1904–1950), and, perhaps best known, Peig Sayers (1873–1958). Ó Giolláin, *Locating Irish Folklore*, 125–28.

52. Ó Duilearga, *Leabhar Sheáin Í Chonaill*, i–xxvii; Irish-language version published by the Educational Council of Ireland in association with Comhairle le Bhéaloideas Éireann (Folklore of Ireland Council) (Dublin, 1948).

53. Ó Duilearga, *Leabhair Sheáin Í Chonaill*, xix.

CHAPTER 3

1. Carlyle, *Reminiscences of My Irish Journey*, a memoir published posthumously in 1882. For details, see Froude, *Froude's Life of Carlyle*, 478–79, 684–85.

2. Carlyle, *Reminiscences of My Irish Journey*, 2.

3. See Froude, *Froude's Life of Carlyle*, 478–79; Heffer, *Moral Desperado*, 256–57; Kaplan, *Thomas Carlyle*, 326. On Young Ireland, see below (Chapter 5).

4. Kinealy, *This Great Calamity*, 262.

5. Ibid., 254–64.

6. Carlyle's views were elaborated in his lectures of 1840 "On Heroes, Hero Worship and the Heroic in History" and in a series of publications: *Chartism* (1839), *Past and Present* (1843), and *Latterday Pamphlets* (1850). See Moran, "Thomas Carlyle"; and Wellek, "Carlyle and the Philosophy of History." On the

question of Carlyle's understanding of and attitude toward modernity, see La Valley, *Carlyle and the Idea of the Modern*.

7. Heffer, *Moral Desperado*, 266–67.

8. Carlyle, *Reminiscences of My Irish Journey*, 2–4.

9. More than half a century later, in an episode that has become emblematic of numerous latter-day colonial encounters (not to mention anthropological reflections thereon), Joseph Conrad's narrator, Marlow, would describe the same waterway as evoking not only the imperial and mercantile might of contemporary London, but also the lingering aftertraces of an earlier time, continuing to impinge, threateningly, on the present, a time of swamps and shadowed, impenetrable forests, populated by murderous "wild men"—"and this too has been one of the dark places of the earth." Conrad, *Heart of Darkness*, 5; Taussig, *Shamanism, Colonialism and the Wild Man*, 10–11; Clifford, "On Ethnographic Self-Fashioning," 97–102.

10. Carlyle, *Reminiscences of My Irish Journey*, 7–9.

11. Ibid., 18.

12. On the United Irishmen, see Whelan, *Fellowship of Freedom*.

13. Carlyle, *Reminiscences of My Irish Journey*, 46.

14. Ibid., 70.

15. Ibid., 114.

16. Ibid., 125.

17. Ibid., 126.

18. Ibid., 130.

19. Ibid., 135.

20. Ibid., 196.

21. The papal bull *Laudabiliter*, issued in 1155 by the English Pope Adrian IV, had proclaimed Henry *dominus* (lord) over Ireland, with responsibility for the reform of Irish morals and Church affairs. See Leerssen, *Mere Irish and Fíor-Ghael*, 34–35.

22. Gerald of Wales, *History and Topography of Ireland*, 101–2. Gerald's account invokes a distinction, subsequently to be enshrined in statutes, between the "wild Irish," classed as the king's enemies, and loyal English subjects residing in Ireland, mostly in the region around Dublin that came to be known from the late fifteenth century as the "Pale." See Leerssen, "Wildness, Wilderness and Ireland." 30–31.

23. Unlike previous English monarchs, who had retained the title of "lord" (as granted by the terms of *Laudabiliter*), Henry proclaimed himself king of Ireland. The Act of Supremacy of 1537 also proclaimed him supreme head of the newly established Church of Ireland. Henry's religious reforms were further consolidated by Elizabeth I, with the religious settlement of 1560, consisting of a renewed Act of Supremacy and an Act of Uniformity, requiring all clergy in Ireland to use the English Book of Common Prayer of 1559, and imposing fines both on clergy who refused to comply and on members of the laity who refused to attend services. See Canny, *Elizabethan Conquest*, 45–92, 117–35; and Ellis, *Ireland in the Age of the Tudors*, 122–24, 207–17.

24. Spenser, *View of the Present State of Ireland*. The Nine Years' War began in April 1593, with a rebellion led by Hugh O'Neill, second earl of Tyrone. The in-

surgents demanded an autonomous Catholic Ireland, run by the native aristocracy and "Old English" (the descendants of Anglo-Norman conquerors, as distinct from more recent settlers, or "New English"). The conflict ended, after an expense of almost 2 million pounds sterling to the English exchequer, with O'Neill's surrender at Mellifont in March 1603. Spenser, himself a New English planter, was to die in poverty in London in 1599 after being driven off his estates in County Cork. See Morgan, *Tyrone's Rebellion.*

25. The Confederate War (1641–1653), which overlapped with the English Civil War (1642–1648), consisted of a general Catholic rising directed against the Ulster Irish and the Old English of the Pale (see Chapter 3, note 22). Cromwell campaigned in Ireland between 1649 and 1650, his best-known engagements being the sieges of Drogheda (September 11, 1649) and Wexford (October 11, 1649), both resulting in the massacre of garrisons refusing to surrender. Cromwell's campaign was followed by the execution, imprisonment, or transportation of numerous Catholic clergy, along with the widespread confiscation of Catholic lands. See Murphy, *Cromwell in Ireland.*

26. Leerssen, *Mere Irish and Fíor-Ghael,* 61–76. Notable among eighteenth-century travelogues are John Bush's *Hibernia Curiosa* (1769) and Arthur Young's two-volume *A Tour in Ireland* (1780). Both bestow extravagant praises on the beauty of the Irish landscape (especially the district around Killarney, County Kerry) while portraying the Irish themselves as hapless victims of spendthrift landlords and extravagant middlemen. Leerssen, *Mere Irish and Fíor-Ghael,* 71; Young, *Tour in Ireland,* 1:152. The view that the Irish rural masses were well-meaning but credulous simpletons, misled by their designing superiors, was later to become a staple of English anti-Repeal propaganda. Lebow, *White Britain and Black Ireland,* 50–63.

27. The racialized portrayal of the Irish Celt is amply documented in the nineteenth-century cartoons and caricatures discussed by Curtis (*Apes and Angels*). Already influenced by contemporary scientific theories of race, such depictions tended, after the publication of Darwin's *Origin of Species* in 1859, to take on a more explicitly evolutionist slant, expressed both by the "simianizing" of Irish features in pictographic representations (already apparent in the early nineteenth century) and by the labeling of the Irish as "chimpanzees" or "the missing link between the Negro and the Gorilla." See Curtis, *Anglo-Saxons and Celts,* 28–48; Lebow, *White Britain and Black Ireland,* 35–70; Gilley, "English Attitudes." On the scientific background to racialized portrayals of the Irish, see Stepan, *Idea of Race in Science;* and Stocking, *Victorian Anthropology,* 186–237.

28. On Carlyle's relationship to German literature, see Vida, *Romantic Affinities.*

29. Kant, *Critique of the Power of Judgement,* 128–59. See also Gibbons, *Kant's Theory of Imagination,* 124–51.

30. Peat bogs, consisting principally of water and compacted vegetable and animal remains, are estimated to have covered up to 3 million acres of Ireland's land surface in the past. They are subdivided by geographers into two kinds: the raised

bogs occupying the lowland areas of the Irish midlands, formed between ten thousand and seven thousand years ago from postglacial lakes, and the blanket bogs of the uplands and west coast, dating from between five and six thousand years before the present, their formation linked, in part, to the waterlogging of soils resulting from early woodland clearances and agricultural land use. Turbary rights (the right to dig peat or "turf" for fuel) traditionally constituted an important element in leasehold agreements between landlords and tenants, and domestic rights of turbary survive to the present, alongside the commercial exploitation of bogs both for horticultural purposes as a source of fuel. Peat production in Ireland was nationalized in 1946, with the creation of Bord na Móna (Turf Board), a state-owned company with a statutory responsibility to produce fuel from Irish peat bogs. Mitchell, *Reading the Irish Landscape*, 204–11; Foss and O'Connell, "Bogland," 191–92; Aalen, Whelan, and Stout, *Atlas*, 106–21.

31. The reports also suggested that during the early years of the century, actual reclamation was, for the most part, carried out by small tenant farmers, under the dual pressure of rent increases on the one hand, and on the other, the desire of landlords to maximize their income from rent on land used for the cultivation of commercial crops, thus forcing their smaller tenants to reclaim areas of bog in order to meet their own subsistence needs. Connell, "Colonization of Waste Land"; Foss and O'Connell, "Bogland," 187–88.

32. Gray, *Famine, Land and Politics*, 56–59, 153–62, 337.

33. Coles and Coles, *People of the Wetlands*, 12–17, 32–34.

34. Glob, *Bog People*, 18–62, 101–18.

35. Benjamin, "Goethe's *Elective Affinities*," 303–4.

36. Benjamin, "Franz Kafka," 130.

37. Bachofen, *Myth, Religion and Mother-Right*, 113. In Benjamin's essay on Bachofen (written in France, with a view to introducing Bachofen's work to the French public), the latter is credited with revealing the *tableau de la préhistoire*—traces of an archaic world (*die unbeweinte Schöpfung*), predating written history and ruled over by the force of Matter (*Stoff*), along with the feminine and Dionysian principles. In the essay "Franz Kafka," figures such as Odradek ("The Cares of a Family Man") are identified with an "intermediate world" (*Zwischenwelt*) corresponding to Bachofen's archaic, telluric realm. See Hanssen, *Walter Benjamin's Other History*, 93.

38. Benjamin, "Franz Kafka," 116–17.

39. For a more extended discussion of this analogy, see Benjamin, "Excavation and Memory"; and Sagnol, "La Méthode Archaeologique de Walter Benjamin."

40. Stüssi, *Erinnerung an die Zukunft*, 25.

41. Heaney, *Death of a Naturalist*, 32–33.

42. Heaney, *North*, 41.

43. For a more critical reading of Heaney's bog poems, see Lloyd, "Pap for the Dispossessed."

44. Carlyle, *Reminiscences of My Irish Journey*, 201. Since the inception of the

Poor Law, the Poor Law commissioners had insisted that work be required of all workhouse inmates, in order to deter unnecessary requests for relief. Stone breaking was frequently chosen as suitable work for paupers, both because it could be easily quantified and superintended and because it did not set them in competition with independent laborers. Kinealy, *This Great Calamity*, 199–201.

45. Carlyle, *Reminiscences of My Irish Journey*, 201.

46. Ibid., 200.	52. Ibid., 247.
47. Ibid., 242.	53. Ibid., 253–54.
48. Ibid., 233.	54. Ibid., 257.
49. Ibid., 248.	55. Ibid., 259.
50. Ibid., 245.	56. Ibid., 261.
51. Ibid., 240.	57. Ibid., 262.

CHAPTER 4

1. Kinealy, *This Great Calamity*, 6–11.

2. *Frazer's Magazine* 36 (March 1847): 373.

3. The argument that "Irish property must pay for Irish poverty" was invoked by Russell's government to justify the passing of the 1847 amendment to the Poor Law. Russell and his supporters sought to create a reinvigorated landlord class, conscious of its responsibilities toward tenants and capable of managing its estates on a profitable basis. See Gray, *Famine, Land and Politics*, 33–34, 182–85, 247–48. James Donnelly's survey of British press coverage of Ireland during the famine years suggests, however, that the tendency of English newspapers to blame Irish landlords for the distress of the Irish poor declined after 1847. Donnelly, "Irish Property," 60–65.

4. The district referred to as "Little Ireland" was situated to the southwest of Manchester's Oxford Road, in the curve of the river Medlock, and was surrounded on all four sides factories and high embankments. It was home to more than four thousand Irish. See Engels, *Condition of the Working Class*, 98, 125–26. On the background to Engels's study, see Marcus, *Engels, Manchester and the Working Class*.

5. Ibid., 126. Engels's account echoes not only the views of the Liberal commentators who are among his principal sources (see Lebow, *White Britain and Black Ireland*, 38–43), but also those of Thomas Carlyle, whose characterization of the "wild Milesian" he quotes at length, concluding that "If we except his exaggerated and one-sided condemnation of the Irish national character, Carlyle is perfectly right." Engels, *Condition of the Working Class*, 123–24.

6. Malthus, "Population," 306–33.

7. Gallagher, "The Body Versus the Social Body," 83–84.

8. *Speenhamland* was the name given to a system of poor relief devised by a meeting of Berkshire magistrates at Speen, near Reading, in 1795, in response to a poor harvest and high food prices. A scale was drawn up to regulate payments to

the poor, taking into consideration the size of the claimant's family and the current price of bread. See Daunton, *Progress and Poverty*, 447–74.

9. Malthus, *First Essay on Population*, 57–71.

10. Gallaher, "The Body Versus the Social Body," 92.

11. Malthus, *First Essay on Population*, 303–27.

12. Malthus, *Essay on the Principle of Population*, 293–300.

13. Ibid., 299–300.

14. Ibid., 127.

15. Malthus, "Newenham and Others on the State of Ireland," 337–39.

16. Ibid., 350.

17. The series of so-called penal laws (or popery laws) introduced after the expulsion from the English throne in 1688 of the Catholic convert James Stuart (James II) included both the banishment of Catholic clergy and a succession of measures aimed at the Catholic laity, including a prohibition on holding public office and restrictions on the purchase and sale of landed property. Between 1774 and 1793, a series of Catholic Relief Acts reversed many of these measures, although by Malthus's time, Catholics remained excluded from judiciary and senior government offices. After a campaign by the Catholic Association (formed in 1823), these restrictions were removed through a final Catholic Relief Act, which became law in April 1829. See Whelan and Power, *Endurance and Emergence*; and O'Ferrall, *Catholic Emancipation*.

18. Malthus, "Newenham and Others on the State of Ireland," 350–55.

19. Malthus, "Newenham on the State of Ireland," 158–70.

20. Kinealy, *This Great Calamity*, 11–20; *Death-Dealing Famine*, 39–40; see also Burke, *People*.

21. Black, *Economic Thought*, 40.

22. Ibid., 11.

23. Kinealy, *This Great Calamity*, 21–22.

24. Ibid., 23–26. These provisions were later supplemented by an act in 1843 that made landlords liable to pay rates on land valued at under £4 per year (principally in the west of Ireland, where land was heavily subdivided) and, in 1847, by the Quarter Acre Clause. In both cases, the desired end was consolidation of holdings, which was usually achieved at the cost of evictions and clearances. Kinealy, *This Great Calamity*, 180–84, 216–27; *Death-Dealing Famine*, 36–41, 123.

25. The Irish Poor Law operated initially under the supervision of the English Poor Law Commission until 1847, when a separate Poor Law Commission for Ireland was created. The commission superintended the election and proceedings of Poor Law boards and was empowered to dissolve boards whose members were incompetent or inactive. In the decades that followed, the Poor Law Commission assumed responsibility for overseeing a range of welfare services, including the management of dispensaries and the appointment of sanitary inspectors. The commission was dissolved in 1872 and its functions transferred to a newly constituted local government. Kinealy, *This Great Calamity*, 23–24, 150–54. See also Burke, *People*, 44–46, 79–100.

26. O'Connor, *Workhouses,* 94–110.

27. Kinealy, *This Great Calamity,* 26–29.

28. Hume, *History of England,* 1:424; quoted in Leerssen, *Mere Irish and Fíor-Ghael,* 65.

29. Gray, *Famine, Land and Politics,* 96–106. For a more wide-ranging account of evangelical currents in nineteenth-century intellectual life, see Hilton, *Age of Atonement.*

30. Repr. Killen, *Famine Decade,* 189–90.

31. *Illustrated London News* 10, no. 256 (March 23, 1847): 201–2. Similar sermons were preached at other London churches, in many cases relying on the same texts and analogies.

32. Gray, *Famine, Land and Politics,* 239. Gray's exhaustive survey of relief policy during the famine years shows Russell as subject to pressure, on the one hand, from "moralists" like Wood and Trevelyan, and on the other, from moderates within his own party, who urged continued government support for relief schemes, including public works (235–39).

33. Nassau Senior, *Journals, Conversations and Essays Relating to Ireland,* 1:67.

34. See Boylan and Foley, *Political Economy,* 2–6, 67–69, and "Nation Perishing." On Whately's life and career, see Donald H. Akenson, *Protestant in Purgatory.*

35. Daniel O'Connell (1775–1848), member of Parliament (1832–1847) and campaigner for repeal of the Act of Union. See Nowlan, *Politics of Repeal,* and Edwards, *Daniel O'Connell.* O'Connell's widely noted skill as an orator was viewed with particular suspicion by English commentators. His addresses to Repeal Association "Monster Meetings" were interpreted (especially by *Punch*) as a form of rabble-rousing, appealing to the all too easily excited passions of his audience, and thus deflecting them from the realization of their true interests, which were taken to coincide with the preservation of the union: "Mr. O'Connell knows too well, it is only by keeping an Irishman's head in ignorance of what his hand and heart are led to do, when he sends round the hat, he can make sure of his shilling." *Punch* 9 (1845): 45.

36. Boylan and Foley, *Political Economy,* 126–27.

37. Ibid., 128–29.

38. Ibid., vii.

39. Quoted in Black, *Economic Thought,* 16.

40. Daly, *Spirit of Earnest Inquiry,* 7–37.

41. "Report of Council" (read at opening of sixth session), *Transactions of the Dublin Statistical Society* 3 (1851–1854): 8; quoted in Boylan and Foley, *Political Economy,* 111.

42. Senior, "Ireland"; see also Gray, "Nassau Senior and the *Edinburgh Review.*"

43. Senior, "Proposals for Extending the Irish Poor Law."

44. Gray, *Famine, Land and Politics,* 239.

45. Gray, *Famine, Land and Politics,* 270–85; Kinealy, *This Great Calamity,* 180–81.

46. Gray, *Famine, Land and Politics*, 231.

47. Trevelyan, "The Irish Crisis"; repr. Killen, *Famine Decade*, 175.

48. *Times* (October 12, 1847); quoted in Kinealy, *Death-Dealing Famine*, 121.

49. It is instructive to consider the role of political economy in nineteenth-century Ireland alongside the theory of "colonial governmentality" outlined by David Scott, who distinguishes between the notion of a "break" with the past as a commonplace of ideologies of modernization and the specific ways in which such a break is configured in contexts of colonial rule so as to undermine preexisting forms of life and facilitate the production of new ones. Scott, "Colonial Governmentality," 26.

50. Quoted in Inglis, *Poverty and the Industrial Revolution*, 235.

51. See Foucault, *History of Sexuality*, 140–41, 143–44.

52. On this point, see Agamben, *Homo Sacer*, 188.

53. Mauss, *Gift*, 3.

54. See Bataille, "Notion of Expenditure" and *Accursed Share*, vol. 1; Derrida, *Given Time*, 6–11. James Boon suggests, rightly, I think, that Derrida's reading fails to give Mauss himself sufficient credit for recognizing the contradictory character of the gift, as attested both by Mauss's opening formulation and by his treatment of an assortment of ethnographic case studies. Derrida's own discussion might thus be read less as a deconstruction of Mauss's argument than as an (unacknowledged) appropriation of possibilities already made available in Mauss's text. Boon, *Verging on Extra-Vagance*, 211–20.

55. Heidegger, *On Time and Being*, 5; Derrida, *Given Time*, 20–22; Bracken, *Potlatch Papers*, 5–31.

56. Bracken, *Potlatch Papers*, 30–31. For a more detailed account of the potlatch, see Boas, *Kwakiutl Ethnography*, 77–104.

57. See Leerssen, *Mere Irish and Fíor-Ghael*, 61–76.

58. Derrida, *Given Time*, 34–70.

59. Nineteenth-century Ireland here parallels numerous other colonial situations in exemplifying what Chatterjee has termed "the colonial rule of difference," whereby the project of colonial rule, undertaken in the name of progress and universal history, could be sustained only if colonized populations were viewed as innately resistant to the imperatives of modernization and progress and therefore suited only to be governed rather than to govern themselves. Chatterjee, *Nation and Its Fragments*, 20. See also Dirks, *Castes of Mind*, 9–10. In the case of Ireland, as I have suggested, matters were further complicated both by the physical proximity of rulers and ruled and by Ireland's status as a titular part of the United Kingdom, factors that made the articulation of colonial differences at once more urgent and more problematic.

CHAPTER 5

1. See Woodham-Smith, *Great Hunger*, 197–200.

2. Mitchel, *Last Conquest*, 219.

3. See Trevelyan, "The Irish Crisis."

4. In more recent years, an understanding of famine as a conjunction of natural and sociological factors has been elaborated in terms of welfare economics by, among others, Amartya Sen, who has argued, famously, that famine should be understood in terms of a crisis of "entitlements" (including access to resources, control over food supplies, and so forth), such that certain groups within a society are unable to obtain enough to eat. Sen's theories have been discussed with reference to nineteenth-century famines (particularly in the colonized world) by Mike Davis. Davis, *Late Victorian Holocausts*, 19–20; Sen, *Poverty and Famines*, 1–9.

5. On the origins of this disciplinary division of labor in the early modern period, see Latour, *We Have Never Been Modern*, 13–48; and Shapin and Schaffer, *Leviathan and the Air Pump*.

6. Storms are mentioned in a number of accounts; fog is recorded in Counties Clare, Galway, and Mayo, IFC 1069, 324–57.

7. Kilkenny West, County Westmeath; IFC 1069, 182–83.

8. Strabally, County Laois, IFC 1075, 1–69; Dromard Parish, County Longford, IFC 1429, 143–45; Eniskeane, County Cork, IFC 1071, 237–41; Rossport, County Mayo, IFC 1072, 65–73.

9. Gregory, *Visions and Beliefs*, 206.

10. Evans-Wentz, *Fairy Faith*, 43.

11. Derrida, *Gift of Death*.

12. Dáithí Ó Ceantabhaill, Croom, County Limerick, IFC 1068, 57.

13. O'Neill, "Peig Sayers and Need Foods," 77–79.

14. Tahilla, County Kerry, IFC 1068, 118; Jimmy Quinn, 76, shoemaker, Kilkeel, County Down, IFC 1072, 393.

15. Drumakill, Castleblayney, County Monaghan, IFC 1069, 34.

16. Tuosist, Kenmare, County Kerry, IFC 1068, 110.

17. Bourke, "Wild Men and Wailing Women"; Nagy, "Liminality and Knowledge" and "Wisdom of the Geilt"; Ó Riain, "Study of the Irish Legend of the Wild Man." Seamus Heaney has produced a modern verse rendition of the Sweeney story, based on J. G. O'Keefe's bilingual edition, first published by the Irish Texts Society in 1913. O'Keefe's text is in turn based on a manuscript written in County Sligo between 1671 and 1674 (now part of the Stowe Collection at the Royal Irish Academy). The editor admits that the text may have been composed at any time between 1200 and 1500, although earlier references to the story are to be found in the tenth-century *Book of Aicill*. Heaney conjectures that traditions relating to Sweeney may date back to the Battle of Moira, where Sweeney (until then king of an area spanning present-day County Antrim and north Down) was alleged to have lost his sanity and been transformed by the curse of Saint Ronan into a bird of the air. Heaney, *Sweeney Astray*, v–viii.

18. Central Relief Committee of the Society of Friends, *Transactions*, 181. The Society of Friends (Quakers) responded to the failure of the potato crop by setting up a Central Relief Committee in Dublin, acting in conjunction with a series of

locally based committees throughout Ireland. The Friends distributed food, clothing, cooking equipment, seeds, and money and established soup kitchens in rural
areas. In addition, the Central Relief Committee sent a number of representatives
to observe and report on conditions in Ireland. Their findings (*Transactions of the
Central Relief Committee of the Society of Friends*) were published in 1852 by Whelan and Chapman of Dublin.

19. For the genealogy of this distinction, see Woolf, *The Poor in Western Europe*, 1–46; and Jutte, *Poverty and Deviance*, 8–20, 158–65, both of whom trace its
origins in early modern Europe to urban centers, where existing poor relief mechanisms were put under pressure by increasing immigration from the countryside,
with the result that those charged with the administration of relief tended to favor
applicants already resident in towns, whereas newcomers were more likely to be
classed as tricksters and frauds.

20. Ó Ciosáin, "Boccoughs and God's Poor," 94–94; O'Neill, "Poverty in Ireland," 22–24. Ó Ciosáin suggests that, contrary to the findings of the Commission
of Inquiry, a distinction analogous to that between "deserving" and "undeserving"
poor was operative in nineteenth-century Ireland. Those perceived as genuinely
needy or destitute, he suggests, were considered "God's poor" and as such, deserving of assistance. The undeserving, in contrast, included those known to be given
to drunkenness, quarreling, or blasphemy, along with "boccoughs" (Ir. *bacach*), a
class of beggars often to be found at fairs and markets and given to using deceptive means in order to elicit charitable donations. The same distinction, reinforced
by the preaching of clergy of all denominations, is echoed in a proverb current in
County Mayo in the early twentieth century: *ní bacach an fear siúil ach bochtán Dé*
(the wandering man is not a boccough but one of God's poor). Ó Máille, *Seanfhocla Chonnacht*, 81.

21. Central Relief Committee of the Society of Friends, *Transactions*, 179.

22. *Illustrated London News* 10, no. 250 (February 13, 1847): 100.

23. Ibid.

24. *Illustrated London News* 10, no. 251 (February 20, 1847): 117–18.

25. Ibid.

26. *Illustrated London News* 10, no. 252 (February 27, 1847): 135.

27. Ibid.

28. Quoted in Woodham-Smith, *Great Hunger*, 164.

29. Ibid., 61–64.

30. Ibid., 95–98.

31. *Illustrated London News* 10, no. 259 (April 17, 1847): 250.

32. Somerville, *Letters from Ireland*, 107. Somerville tended to blame conditions
in Ireland on the negligence of Irish landlords and remained convinced that political economy was "the very essence of humanity, benevolence and justice" (134).

33. Ibid., 107–8. For details of the history, archaeology and geology of the region, see O'Hara, *Mayo*.

34. For a description of Erris, see Ní Cheannain, *Heritage of Mayo*, 15–19.

35. Central Relief Committee of the Society of Friends, *Transactions*, 205.

36. Ibid., 205–6.

37. Ibid, 163.

38. Ibid., 164.

39. Ibid., 168.

40. Ibid., 165.

41. Ibid., 166.

42. Ibid., 167.

43. Lee, "Ribbonmen"; O'Farrell, "Millenialism"; Donnelly, "Pastorini and Captain Rock."

44. In the see of Limerick, millenarian excitement at the time was perceived to be so high that the Roman Catholic bishop had felt it necessary to issue a pastoral letter contraverting Pastorini. Donnelly, "Pastorini and Captain Rock," 136.

45. Donnelly suggests that the success of the Repeal Association during this period may owe much to the (qualified) support of many Roman Catholic clergy, despite the officially anti-Repeal stance of the Vatican, the Catholic hierarchy having always been unequivocal in its condemnation of Pastorini. Donnelly, "Pastorini and Captain Rock," 136–37.

46. Eiriksson, "Food Supply," 88–89. The Office of Public Works, or Board of Works, was established by an Act of Parliament of 1831 (Act for the Extension and Promotion of Public Works in Ireland). The board's response to the potato failure was to focus on providing employment for the destitute poor under the terms of a series of acts passed early in the parliamentary session of 1846, for the specific purpose of providing relief by employment (road building, land drainage, construction of piers and harbors, etc.). In August of that year, the government was given additional powers to employ the laboring poor by means of treasury loans, resulting in a daily average of ninety thousand people being employed in that year, the number rising to a hundred thousand by the autumn of 1847. Details of the board's activities were set out in monthly reports submitted to Parliament. See Griffiths, "Irish Board of Works."

47. *House of Commons Papers* (1847), 764; quoted in Eiriksson, "Food Supply," 89.

48. Ibid., 78–79.

49. *Limerick Reporter* (11 May, 14 May, 1847); quoted in Eiriksson, "Food Supply," 85–86.

50. Ibid., 87.

51. Gray notes that in the final months of 1847 the nonappearance of the potato blight, an unexpectedly productive Irish grain harvest, and a financial recession combined to produce a hardening of attitudes toward Ireland on the part of both politicians and press. Gray, *Famine, Land and Politics*, 285.

52. *Illustrated London News* 11, no. 280 (September 11, 1847): 167.

53. *Illustrated London News* 11, no, 281 (September 18, 1847): 287.

54. *Illustrated London News* 11, no. 285 (October 16, 1847): 254.

55. *Illustrated London News* 11, no. 286 (October 23, 1847): 270.

56. *Times* (February 7, 1848); quoted in Woodham-Smith, *Great Hunger*, 329.

57. Hill, "Intelligentsia and Irish Nationalism"; Ryder, "Reading Lessons." The *Nation* was founded in 1842 by Duffy, Dillon, and Davis. Their stated aim—leg-

islative independence under the British crown—was one that Smith O'Brien continued to endorse until the end, while Mitchel and others came to favor the severance of all political ties with Britain. Gwynn, *Young Ireland and 1848*, 7–8; Davis, *Young Ireland Movement*, 9–36.

58. Quoted in Ryder, "Reading Lessons," 156.

59. Ibid.

60. *Nation*, 5, no. 224 (January 23, 1847): 251.

61. Ibid.

62. *Nation* 5, no. 225 (January 30, 1847): 265.

63. Duffy, *Four Years of Irish History*, 217–72; Gwynn, *Young Ireland and 1848*, 67–78; Donnelly, "Famine in Irish Politics," 360–61; Davis, *Young Ireland Movement*, 82–116.

64. Duffy, *Four Years of Irish History*, 357–407; Gwynn, *Young Ireland and 1848*, 79–86, 98–113.

65. Gwynn, *Young Ireland and 1848*, 138–53.

66. Ibid., 154–70; Duffy, *Four Years of Irish History*, 533–87.

67. Duffy, *Four Years of Irish History*, 600–40; Gwynn, *Young Ireland and 1848*, 185–215; Nowlan, *Politics of Repeal*, 194–96, 202–5; Donnelly, "Famine in Irish Politics," 366–68; Davis, *Young Ireland Movement*, 159–62.

68. Gwynn, *Young Ireland and 1848*, 215–27; Woodham-Smith, *Great Hunger*, 349–56.

69. Duffy, *Four Years of Irish History*, 641–700; Gwynn, *Young Ireland and 1848*, 250–68; Woodham-Smith, *Great Hunger*, 356–9; Donnelly, "Famine in Irish Politics," 368–9. Smith O'Brien and Meagher were convicted of high treason and sentenced to transportation for life to Tasmania. Smith O'Brien was released in 1854, on grounds of ill health, and lived at Bangor, North Wales, until his death in 1854. Meagher escaped in 1852 to the United States. Mitchel was transported first to Bermuda and, subsequently, to Van Diemen's Land. He escaped to the United States in 1853. Duffy, who had been remanded in Newgate Prison at the time of the rising, was tried five times under the Treason Felony Act. The prosecution case was dropped in 1849, after successive failures to obtain a conviction. In 1852, he was elected member of Parliament for New Ross and tried, unsuccessfully, to introduce a bill giving tenants the right to compensation for improvements made on their holdings. In 1854, he emigrated to Australia, where he rose to become minister of the province of Victoria. He was knighted in 1873. Duffy, *Four Years of Irish History*, 700–80; Gwynn, *Young Ireland and 1848*, 268–73; Woodham-Smith, *Great Hunger*, 417–18; Sloan, *William Smith O'Brien*, 291–303; Donnelly, "Famine in Irish Politics," 370–71.

70. Such an interpretation was both reiterated and, in part, challenged by the 1998 conference of the Society for the Study of Nineteenth Century Ireland, held at University College, Cork, and entitled "1798, 1848, 1898: Revolution, Renewal and Commemoration." The proceedings have since been published under the editorship of Laurence M. Geary as *Rebellion and Remembrance in Modern Ireland*.

Several of the contributions set out explicitly to reexamine the relationship between politics and forms of popular protest. Gary Owens's "Popular Mobilization and the Rising of 1848: The Clubs of the Irish Confederation" (51–63) considers the ways in which the network of Confederate Clubs departed from and transformed earlier forms of popular protest, including agrarian secret societies. James Donnelly's "Sectarianism in 1798 and in Catholic Nationalist Memory" (15–37) argues that the earlier rising of 1798 shows the persistence of sectarian idioms and popular belief at local level despite the avowedly antisectarian aims of the Society of United Irishmen themselves. Two further contributions consider the afterlife of historical events in popular memory: Tom Dunne's "*Tá Gaedhil bhocht cráidhte*: Memory, Tradition and the Politics of the Poor in Gaelic Poetry and Song" (93–111) and Maura Cronin's "Memory, Story and Balladry: 1798 and Its Place in Popular Memory in Prefamine Ireland" (112–34). At the same time, the volume as a whole arguably affirms the canonical status of the 1848 rising by placing it alongside the events of 1798 and the acts of commemoration linked to the latter's hundredth anniversary in 1898. The conference itself was timed to coincide with both the two hundredth anniversary of 1798 and the hundred fiftieth anniversary of 1848. A discussion of the significance assumed by 1798 in the writings of the Young Irelanders themselves is to be found in Seán Ryder's contribution, "Young Ireland and the 1798 Rebellion" (135–47).

71. Quoted in Duffy, *Four Years of Irish History*, 390.

72. Quoted in Ryder, "Reading Lessons," 162.

CHAPTER 6

1. Johnny Bat Sullivan, aged 80, Tuosist, Kenmare, County Kerry, recorded by Seán Ó Súilleabháin, IFC 1068, 109.

2. *Nation*, 5, no. 310 (February 13, 1847).

3. Kristeva, *Powers of Horror*, 2–4.

4. Carlyle, *Reminiscences of My Irish Journey*, 206.

5. *Illustrated London News* 11, no. 234 (April 3, 1847): 234.

6. Artaud, "Theatre of Cruelty," 57.

7. Schechner, *Future of Ritual*, 1.

8. Kristeva, "Word, Dialogue, Novel," 50.

9. Dromintee Parish, County Armagh, IFC 1072, 333.

10. Crossmaglen, County Armagh, IFC 1072, 314.

11. Ballina, County Mayo, IFC 1069, 376; Aunascaul, County Kerry, IFC 354, 315–16.

12. Martin O'Malley, aged 85, Mulranny, Westport, County Mayo, IFC 1072, 106.

13. Ibid.

14. Golden and Kilfeakle, County Tipperary, IFC 1068, 41–42.

15. Dáithí Ó Ceantabhaill, Croom, County Limerick, IFC 1068, 50–51.

16. Ballina, County Mayo, IFC 1069, 357.

17. An uncoffined burial is described in an account from County Galway in

the 1820s: "the body was not in a coffin, but on a bier, with a linen cloth thrown over it, and confined at the four corners, to prevent its being blown away." The writer observes, however, that this was not a common practice, the majority of people being buried in coffins. Another account from the same period, from Donegal, states that the body was wrapped in a piece of flannel, placed on a bier constructed of wooden slats joined by ropes, and the wooden structure placed on a mat of plaited straw with holes at each corner. Ropes were threaded through each hole and placed over the shoulders of four men, who in this way carried the corpse to the graveyard. Ballard, "Before Death and Beyond," 21.

18. In their published narrative of their journey, Crossfield and Forster recall a visit to Carrick-on-Shannon, where they saw large numbers of people seeking admission to the workhouse, many of them in the last stages of starvation. Central Relief Committee of the Society of Friends, *Transactions*, 145.

19. Ibid., 155. Refers to a visit to Clifden, County Galway, January 20, 1847.

20. Central Relief Committee of the Society of Friends, *Transactions*, 198.

21. Peter Brown draws attention to the centrality of death and death ritual to the dissemination of the Church's power and influence in late antiquity through the cult of the saints, many of whom were martyrs whose status, including the power attributed to their relics, was defined in part by the manner of their deaths. Lawrence Taylor notes, however, that martyrs were not to be found among the early Celtic saints in Ireland, who tended rather to live to an advanced age and to continue to be associated after death with features of the local landscapes in which their lives had been spent. From the early twelfth century onward, attempts were made by the Anglo-Norman clergy (who by this time had gained control of the Irish church) to promote saints' cults on the model of continental Europe. It was this period that witnessed the "discovery" of the remains of Saints Patrick, Brigid, and Columcille. Nonetheless, although saints' relics were widely resorted to for healing purposes, their use did not become focused on particular institutional centers, as it had in continental Europe, and thus failed to provide the desired means of reinforcing Church power. Taylor links these developments to the Church's failure, up to and including the nineteenth century, to establish an unchallenged monopoly over death and mortuary rites in Ireland. Brown, *Cult of the Saints*, 69–85; Taylor, "Bas InÉirinn," 179–83.

22. Hertz, "Collective Representation," 85.

23. Ariès, *Hour of Our Death*, 5–29, 559–601.

24. Baudrillard, *Symbolic Exchange*, 126–27.

25. Spenser elaborates on the supposedly pagan character of such laments: "For yt is the manner of all *Pagans*. And *Infidells*, to be yntemperate in there waylinges, of theire dead, for that they had no faith nor hope of salvacion." Spenser, *View of the Present State of Ireland*, 72–73.

26. See, for example, Morris, "Irish Wake Games"; and Ó Súilleabháin, *Irish Wake Amusements*.

27. Witoszek and Sheeran, *Talking to the Dead*. See also Witoszek, "Ireland: A Funerary Culture?"

28. Taylor suggests that death and death ritual in Ireland have been the locus of an ongoing struggle between institutionalized religion (represented by the Catholic Church) and popular belief, a struggle manifested, for example, in the long-standing rivalry between the community-based wake and the priest-controlled funeral. If the Church has, to a large extent, succeeded over the years in domesticating wake observances, Taylor notes that older forms and practices continue to resurface in a contemporary context. At the same time, elements of Church rites have sometimes been appropriated by local communities to serve other purposes: for example, IRA funerals in Northern Ireland during the 1970s and 1980s, where large-scale processions of mourners (along with the inevitable presence of British security forces) became a form of political theater, aimed at attracting public and media attention to the Republican cause. Taylor, "Bas In-Éirinn," 183–84.

29. Ballard, "Before Death and Beyond," 24–26. See also Anne O'Connor, "Placeless Dead," 36.

30. Newfield, County Mayo, IFC 1072, 103.

31. Skibbereen, County Cork, IFC 1071, 310.

32. Skibbereen, County Cork, IFC 1068, 246. Another, less detailed version of the story is recorded, also from West Cork: "When the bodies were being pushed into the huge open-grave—the story goes—a little child's body was in the way and one of the grave diggers pushed it with a spade or shovel. In doing so, he broke both knees of the child with the result that the child woke up—it wasn't really dead! The child who had this marvelous escape from being buried alive was taken to the local workhouse. He grew strong and healthy but was severely 'knock-kneed' for the rest of his life." Macroom, County Cork, IFC 1068, 274.

33. Drimoleague, County Cork, IFC 1068, 246.

34. Johnny Callaghan, aged 90, Castlerea, County Roscommon, recorded by Kathleen Hurley, Ballymoe, County Galway, IFC 1069, 255.

35. Macalister, *Lebor Gabála Érenn*. On the Tuatha Dé Danaan, see Ó hÓgáin, *Myth, Legend and Romance*, 407–9.

36. McCone, *Pagan Past and Christian Present*, 65–72.

37. See Spence, *British Fairy Origins*, 53–64.

38. Flanagan notes that the term "fairy forts" has often been misapplied to earthen ring forts, which are, in fact, Iron Age defended farmsteads. So-called fairy mounds are identified with Passage Tombs, dating from the Neolithic period and spread throughout Ireland, but most concentrated in areas such as the Boyne Valley and County Sligo. These tombs, often described in Irish as *sí*, or fairy dwellings, are characterized by round cairns, sometimes of considerable diameter, and an entranceway terminating in a cruciform chamber, as at Newgrange, County Meath, probably the best-known example. Flanagan, *Dictionary of Irish Archaeology*, 182–83.

39. Ó hÓgáin, *Myth, Legend and Romance*, 185–90. See also Spaan, *Otherworld*.

40. See Ballard, "Before Death and Beyond," 24.

41. See Brindley, *Irish Prehistory*, 13, 20.

42. Dáithí Ó Ceantabhail, Croom, County Limerick, IFC 1068, 52.

43. Kilcommon, County Mayo, IFC 1069, 340.

44. Johnny Bat Sullivan, Tuosist, Kenmare, County Kerry, IFC 1068, 109.

45. Croom, County Limerick, IFC 1068, 50–51.

46. Killarney, County Kerry, IFC 1068, 132.

47. Erris, County Mayo, IFC 1072, 61.

48. Ibid., 74.

49. West Donegal, IFC 353, 30; trans. Máire MacNeill, "Wayside Death Cairns," 55. Similar responses are recorded from the Mullet peninsula and Castlebar, County Mayo. In Fanad, County Donegal, for example, is a cairn known as the "Madman's Grave" and attributed to pre-Christian times. It is told how the dead man used to rise periodically and harass the living, until Saint Columcille laid him to rest. At the time of the Irish Folklore Commission's survey of death cairn customs in the late 1930s, passersby were still accustomed to add a stone, the reason given being: "ní le h-onóir dó ach le trom a chur air ar eagla go n-eireochadh sé" (not to honor him, but to weigh him down lest he would rise again). IFC 653, 48; trans. MacNeill, "Wayside Death Cairns," 54. MacNeill's article is based on the questionnaire on death cairn customs sent out by the Irish Folklore Commission (1938–1939) on the catalogued portion of the Commission's manuscripts and on the collection of folklore made by Irish primary schools, 1937–1938.

50. For example, a story is told relative to a "leacht" on the land of Mrs. Bridget Corduff, 2 miles from Rossport, County Mayo: a boy, Thomas Rooney, was out tending sheep when he saw a man staggering. He notified his father and elder brother, who in turn told the landlord. They established that the man was a Catholic and summoned a priest to perform the last rites. The man was buried in the local graveyard (Kilcommon) and a leacht was erected where he fell. Mrs. Bridget Corduff, 60, Erris, County Mayo (heard the story from her father, who was the first person to come to the dying man's aid), IFC 1072, 61–63.

51. Galway, IFC 653, 444; trans. MacNeill, "Wayside Death Cairns," 58–59.

52. Erris, County Mayo, IFC 653, 275; quoted in MacNeill, "Wayside Death Cairns," 59.

53. Knockabanna, County Clare, IFC 433, 68.

54. Frazer, *Golden Bough*, 1:52.

55. See Douglas, *Purity and Danger*, 140–58.

56. Loughrea, County Galway, IFC 627, 9; trans. MacNeill, "Wayside Death Cairns," 58.

57. For example, of the Maori practice of gift exchange as a system of total services, Mauss writes: "In this system of ideas one clearly and logically realized that one must give back to another person what is really part and parcel of his nature and substance, because to accept something from somebody is so accept some part of his spiritual essence, his soul." Such a conception, Mauss notes, appears to differ from the strict distinction made between real rights and personal rights, or

between things and persons, in the western legal tradition. This distinction, however, Mauss argues, can be shown to be of relatively recent origin and to have developed out of antecedent practices of exchange, "in which persons and things merge." The point is developed via a comparison of Roman, Germanic, and Sanskrit legal texts and through an analysis of the theory of the *nexum* in archaic and later Roman law. Mauss contends that the separation of persons and things instituted in contemporary European law can be shown to have its origin in an earlier dispensation under the terms of which persons and things were not so distinguished and which survives to the present in fragmentary and vestigial guise in European legal theory, as well as in more elaborated form in other, nonwestern traditions. Mauss, *Gift*, 12, 47–64.

58. Bataille, *Theory of Religion*.

59. MacNeill, "Wayside Death Cairns," 58.

CHAPTER 7

1. Jacques Derrida, *Specters of Marx*, 39. For a more extended discussion of spectrality as a social-cultural analytic, see Gordon, *Ghostly Matters*.

2. Gregory, *Visions and Beliefs*, 195; County Leitrim IFC 1069, 459.

3. Golden and Kilfeakle, County Tipperary, IFC 1068, 41–42.

4. Kenmare, County Kerry, IFC 1070, 313.

5. Mulranny, County Mayo, IFC 1072, 165. The practice of burying corpses on offshore islands is recorded in a mid-eighteenth-century account of the Rosses, County Donegal, reprinted in the journal *Ulster Folklife*. The correspondent, known as "A.B.," was originally writing to Joseph Cooper Walker, and his letter was published as appendix 1 to the latter's *An Historical Essay on the Dress of the Ancient and Modern Irish* (Dublin, 1788). The description, dating from the period 1753–1754, is second-hand, deriving from the correspondence and verbal accounts of a friend, "Mr. N," a native of Donegal and a speaker of Irish: "Wrapped in a coarse woolen cloth, . . . the corpse was put into a curragh, with his feet and legs hanging over the side; and [with it] a man with a paddle, to conduct the whole train to the Isle of Aran [Aranmore?] where their burial ground was: this curragh was followed by that, which carried the priest; next him went the relations of the deceased, in order of their proximity in kindred; and then as many as had curraghs; and of these, Mr. N saw sixty or eighty in a train." "A.B.," "The Rosses, County Donegal, in 1753–4," 20–23. Note that the burial described appears to have been coffinless.

6. *Illustrated London News* (February 13, 1847); repr. Killen, *Famine Decade*, 113.

7. Ibid.

8. Ibid., 112.

9. *Times* (December 24, 1846); quoted in Woodham-Smith, *Great Hunger*, 162–63.

10. Somerville, *Letters from Ireland*, 56.

11. Ibid., 87.

12. Ibid., 152.

13. Ibid., 153.

14. Žižek, "Taking Sides," 210–11; see also Ellmann, *Hunger Artists*, 54.

15. Ó Gráda, *Black '47 and Beyond*, 61–63.

16. Repr. Killen, *Famine Decade*, 86.

17. Ibid., 101.

18. Horkheimer and Adorno, *Dialectic of Enlightenment*, 2–7.

19. Agamben relates such a condition of human "infancy" (or "what comes before the subject") to Benjamin's notion of "experience in the strict sense of the term" [*Erfahrung*], which is, similarly, seen to involve a state of self-forgetfulness. Agamben, *Infancy and History*, 13–63; Benjamin, "Storyteller," 91.

20. Repr. *Nation* (January 2, 1847), 5, no. 221, 197.

21. See above (Chapter 6). Carleton's title plays on the near homographs *féar gortach* (hungry grass) and *fear gortach* (hungry or miserly man).

22. Carleton, "Fair Gurtha," 119–20.

23. See Morash, *Writing the Irish Famine*. In the preface to the single-volume edition of *Black Prophet*, published in February 1847, Carleton drew explicit parallels between these earlier disasters and contemporary events in Ireland. Carleton, *Black Prophet*, 344.

24. According to twentieth-century medicine, this condition, produced by starvation in its last stages, has no connection with the ailment usually referred to today as "dropsy." In the mid-nineteenth century, hunger edema was often (mis)diagnosed as a symptom of fever. Thus Dr. Taylor of the Kenmare workhouse (County Kerry), in a medical report of 1847, cited diarrhea, dysentery and anascara, and dropsical swelling of the limbs alike as symptoms of "fever." Woodham-Smith, *Great Hunger*, 194.

25. Ibid., 144.

26. Kilkenny West, County Westmeath, IFC 1069, 184; Sneem, County Kerry (story attributed to fellow worker of the dead man), IFC 1070, 307.

27. Bakhtin, *Rabelais and His World*, 317.

28. Central Relief Committee of the Society of Friends, *Transactions*, 164.

29. Ibid., 39.

30. Quoted in Woodham-Smith, *Great Hunger*, 195–96. Known by the medical name *lanugo*, and recognized as a symptom of the eating disorder anorexia nervosa, such hair is the body's attempt to keep warm in the absence of sufficient food. The same term also refers to the covering of fine, soft hair found on the body of a human fetus. See Bhanji and Mattingly, *Medical Aspects*.

31. Webb, "A Tour Through Mayo and Galway," MSS Historical Collection of the Society of Friends; quoted in Woodham-Smith, *Great Hunger*, 196.

32. See Curtis, *Apes and Angels*, 29–57.

33. See Piña-Cabral, "The Gods of the Gentiles Are Demons."

34. Bakhtin notes the influence of Celtic, specifically Irish, tradition in shaping this repertoire of images. The story of the "Purgatory of Saint Patrick," which

attained wide currency from the twelfth century onward through the versions of Marie de France and others, identifies the entrance to purgatory as a hole in the ground (identified as a cavern on an island in Lough Derg, County Donegal, still a popular pilgrimage site), with further connotations of anal orifice. Similarly, the "Travels of Saint Brendan" (*Navigatio Sancti Brendani*), which enjoyed immense popularity in medieval Europe, describes the entrance to hell as a gaping mouth from which a cloud of fire rises. Rabelais's appropriation of popular imagery draws explicitly on both of these traditions. Bakhtin, *Rabelais and His World*, 389; Hopkin, *Living Legend*, 84–105; Kenney, *Sources for the Early History of Ireland*, 319–56, 406–21.

35. Taussig, *Shamanism, Colonialism and the Wild Man*, 5.

36. Central Relief Committee of the Society of Friends, *Transactions*, 205–6.

37. According to Derrida, Marx lacks the courage of his own insights as a theorist of both materialism and the specter, because he insists on the necessity of distinguishing between the spectral and the real. Derrida argues that an analytic of spectrality should take as its starting point not the assumed knowability of society's material base, but a moment prior to the institution of any conceptual distinction between substance and phantasm, or between life-as-such and death-as-such. Derrida, *Specters of Marx*, 166–70.

CHAPTER 8

1. *Illustrated London News* 15, no. 404 (December 22, 1849): 404–5.

2. Ibid., 406. Bridget O'Donnell's picture has been one of the most frequently reproduced of contemporary images of the famine years, appearing as the frontispiece to a recent collection of contemporary accounts from the 1840s (Killen, *Famine Decade*) and, many times enlarged, as a Republican mural on West Belfast's Falls Road during the summer of 1997.

3. For examples of specific case studies, see Hubbs, *Mother Russia*; Landes, *Visualizing the Nation*; Herminghouse and Mueller, *Gender and Germanness*.

4. McClintock, "No Longer in a Future Heaven," 263–64.

5. Macalister, *Lebor Gabála Érenn*; Ó hÓgáin, *Myth, Legend and Romance*, 407–9.

6. Ní Bhrolcháin, "Women in Early Irish Myths and Sagas"; MacCana, "Aspects of the Theme of King and Goddess in Irish Literature" and "Aspects of the Theme of King and Goddess in Irish Literature, Continued." The story of Niall Noigiallach (Niall of the Nine Hostages) dates from the fifth century and is recorded in the *Annals of Ulster*, where he is described as the last king of Ireland before the introduction of Christianity. See O'Rahilly, *Early Irish History and Mythology*, 209–34.

7. The term *banshee* derives from the Irish *bean sí* (fairy woman). Patricia Lysaght identifies the folkloric banshee as a figure whose attributes and functions, including wailing and lamentation and a particular association with violent deaths, recall aspects of the sovereignty goddess of early Irish literature. She notes both the

banshee's role as a harbinger of death and her sometime connection to native landowning families. Lysaght, *Banshee*, 191–218. Allen Feldman refers to more recent banshee stories told in connection with sectarian killings in Northern Ireland. Feldman, *Formations of Violence*, 65–68.

8. Breathnach, "Sovereignty Goddess"; Dalton, "Tradition of Blood Sacrifice." O'Rahilly suggests that the *bruiden* (hostel) is itself situated in a *sí* mound and thus represents a gateway to the Otherworld, in which case the two hags would occupy the familiar mythological role of women as intermediaries between the human and supernatural realms. O'Rahilly, *Early Irish History and Mythology*, 117.

9. In the twentieth century, this motif found one of its most widely disseminated expressions in the political iconography of the unsuccessful rising against British rule of Easter 1916: in the pronouncements of the insurgents, affirming the necessity of a blood "sacrifice" to throw off foreign domination, and in the postexecution posters, showing the dead poet-patriot Patrick Pearse, resting on the bosom of a mythic woman who brandishes a tricolor, the Irish national flag. Here the woman appears both as the embodiment of the national past, on behalf of which Pearse and his confederates have given their lives, and as the tutelary spirit of the violence upon which the national struggle has been founded and which would subsequently find its place in the self-spun origin story of a newly independent Ireland. Noteworthy too is the gendered division of labor that the poster depicts: the woman furnishes the visual icon and supernatural charter for an action in which she herself does not participate. It is, rather, Ireland's "sons" who are called upon to sacrifice themselves in her name. Kearney, *Myth and Motherland*, 10; Edwards, *Patrick Pearse*, 275–344; Moran, *Patrick Pearse*, 174–202.

10. On the high social standing enjoyed by poets (*filí*) and on the system of literary patronage that survived in Gaelic Ireland until the seventeenth century, see Leerssen, *Mere Irish and Fíor-Ghael*, 153, 190–253.

11. Ó Rathaille's own biography exemplifies the downward social mobility characteristic of poets in seventeenth-century Ireland. When the lands of his patron were confiscated, Ó Rathaille, whose family had previously held the lease on a large parcel of land in the vicinity of Killarney, County Kerry, belonging to the Browne estates, was forced to relocate to Castlemaine Harbor, 12 miles to the west, where he lived in greatly reduced circumstances. Ó Tuama and Kinsella, *An Duanaire 1600–1900*, 139.

12. Ó Tuama and Kinsella, *An Duanaire 1600–1900*, 153, 156–60.

13. Ibid., 179.

14. *Cork Magazine* 2, no. 13 (November 1848); repr. Morash, *Hungry Voice*, 57–58.

15. O'Ryan, *Tipperary Minstrel*, 15.

16. *Irishman* (March 25, 1849), 1, no. 18; repr. Morash, *Hungry Voice*, 165–66.

17. *Irishman* 1, no. 25 (June 23, 1849): 25; repr. Morash, *Hungry Voice*, 62–64.

18. Kelleher, "Irish Famine in Literature," 259.

19. *Irishman* 1, no. 18 (May 5, 1849); repr. Morash, *Hungry Voice*, 166.

20. See also accounts from Carrick, County Donegal (IFC 1069, 169–71), and Drimoleague, County Cork (IFC 1068, 244–50). A number of accounts indicate that in the absence of able-bodied men, it was often women who were left with the responsibility of burying the dead.

21. In an Irish-language account from Cape Clear Island, County Cork, a woman snatches a potato from her child and eats it all, leaving none for the child. The child dies, but the mother survives and is haunted by the memory of her action. IFC 1071, 198–99.

22. Gliasc, Glenbeigh, County Kerry, IFC 462, 8–11.

23. Redbray, Tullaghan, County Leitrim, IFC 1072, 185–230.

24. Ibid. Many contemporary journalistic accounts make reference also to the consumption of entrails and other foods more commonly associated with stray dogs and other scavengers. The following first appeared in the *Cork Constitution* (January 10, 1847) and relates to the district of Skibbereen: "Going into the hotel yard, I perceived an unfortunate woman rush by me and take up some fish guts which lay in a fetid pool, and retiring, she ate them, ravenously. On getting outside the gateway, she reeled for a few paces and then fell, but, while lying exhausted on the street, with the most savage ferocity she continued to gnaw the disgusting entrails." *Times* (January 12, 1847), 5. Although similar references are to be found in the Irish Folklore Commission accounts (for example, County Kerry, IFC 1070, 345–46, 384), equal emphasis is usually placed in the latter on the women's efforts to procure food for their children.

25. Police records from the period focus on the increasing numbers of destitute women who had taken to prostitution on the streets of Irish cities. Under the Dublin Police Act of 1842, all that was needed to secure a conviction for prostitution was for a policeman to state that a woman was known to him as a prostitute and that he had seen her approach men. While the act remained in force, the greatest number of arrests took place during the famine years. McLoughlin, "Workhouses and Irish Female Paupers"; Luddy, *Women and Philanthropy*, 9–20.

26. Luddy, *Women and Philanthropy*, 187.

27. Ibid.

28. On Benjamin's relationship to psychoanalysis, see Weigel, *Body and Image Space*, 116–17.

29. Benjamin, "Franz Kafka," 133–34.

30. Ibid., 115.

31. Weigel, *Body and Image Space*, 74–79.

32. Quoted in Weigel, *Body and Image Space*, 83.

33. Quoted in Weigel, *Body and Image Space*, 85.

34. Weigel, *Body and Image Space*, 86.

35. Benjamin, "Berlin Chronicle," 11.

36. O'Flaherty, *Famine*, 139.

37. Ibid., 197–98.

38. Ibid., 199. O'Flaherty's fictionalized account of the keen (*caoine*) can be

compared with the description given by the playwright John Millington Synge, recounting a visit made in 1898 to the Aran Islands, off Galway Bay. Synge, *Aran Islands*, 36–37. O'Flaherty himself was a native of Inis Mór, the largest of the Aran Islands.

39. Angela Bourke has pointed out that laments sung by women, both at funerals and on the occasion of a death, were, in many cases, critical reflections on the existing state of gender relations in Irish society, including instances of domestic violence. Such sentiments would, however, be audible only to the women gathered around the corpse, male mourners remaining at a distance. Bourke, "More in Anger than in Sorrow," 163, 170–75.

40. *Times* (January 20, 1847), 8.

41. Ibid.

42. Central Relief Committee of the Society of Friends, *Transactions*, 163.

43. Benjamin, "On the Mimetic Faculty," 331. On the question of the mimetic faculty's contemporary resurfacing via new media and representational technologies, see Taussig, *Mimesis and Alterity*, 19–43. For a review of the concept of mimesis, see Gebauer and Wulf, *Mimesis*.

44. Ballina, County Mayo, IFC 1069, 353.

45. See Lysaght, "Perspectives on Women." Tom Peete Cross's encyclopedic *Motif Index of Early Irish Literature* points to the Europe-wide and worldwide provenance of the figure of the charitable woman. Economic historian Cormac Ó Gráda, meanwhile, finds a more immediate antecedent in a story told concerning Saint Brigid, probably the best known of Irish female saints and a figure widely portrayed as an exemplification of Christian charity. Ó Gráda, *An Drochshaol*, 30–31. On traditions relating to Brigid, see Ó Catháin, *Festival of Brigit*.

46. Lissyconnor, County Kerry, IFC 1071, 133.

47. Ireland adopted the euro as its official currency in January 2002.

48. Luddy, *Women and Philanthropy*, 27–28.

49. Boherbue, Newmarket, County Cork, IFC 1068, 251–69; see also Macroom, County Cork, IFC 1068, 272–77.

50. Many accounts refer to the stigmatization of those remembered as having yielded to the overtures of the "soupers" and embraced Protestantism in exchange for a meal. Cathal Póirtéir's recent anthologies of Irish- and English-language famine folklore (based on materials collected by the Irish Folklore Commission) include a number of stories relating to such individuals. Historians, meanwhile, continue to debate the extent to which souperism was an actual and widespread phenomenon. Póirtéir, *Famine Echoes*, 166–81; *Glórtha ón Ghorta*, 192–212; Whelan, "Stigma of Souperism."

51. Derrida, *Given Time*, 34–37.

52. See, for example, Cixous and Clément, *Newly Born Woman*, 63–132.

53. Irigaray, *Speculum of the Other Woman*, 243–364.

CHAPTER 9

1. Dening, *Performances*, 37.

2. On questions of governmental culpability and the long-term impact of the famine, see Kinealy, *This Great Calamity* and *Death-Dealing Famine*; Ó Gráda, *Ireland Before and After the Famine* and *Black '47 and Beyond*; Gray, *Famine, Land and Politics*; Scally, *End of Hidden Ireland*. Like Scally's study, a number of recent works deal specifically with the effects of emigration: Fanning, *New Perspectives*; Gilman, *Receiving Erin's Children*; Gribben, *Great Famine*; Keneally, *Great Shame*; Laxton, *Famine Ships*; Crawford, *Hungry Stream*; Guinnane, *Vanishing Irish*; Hollett, *Passage to the New World*; Rees, *Farewell to Famine*. A collection of contemporary narratives of the emigrant experience, focusing on the postfamine decades, is to be found in Fitzpatrick, *Oceans of Consolation*.

3. See, for example, Killen, *Famine Decade*; and Kissane, *Irish Famine*. New editions of contemporary accounts included Central Relief Committee of the Society of Friends, *Transactions*; and individual narratives by, among others, the American traveler Asenath Nicholson, *Annals of the Famine*; and Thomas Colville Scott, *Connemara After the Famine*.

4. Ó Cathaoir, *Famine Diary*.

5. The "Thomas Davis Lectures" of 1995 (named after the Young Ireland leader and broadcast annually since 1953) were published as Póirtéir, *Great Irish Famine*. The television drama *The Hanging Gale* (1995), directed by Diarmuid Lawrence and produced by the Dublin-based company Little Bird, was broadcast both in Ireland and the United Kingdom.

6. Two famine-related Web sites have proven particularly helpful in the course of my own researches: a site maintained by the National Archives of Ireland (http://www.nationalarchives.ie/famine.html), and "Views of the Famine," compiled by Steve Taylor, comprising a selection of contemporary newspaper articles and illustrations, along with a list of other sites (http://vassun.vassar.edu/sttaylor/FAMINE/).

7. See Campbell, *Great Irish Famine*. Further information on the Famine Museum is available on its official Web site (http://www.strokestownpark.ie/museum.html). Strokestown Park achieved notoriety in 1847 with the murder of the landlord, Major Dennis Mahon, after he had attempted to clear eight thousand destitute tenants from his estates through evictions and assisted emigration.

8. Robinson's address to the Oireachtas, entitled "Cherishing the Diaspora," called for increased dialogue with the Irish diaspora and referred to initiatives such as the Irish Genealogical Project, jointly sponsored by the governments of Ireland and the United States, intended to enable men and women of Irish descent living overseas to "reclaim" their history by tracing their family origins. She also drew a number of explicit parallels between the Irish experience of famine and emigration and present-day instances of poverty and hunger, suggesting that commemorations of the 1840s might provide an impetus toward greater Irish involvement in contemporary famine relief.

9. A similar point is made by the visual display that greets travelers waiting to board flights to the United States at Dublin airport, where reproductions of contemporary illustrations of the famine (including, once again, Bridget O'Donnell and her children) are juxtaposed with images and verbal accounts of the Irish in America.

10. Arjun Appadurai has used the term *ethnoscape* to denote the spatial and territorial dispersal of group identifications in the contemporary world, suggesting that such developments prefigure the emergence of postnational forms of political consciousness through the medium of "diasporic public spheres." If commemorations of the famine's one hundred fiftieth anniversary appear to invoke and utilize precisely such transnational flows of people and information (with a strong emphasis on the Irish diaspora in the United States), the terms of recent debates appear to testify equally to the seeming durability of conceptions of nationhood as a reference point for the mobilization of identity claims and historical interpretations on the part of groups that are themselves no longer territorially bounded. See Appadurai, *Modernity at Large*, 21, 48.

11. *Irish Times* (http://www.ireland.com/newspaper/archive), Monday, July 21, 1997.

12. Unfortunately, the Battery Park Hunger Memorial opened too late to be described at length here. I plan to provide a more detailed account in a separate study.

13. *Irish Times* (http://www.ireland.com/newspaper/archive), May 22, 1997.

14. *Irish Times* (http://www.ireland.com/newspaper/archive), October 28, 1998. On more recent criticisms of the Irish Famine Commemoration Fund, specifically the high level of administrative expenditure revealed by a recent audit and its alleged failure (at the time of writing) to deliver on many of its philanthropic commitments, see *Ireland on Sunday* (http://www.irelandonsunday.com), September 30, 2001.

15. O'Connor, "Famine."

16. For an anthropological account of mental illness in twentieth-century Ireland, see Scheper-Hughes, *Saints, Scholars and Schizophrenics*.

17. Waters, "Confronting the Ghosts of Our Past," 28.

18. Borch-Jacobsen, *Remembering Anna O.*, 2.

19. Van der Kolk, McFarlane, and Weisath, *Traumatic Stress*; Caruth, *Unclaimed Experience*.

20. Felman and Laub, *Testimony*.

21. See Caruth, *Trauma*, 10. For a critical appraisal of this position see Michaels, "You Who Never Was There."

22. Leys, *Trauma*. Leys draws extensively on Borch-Jacobsen's work concerning the place of hypnotic suggestion and imitation in Freud's writings, particularly the implied loss of identity and the dedifferentiation between subject and object against which Freud's texts are seen to struggle. Leys suggests that post-Freudian trauma theory (particularly the work of Freud's one-time student Sándor Ferenczi)

has hesitated between "mimetic" and "antimimetic" impulses, between a view of traumatic experience as impacting on an already constituted subjectivity and a view of "originary" trauma as constitutive of the subject through a break with a prior condition of presubjectival undifferentiation. Leys, *Trauma*, 120–89. See Borch-Jacobsen, *Freudian Subject* and *Emotional Tie*.

23. *Irish Times* (http://www.ireland.com/newspaper/archive), June 2, 1997.

24. On the contemporary role of the Catholic Church, see Inglis, *Moral Monopoly*.

25. On the contemporary distribution of poverty in Ireland, see Pringle, Walsh, and Hennessy, *Poor People, Poor Places*.

26. Chakrabarty, *Provincializing Europe*, 108–13.

27. Evans, *Irish Folk Ways*, 282.

28. On corporeal symbolism, see Douglas, *Purity and Danger*, 114–28. On "embodiment," see Csordas, *Embodiment and Experience*, 1–24.

29. Latour, *We Have Never Been Modern*.

30. It is worth noting that Benjamin makes a sharp distinction between instrumentalized "vulgar-Marxist" conceptions of mastery over nature and the very different vision of human-nature symbiosis expounded in the socialist utopias of Fourier and his contemporaries: "According to Fourier, as a result of efficient cooperative labor, four moons would illuminate the earthly night, the ice would recede from the poles, sea water would no longer taste salty, and beasts of prey would do man's bidding. All this illustrates a kind of labor which, far from exploiting nature, is capable of delivering her of the creations which lie dormant in her womb as potentials." Benjamin, "Theses on the Philosophy of History," 259.

On Benjamin's debt to Fourier, see Buck-Morss, *Dialectics of Seeing*, 275–76, 303–5.

31. See Lloyd, *Ireland After History*, 19–36.

Bibliography

Aalen, F. H. A., Kevin Whelan, and Matthew Stout, eds. *Atlas of the Irish Rural Landscape*. Toronto: University of Toronto Press, 1997.

"A.B." "The Rosses, County Donegal, in 1753–4." *Ulster Folklife* 22 (1973): 20–23.

Abrams, M. H. *Natural Supernaturalism: Tradition and Renovation in Romantic Literature*. New York: Norton, 1971.

Adorno, Theodor W. "The Idea of Natural History" (1932). Translated by Robert Hullot-Kentor. *Telos* 60 (1984): 111–24.

Agamben, Giorgio. *Homo Sacer: Sovereign Power and Bare Life*. Translated by Daniel Heller-Roazen. Stanford, CA: Stanford University Press, 1998.

———. *Infancy and History: Essays on the Destruction of Experience*. Translated by Liz Heron. New York: Routledge, 1993.

Akenson, Donald H. *A Protestant in Purgatory: Richard Whately, Archbishop of Dublin*. North Haven, CT: Archon Books, 1981.

Almqvist, Bo. "The Irish Folklore Commission: Achievement and Legacy." *Béaloideas* 45–47 (1977–1979): 6–27.

Anderson, Benedict. *Imagined Communities: Reflections on the Origin and Spread of Nationalism*. London: Verso, 1991.

Appadurai, Arjun. *Modernity at Large: Cultural Dimensions of Globalization*. Minneapolis: University of Minnesota Press, 1996.

Ariès, Philippe. *The Hour of Our Death*. Translated by Helen Weaver. London: Penguin, 1982.

Artaud, Antonin. "The Theatre of Cruelty." In *The Theory of the Modern Stage: An Introduction to Modern Theatre and Drama*, edited by Eric Bentley, 55–65. Harmondsworth: Penguin Books, 1968.

Asad, Talal. *Genealogies of Religion: Discipline and Reasons of Power in Christianity and Islam*. Baltimore: Johns Hopkins University Press, 1993.

Bachofen, J. J. *Myth, Religion and Mother-Right: Selected Writings of J. J. Bachofen*. Translated by Ralph Mannheim. Princeton, NJ: Princeton University Press, 1992.

Bakhtin, Mikhail. *Rabelais and His World.* Translated by Helene Iswolsky. Bloomington: Indiana University Press, 1984.

Ballard, Linda-May. "Before Death and Beyond: Death and Ghost Traditions with Particular Reference to Ulster." In *The Folklore of Ghosts,* edited by Hilda Ellis Davidson and W. M. S. Russell, 13–42. The Folklore Society Mistletoe Series, vol. 15. Cambridge: D. S. Brewer, 1981.

Bataille, Georges. *Accursed Share: An Essay on General Economy.* 2 vols. Translated by Robert Hurley. New York: Zone Books, 1989–1991.

———. "The Notion of Expenditure." In *Visions of Excess: Selected Writings, 1927–1939,* edited by Allan Stoekl, 116–29. Minneapolis: University of Minnesota Press, 1985.

———. *Theory of Religion.* Translated by Robert Hurley. New York: Zone Books, 1989.

Baudrillard, Jean. *Symbolic Exchange and Death.* London: Sage Publications, 1993.

Benitez-Rojo, Antonio. *The Repeating Island: The Caribbean and the Postmodern Perspective.* Durham, NC: Duke University Press, 1992.

Benjamin, Walter. "Berlin Chronicle," and "On the Mimetic Faculty." In *Reflections: Essays Aphorisms, Autobiographical Writings,* edited by Peter Demertz, translated by Edmund Jephcott, 3–60, 314–32, 333–36. New York: Harcourt Brace Jovanovich, 1979.

———. "Excavation and Memory." In *Selected Writings,* vol. 2, *1927–1934,* edited by Michael W. Jennings, Howard Eliand, and Gary Smith, translated by Rodney Livingstone et al., 576. Cambridge: Belknap Press, 1999.

———. "Goethe's *Elective Affinities.*" In *Selected Writings,* vol. 1, *1913–1926,* edited by Marcus Bullock and Michael W. Jennings, 100–111, 297–360. Cambridge: Belknap Press, 1997.

———. *The Origin of German Tragic Drama.* Translated by John Osborne. London: New Left Books, 1977.

———. "The Storyteller," "Franz Kafka," and "Theses on the Philosophy of History." In *Illuminations,* edited by Hannah Arendt, translated by Harry Zohn, 83–110, 111–40, 253–67. New York: Schocken, 1969.

Bhabha, Homi K. "DissemiNation." In *Nation and Narration,* edited by Homi K. Bhabha, 291–320. London: Routledge, 1989.

Bhanji, S., and David Mattingly. *Medical Aspects of Anorexia Nervosa.* London: Wright, 1988.

Biersack, Aletta, ed. *Clio in Oceania: Towards a Historical Anthropology.* Washington, DC: Smithsonian Institution Press, 1991.

Black, R. D. Collison. *Economic Thought and the Irish Question, 1817–1870.* Cambridge: Cambridge University Press, 1960.

Blanchot, Maurice. *The Writing of the Disaster.* Translated by Ann Smock. London: University of Nebraska Press, 1995.

Boas, Franz. *Kwakiutl Ethnography.* Edited by Helen Codere. Chicago: University of Chicago Press, 1966.

Boon, James A. *Verging on Extra-Vagance: Anthropology, History, Religion, Literature, Arts . . . Showbiz.* Princeton, NJ: Princeton University Press, 1999.

Borch-Jacobsen, Mikkel. *The Emotional Tie: Psychoanalysis, Mimesis and Affect.* Stanford, CA: Stanford University Press, 1993.

———. *The Freudian Subject.* Stanford, CA: Stanford University Press, 1988.

———. *Remembering Anna O.: A Century of Mystification.* New York: Routledge, 1996.

Borofsky, Robert. *Making History: Anthropological and Pukapukan Constructions of Knowledge.* Cambridge: Cambridge University Press, 1987.

Bourke, Angela. "The Baby and the Bathwater: Cultural Loss in Nineteenth Century Ireland." In *Ideology and Ireland in the Nineteenth Century,* edited by Tadgh Foley and Sean Ryder, 79–92. Dublin: Four Courts Press, 1998.

———. "More in Anger than in Sorrow: Irish Women's Lament Poetry." In *Feminist Messages: Coding in Women's Folk Culture,* edited by J. N. Radner, 160–82. Urbana: University of Illinois Press, 1993.

———. "Wild Men and Wailing Women." *Éigse* 17 (1980–1981): 25–37.

Boylan, Thomas, and Timothy P. Foley. "A Nation Perishing of Political Economy?" In Morash and Hayes, *Fearful Realities,* 138–50.

———. *Political Economy and Colonial Ireland: The Propagation and Ideological Function of Economic Discourse in Nineteenth Century Ireland.* London: Routledge, 1992.

Bracken, Christopher. *The Potlatch Papers: A Colonial Case History.* Chicago: University of Chicago Press, 1997.

Bradshaw, Brendan. "Nationalism and Historical Scholarship in Modern Ireland." *Irish Historical Studies* 26, no. 104 (1994): 329–51.

Breathnach, Máire. "The Sovereignty Goddess as Goddess of Death." *Zeitschift für Celtische Philologie* 39 (1982): 243–60.

Brindley, Anna. *Irish Prehistory: An Introduction.* Dublin: Ard-Mhusaem na hÉireann (National Museum of Ireland)/Trinity House, 1994.

Brown, Peter. *The Cult of the Saints: Its Rise and Function in Latin Christianity.* Chicago: University of Chicago Press, 1981.

Buck-Morss, Susan. *The Dialectics of Seeing: Walter Benjamin and the Arcades Project.* Cambridge, MA: MIT Press, 1989.

Burke, Edmund. *A Philosophical Inquiry into the Origin of Our Ideas of the Sublime and Beautiful.* Oxford: Basil Blackwell, 1987.

Burke, Helen. *The People and the Poor Law in Nineteenth Century Ireland.* Dublin: Women's Education Bureau, 1987.

Burke, Peter. *Popular Culture in Early Modern Europe.* New York: New York University Press, 1978.

Bury, John Bagnell. *The Idea of Progress: An Inquiry into Its Origins and Growth.* New York: Dover Publications, 1960.

Butler, Marilyn. *Romantics, Rebels and Reactionaries: English Literature and Its Background, 1760–1830.* New York: Oxford University Press, 1982.

Caillois, Roger. *Man and the Sacred.* Glencoe, IL: Free Press of Glencoe, 1960.

Campbell, Stephen J. *The Great Irish Famine.* Strokestown, County Roscommon: Famine Museum, Strokestown Park, 1994.

Canny, Nicholas. *The Elizabethan Conquest of Ireland: A Pattern Established 1565–76.* Hassocks, Sussex: Harvester Press, 1976.

Carleton, William. *The Black Prophet.* Shannon: Irish University Press, 1972.

———. "Fair Gurtha: Or the Hungry Grass; A Legend of the Dumb Hill." *Dublin University Magazine* 47, no. 250 (April 1856): 414–35.

Carlyle, Thomas. *Reminiscences of My Irish Journey in 1849.* London: Sampson Low, Marston, Searle, 1882.

Caruth, Cathy. *Unclaimed Experience: Trauma, Narrative and History.* Baltimore: Johns Hopkins University Press, 1996.

Caruth, Cathy, ed. *Trauma: Explorations in Memory.* Baltimore: Johns Hopkins University Press, 1995.

Central Relief Committee of the Society of Friends. *Transactions of the Central Relief Committee of the Society of Friends.* Dublin: Whelan and Chapman, 1852.

Chakrabarty, Dipesh. *Provincializing Europe: Postcolonial Thought and Historical Difference.* Princeton, NJ: Princeton University Press, 2000.

Chatterjee, Partha. *The Nation and Its Fragments: Colonial and Postcolonial Histories.* Princeton, NJ: Princeton University Press, 1993.

Cixous, Hélène, and Catherine Clément. *The Newly Born Woman.* Translated by Betsy Wing. Minneapolis: University of Minnesota Press, 1986.

Clifford, James. "On Ethnographic Self-Fashioning: Conrad and Malinowski." In *The Predicament of Culture: Twentieth Century Literature, Ethnography and Art.* Cambridge: Harvard University Press, 1988, 92–113.

Cocchiara, Giuseppe. *The History of Folklore in Europe.* Translated by John M. McDaniel. Philadelphia: Institute for the Study of Human Issues, 1981.

Coleman, Steve. "A Cat and a Mouse in a Box: Máirtín Ó Cadhain and the Irish State." Unpublished MS.

———. "Return from the West: A Poetics of Voice in Irish." PhD diss., University of Chicago, 1999.

Coles, Bryony and John Coles. *People of the Wetlands: Bogs, Bodies and Lake-Dwellers.* London: Thames and Hudson, 1980.

Collingwood, R. G. *The Idea of History.* Oxford: Clarendon Press, 1993.

Comaroff, Jean, and John L. Comaroff. "Occult Economies and the Violence of Abstraction: Notes from the South African Post-Colony." *American Ethnologist* 26, no. 2 (February 1999): 279–303.

Comaroff, Jean, and John L. Comaroff, eds. *Modernity and Its Malcontents: Ritual and Power in Postcolonial Africa.* Chicago: University of Chicago Press, 1993.

Connell, K. H. "The Colonization of Waste Land in Ireland, 1780–1845." *Economic History Review* 3 (2nd ser., 1950–1951): 44–71.

Conrad, Joseph. *Heart of Darkness.* London: Penguin Classics, 1995.

Crawford, Margaret, ed. *The Hungry Stream: Essays on Emigration and Famine.* Belfast: Center for Emigration Studies, Ulster-American Folk Park/Institute of Irish Studies, Queen's University, Belfast, 1997.

Cross, Tom Peete. *Motif Index of Early Irish Literature.* Bloomington, Indiana: University of Indiana Press, 1952.

Csordas, Thomas, ed. *Embodiment and Experience: The Existential Ground of Culture and Self.* Cambridge: Cambridge University Press, 1994.

Curran, Joseph M. *The Birth of the Irish Free State.* University: University of Alabama Press, 1980.

Curtin, Chris, and Thomas M. Wilson, eds. *Ireland from Below: Social Change and Local Communities.* Galway: Galway University Press, 1987.

Curtin, Nancy, and Marilyn Cohen, eds. *Reclaiming Gender: Transgressive Identities in Modern Ireland.* New York: St. Martin's Press, 1999.

Curtis, L. P. *Anglo-Saxons and Celts: A Study of Anti-Irish Prejudice in Victorian England.* Bridgeport, CT: Conference on British Studies at the University of Bridgeport/New York: New York University Press, 1968

———. *Apes and Angels: The Irishman in Victorian Cariacature.* Newton Abbot: David and Charles, 1971.

Dalton, G. F. "The Tradition of Blood Sacrifice to the Goddess Eire." *Studies: An Irish Quarterly Review of Letters, Philosophy and Science* 63 (Winter 1974): 343–54.

Daly, Mary. *The Famine in Ireland.* Dublin: Dublin Historical Association/Dundalgan Press, 1986.

———. "The Operations of Famine Relief." In *The Great Irish Famine,* edited by Cathal Póirtéir, 123–34. Dublin: Mercier Press, 1995.

———. "Revisionism and Irish History: The Great Famine." In *The Making of Modern Irish History: Revisionism and the Revisionist Controversy,* edited by D. George Boyce and Alan O'Day, 71–89. London: Routledge, 1996.

———. *The Spirit of Earnest Inquiry: The Statistical and Social Inquiry Society of Ireland, 1847–1997.* Dublin: Statistical and Social Inquiry Society of Ireland, 1996.

Daunton, Martin J. *Progress and Poverty: An Economic and Social History of Britain, 1700–1850.* Oxford: Oxford University Press, 1995.

Davis, Mike. *Late Victorian Holocausts: El Niño Famines and the Making of the Third World.* London: Verso, 2001.

Davis, Richard. *The Young Ireland Movement.* Dublin: Gill and Macmillan, 1987.

De Certeau, Michel. *The Writing of History.* Translated by Tom Conley. New York: Columbia University Press, 1988.

De Landa, Manuel. *A Thousand Years of Non-Linear History.* New York: Zone Books, 1997.

De Man, Paul. *Allegories of Reading.* New Haven: Yale University Press, 1979.

————. *The Rhetoric of Romanticism.* New York: Columbia University Press, 1984.

Dening, Greg. *Performances.* Chicago: University of Chicago Press, 1996.

Derrida, Jacques. *Archive Fever: A Freudian Impression.* Translated by Eric Prenowitz. Chicago: University of Chicago Press, 1995.

————. *The Gift of Death.* Translated by David Wills. Chicago: University of Chicago Press, 1995.

————. *Given Time: I Counterfeit Money.* Translated by Peggy Kamuf. Chicago: University of Chicago Press, 1993.

————. *Specters of Marx: The State of the Debt, the Work of Mourning and the New International.* Translated by Peggy Kamuf. New York: Routledge, 1994.

Dirks, Nicholas B. *Castes of Mind: Colonialism and the Making of Modern India.* Princeton, NJ: Princeton University Press, 2001.

————. "History as a Sign of the Modern." *Public Culture* 2, no. 2 (1990): 25–31.

Donnelly, James S. "Famine and Government Response, 1845–6" and "A Famine in Irish Politics." In *A New History of Ireland,* edited by W. E. Vaughan, 5:272–85, 5:257–71. Oxford: Clarendon Press, 1988.

————. "Irish Property Must Pay for Irish Poverty: British Public Opinion and the Great Famine." In Morash and Hayes, *Fearful Realities,* 60–75.

————. "Pastorini and Captain Rock: Millenarianism and Sectarianism in the Rockite Movement of 1821–4." In *Irish Peasants: Violence and Political Unrest 1780–1914,* edited by Samuel Clark and James S. Donnelly, 102–39. Madison: University of Wisconsin Press, 1983.

Dorson, Richard. *The British Folklorists: A History.* Chicago: University of Chicago Press, 1968.

Douglas, Mary. *Purity and Danger: An Analysis of the Concepts of Pollution and Taboo.* New York: Praeger, 1966.

Duffy, Charles Gavan. *Four Years of Irish History, 1845–1849.* New York: Cassell, Petter, Galpin, 1882.

Eade, John Christopher, ed. *Romantic Nationalism in Europe.* Canberra: Australian National University, 1983.

Edwards, Robert Dudley. *Daniel O'Connell and His Times.* London: Thames and Hudson, 1975.

Edwards, Ruth Dudley. *Patrick Pearse: The Triumph of Failure.* London: Gollancz, 1977.

Eiriksson, Andres. "Food Supply and Food Riots." In *Famine 150: Commemorative Lecture Series,* edited by Cormac Ó Gráda, 67–93. Dublin: Teagasc/University College, Dublin, 1996.

Ellis, Steven G. *Ireland in the Age of the Tudors, 1447–1603: English Expansion and the End of Gaelic Rule.* New York: Longman, 1998.

Ellmann, Maud. *The Hunger Artists: Starving, Writing and Imprisonment.* Cambridge: Harvard University Press, 1993.

Engels, Friedrich. *The Condition of the Working Class in England.* New York: Viking Penguin, 1987.

Escobar, Arturo. *Encountering Development: The Making and Unmaking of the Third World.* Princeton, NJ: Princeton University Press, 1995.

Evans, E. Estyn. *Irish Folk Ways.* London: Routledge, 1988.

Evans-Wentz, Walter Yeeling. *The Fairy Faith in Celtic Countries.* Atlantic Highlands, NJ: Humanities Press, 1978.

Fanning, Charles, ed. *New Perspectives on the Irish Diaspora.* Carbondale: Southern Illinois University Press, 2000.

Feldman, Allen. *Formations of Violence: The Narrative of the Body and Political Terror in Northern Ireland.* Chicago: University of Chicago Press, 1991.

Felman, Shoshana, and Dori Laub. *Testimony: Crises of Witnessing in Literature, Psychoanalysis and History.* London: Routledge, 1992.

Ferguson, James. *The Anti-Politics Machine: "Development," Depoliticization and Bureaucratic Power in Lesotho.* Minneapolis: University of Minnesota Press, 1994.

Fitzpatrick, David, ed. *Oceans of Consolation: Personal Accounts of Irish Emigration to Australia.* Ithaca, NY: Cornell University Press, 1994.

Flanagan, Lawrence. *A Dictionary of Irish Archaeology.* Dublin: Gill and Macmillan, 1993.

Ford, Alan, James I. McGuire, and Kenneth Milne, eds. *As by Law Established: The Church of Ireland Since the Reformation.* Dublin: Lilliput Press, 1995.

Foss, Peter, and Catherine O'Connell. "Bogland: Study and Utilization." In *Nature in Ireland: A Scientific and Cultural History,* edited by John Wilson Foster, 184–98. Dublin: Lilliput Press, 1997.

Foster, Roy F. *Modern Ireland, 1600–1972.* London: Viking Penguin, 1988.

———. "We Are All Revisionists Now." *Irish Review* 1, no. 3 (1986): 1–5.

Foucault, Michel. *The History of Sexuality,* vol. 1, *Introduction.* Translated by Robert Hurley. New York: Pantheon Books, 1978.

Frazer, Sir James George. *The Golden Bough: A Study in Magic and Religion.* Vol. 1. London: Macmillan, 1912.

Froude, James Anthony. *Froude's Life of Carlyle.* Abridged and edited by John Clubbe. Columbus: Ohio State University Press, 1979.

Gallagher, Catherine. "The Body Versus the Social Body in the Works of Thomas Malthus and Henry Mayhew." In *The Making of the Modern Body: Sexuality and Society in the Nineteenth Century,* edited by Catherine Gallagher and Thomas Laqueur, 83–106. Berkeley: University of California Press, 1987.

Garvin, Tom. *The Evolution of Irish Nationalist Politics.* New York: Holmes and Meier, 1981.

Geary, Laurence M., ed. *Rebellion and Remembrance in Modern Ireland.* Dublin: Four Courts Press, 2001.

Gebauer, Gunter, and Christoph Wulf. *Mimesis: Culture, Art, Society.* Translated by Don Reneau. Berkeley: University of California Press, 1995.

Gerald of Wales. *History and Topography of Ireland.* Translated by John J. O'Meara. Harmondsworth: Penguin Books, 1981.

Geschiere, Peter. *The Modernity of Witchcraft: Politics and the Occult in Postcolonial Africa.* Charlottesville: University of Virginia Press, 1997.

Gibbons, Sarah L. *Kant's Theory of Imagination: Bridging Gaps in Judgement and Experience.* Oxford: Clarendon Press, 1995.

Giddens, Anthony. *The Nation State and Violence.* Berkeley: University of California Press, 1987.

Gilley, Sheridan. "English Attitudes to the Irish in England, 1780–1900." In *Immigrants and Minorities in British Society,* edited by Colin Homes, 81–110. London: Allen and Unwin, 1978.

Gilman, J. Matthew. *Receiving Erin's Children: Philadelphia, Liverpool and the Irish Famine Migration.* Chapel Hill: University of North Carolina Press, 1999.

Glob, P. V. *The Bog People: Iron Age Man Preserved.* Ithaca, NY: Cornell University Press, 1970.

Gomme, George L. *Ethnology in Folklore.* Detroit: Singing Tree Press, 1969.

Goody, Jack. *The Domestication of the Savage Mind.* Cambridge: Cambridge University Press, 1977.

———. *The Interface Between the Written and the Oral.* Cambridge: Cambridge University Press, 1987.

Gordon, Avery. *Ghostly Matters: Haunting and the Sociological Imagination.* Minneapolis: University of Minnesota Press, 1996.

Goux, Jean-Joseph. *Oedipus Philosopher.* Translated by Catherine Porter. Stanford, CA: Stanford University Press, 1993.

Gramsci, Antonio. "Notes on Italian History." In *Selections from the Prison Note-*

books of Antonio Gramsci, edited by Quentin Hoare and Geoffrey Nowell-Smith, 44–120. New York: International Publishers, 1971.

Gray, Peter. *Famine, Land and Politics: British Government and Irish Society, 1843–50.* Blackrock, County Dublin: Irish Academic Press, 1999.

———. "Nassau Senior and the *Edinburgh Review*." In *Ideology and Ireland in the Nineteenth Century*, edited by Tadgh Foley and Sean Ryder, 130–42. Dublin: Four Courts Press, 1996.

Gregory, Augusta. *Visions and Beliefs in the West of Ireland, Collected and Arranged by Lady Gregory. With Two Essays and Notes by W. B. Yeats.* New York: Oxford University Press, 1970.

Gribben, Arthur, ed. *The Great Famine and the Irish Diaspora in America.* Amherst: University of Massachusetts Press, 1999.

Griffiths, A. R. G. "The Irish Board of Works in the Famine Years." *Historical Journal* 13, no. 4 (1970): 634–52.

Guha, Ranajit. "The Prose of Counter-Insurgency." In *Selected Subaltern Studies*, edited by Ranajit Guha and Gayatri Chakravorty Spivak, 45–84. New York: Oxford University Press, 1988.

Guinnane, Timothy. *The Vanishing Irish: Households, Migration and the Rural Economy in Ireland, 1880–1914.* Princeton, NJ: Princeton University Press, 1997.

Gwynn, Denis. *Young Ireland and 1848.* Cork: Cork University Press, 1949.

Hacking, Ian. *The Emergence of Probability: A Philosophical Study of Ideas of Probability, Induction and Statistical Inference.* Cambridge: Cambridge University Press, 1975.

———. *The Taming of Chance.* Cambridge: Cambridge University Press, 1990.

Hanssen, Beatrice. *Walter Benjamin's Other History: Of Stones, Animals, Human Beings and Angels.* Berkeley: University of California Press, 1998.

Hayles, N. Katherine. *Chaos Bound: Orderly Disorder in Contemporary Literature and Science.* Ithaca, NY: Cornell University Press, 1990.

Heaney, Seamus. *Death of a Naturalist.* London: Faber and Faber, 1966.

———. *North.* London: Faber and Faber, 1992.

———. *Sweeney Astray.* New York: Farrar Straus Giroux, 1984.

Heffer, Simon. *Moral Desperado: A Life of Thomas Carlyle.* London: Weidenfeld and Nicolson, 1995.

Hegel, Georg Wilhelm Friedrich. *Reason in History: A General Introduction to the Philosophy of History.* Indianapolis: Bobbs-Merrill, 1953.

Heidegger, Martin. *On Time and Being.* Translated by Joan Stambaugh. New York: Harper and Row, 1972.

Herminghouse, Patricia, and Magda Mueller, eds. *Gender and Germanness: Cultural Productions of Nation.* Providence, RI: Berghahn Books, 1997.

Hertz, Robert. "The Collective Representation of Death." In *Death and the Right Hand*, translated by Rodney and Claudia Needham, 25–86. Aberdeen: Cohen and West, 1960.

Herzfeld, Michael. *Cultural Intimacy: Social Poetics in the Nation State*. London: Routledge, 1997.

———. *Ours Once More: Folklore, Nationalism and the Making of Modern Greece*. New York: Pella, 1986.

Hill, Jacqueline R. "The Intelligentsia and Irish Nationalism in the 1840s." *Studia Hibernica* 20 (1980): 73–109.

Hilton, Boyd. *The Age of Atonement: The Influence of Evangelicalism on Social and Economic Thought, 1785–1865*. Oxford: Clarendon Press, 1991.

Hobsbawm, Eric. *Primitive Rebels: Studies in Archaic Forms of Social Movements in the Nineteenth and Twentieth Centuries*. New York: Praeger, 1963.

Hollett, Dave. *Passage to the New World: Packet Ships and Irish Emigrants, 1845–1851*. Abergavenny: P. M. Heaton, 1995.

Hopkin, Alannah. *The Living Legend of St. Patrick*. London: Grafton, 1987.

Horkheimer, Max, and Theodor W. Adorno. *Dialectic of Enlightenment*. Translated by Edmund Jephcott. Stanford: Stanford University Press, 2002.

Hosking, Geoffrey A., and George Schopflin, eds. *Myth and Nationhood*. London: Hurst, 1992.

Hubbs, Joanna. *Mother Russia: The Feminine Myth in Russian Culture*. Bloomington: Indiana University Press, 1988.

Hutchinson, John. *The Dynamics of Irish Cultural Nationalism*. London: Allen and Unwin, 1987.

IFC. Irish Folklore Commission. Volume and page numbers refer to Main Manuscript Collection, Department of Irish Folklore, University College, Dublin.

Inglis, Brian. *Poverty and the Industrial Revolution*. London: Hodder and Stoughton, 1971.

Inglis, Tom. *Moral Monopoly: The Catholic Church in Modern Irish Society*. Dublin: Gill and Macmillan, 1997.

Irigaray, Luce. *Speculum of the Other Woman*. Translated by Gillian C. Gill. Ithaca, NY: Cornell University Press, 1985.

Irish Folklore Commission. *Irish Folklore and Tradition*. Dublin: Irish Folklore Commission/Department of Education, 1938.

Ivy, Marilyn. *Discourses of the Vanishing: Modernity, Phantasm, Japan*. Chicago: University of Chicago Press, 1995.

Jutte, R. *Poverty and Deviance in Early Modern Europe*. Cambridge: Cambridge University Press, 1994.

Kaiser, David Aram. *Romanticism, Aesthetics and Nationalism*. Cambridge: Cambridge University Press, 1999.

Kant, Immanuel. *The Critique of the Power of Judgement.* Translated by Paul Guyes and Eric Matthews. Cambridge: Cambridge University Press, 2000.

Kaplan, Fred. *Thomas Carlyle: A Biography.* Ithaca, NY: Cornell University Press, 1983.

Kearney, Richard. *Myth and Motherland.* Field Day Pamphlet No. 5. Derry: Field Day Theatre Co., 1984.

Kelleher, Margaret. *The Feminization of Famine: Expressions of the Inexpressible.* Durham, NC: Duke University Press, 1997.

———. "Irish Famine in Literature." In *The Great Irish Famine,* edited by Cathal Póirtéir, 232–47. Dublin: Mercier Press, 1995.

Keneally, Thomas. *The Great Shame: A Story of the Irish in the Old World and the New.* London: Chatto and Windus, 1998.

Kenney, James F. *The Sources for the Early History of Ireland: An Introduction and Guide.* New York: Columbia University Press, 1929.

Killen, John, ed. *The Famine Decade: Contemporary Accounts 1841–1851.* Belfast: Blackstaff Press, 1995.

Kinealy, Christine. *A Death-Dealing Famine: The Great Hunger in Ireland.* London: Pluto Press, 1997.

———. *This Great Calamity: The Irish Famine, 1845–52.* Dublin: Gill and Macmillan, 1994.

Kissane, Noel, ed. *The Irish Famine: A Documentary History.* Dublin: National University of Ireland, 1995.

Kristeva, Julia. *Powers of Horror: An Essay on Abjection.* New York: Columbia University Press, 1982.

———. "Word, Dialogue, Novel." In *The Kristeva Reader,* edited by T. Moi, 34–61. New York: Columbia University Press, 1986.

Laclau, Ernesto, and Chantal Mouffe. *Hegemony and Socialist Strategy: Towards a Radical Democratic Politics.* London: Verso, 1985.

Landes, Joan B. *Visualizing the Nation: Gender, Representation and Revolution in Eighteenth Century France.* Ithaca, NY: Cornell University Press, 2000.

Laplanche, J., and J.-B. Pontalis. *The Language of Psychoanalysis.* Translated by Donald Nicholson Smith, with an introduction by Daniel Lagache. New York: Norton, 1973.

Larkin, Emmet. "The Devotional Revolution in Ireland." *American Historical Review* 77, no. 3 (1972): 625–52.

Lash, Scott. *Another Modernity, a Different Rationality.* Oxford: Blackwell, 1999.

Laslett, Peter. *The World We Have Lost.* London: Methuen, 1965.

Latour, Bruno. *We Have Never Been Modern.* Cambridge: Harvard University Press, 1993.

La Valley, Albert J. *Carlyle and the Idea of the Modern.* New Haven, CT: Yale University Press, 1968.

Laxton, Edward. *The Famine Ships: The Irish Exodus to America.* New York: Holt, 1997.

Leach, Edmund. "Two Essays Concerning the Symbolic Representation of Time." In *Rethinking Anthropology,* 124–36. London: Athlone Press, 1966.

Lebow, Richard Ned. *White Britain and Black Ireland: The Influence of Stereotypes on Colonial Policy.* Philadelphia: Institute for the Study of Human Issues, 1976.

Lee, Joseph. "The Famine as History." In *Famine 150: Commemorative Lecture Series,* edited by Cormac Ó Gráda, 159–77. Dublin: Teagasc/University College, Dublin, 1997.

———. "The Ribbonmen." In *Secret Societies in Ireland,* edited by T. D. Williams, 26–35. Dublin: Gill and Macmillan, 1976.

Leerssen, Joseph Theodor. *Mere Irish and Fíor-Ghael: Studies in the Idea of Irish Nationality, Its Development and Literary Expression Prior to the Nineteenth Century.* Cork: Cork University Press, 1997.

———. "Wildness, Wilderness and Ireland: Patterns in the Medieval and Early Modern Demarcation of Civility." *Journal of the History of Ideas* 56, no. 1 (1995): 25–39.

Lévy-Bruhl, Lucien. *Primitive Mythology: The Mythic World of the Australian and Papuan Natives.* Translated by Brian Elliott. St. Lucia: University of Queensland Press, 1983.

Leys, Ruth. *Trauma: A Genealogy.* Chicago: University of Chicago Press, 2000.

Lloyd, David. *Ireland After History.* Cork: Cork University Press, 1999.

———. *Nationalism and Minor Literature: James Clarence Mangan and the Emergence of Irish Cultural Nationalism.* Berkeley: University of California Press, 1986.

———. "Pap for the Dispossessed: Seamus Heaney and the Politics of Identity." In *Anomalous States: Irish Writing and the Post-Colonial Moment.* Dublin: Lilliput Press, 1993, 13–40.

Luddy, Maria. *Women and Philanthropy in Nineteenth Century Ireland.* Cambridge: Cambridge University Press, 1995.

Lyons, F. S. L. Review of Cecil Woodham-Smith, *The Great Hunger. Historical Studies* 14 (1964–1965): 76–78.

Lyotard, Jean-Francois. *The Inhuman: Reflections on Time.* Translated by Geoffrey Bennington and Rachel Bowlby. Cambridge: Polity Press, 1991.

Lysaght, Patricia. *The Banshee: The Irish Supernatural Death Messenger.* Dublin: O'Brien Press, 1996.

———. "Perspectives on Women During the Great Irish Famine from Oral Tradition." *Béaloideas* 64–65 (1996): 63–130.

Macalister, R. A. S. *Lebor Gabála Érenn* [The book of the invasions of Ireland]. 5 vols. Dublin: Irish Texts Society, 1938–1954.

MacCana, Proinsias. "Aspects of the Theme of King and Goddess in Irish Literature." *Études Celtiques* 7 (1955–1956): 76–114.

———. "Aspects of the Theme of King and Goddess in Irish Literature, Continued." *Études Celtiques* 8 (1958–1959): 59–65.

McClintock, Anne. "No Longer in a Future Heaven: Nationalism, Gender and Race." In *Becoming National: A Reader*, edited by Geoff Eley and Ronald Grigor Suny, 260–84. New York: Oxford University Press, 1996.

McCone, Kim. *Pagan Past and Christian Present in Early Irish Literature*. Maynooth: An Sagart, 1990.

McHugh, Roger. "The Famine in Irish Oral Tradition." In *The Great Famine*, edited by R. D. Edwards and T. D. Williams, 391–404. Dublin: Lilliput Press, 1994.

McLoughlin, Dympna. "Workhouses and Irish Female Paupers, 1840–70." In *Women Surviving: Studies in Irish Women's History in the Nineteenth and Twentieth Centuries*, edited by Maria Luddy and Cliona Murphy, 117–47. Swords, County Dublin: Poolbeg Press, 1989.

MacNeill, Maire. "Wayside Death Cairns in Ireland" *Béaloideas* 16 (1946): 49–63.

Malthus, Thomas. *An Essay on the Principle of Population, or, A View of Its Past and Present Effects on Human Happiness: With an Inquiry into Our Prospects Respecting the Future Removal or Mitigation of the Evils which It Occasions*. Based on 1803 edition, showing additions and corrections made in the 1806, 1807, 1817, and 1826 editions. Cambridge: Cambridge University Press, 1992.

———. *First Essay on Population*. New York: Kelley, 1965.

———. "Newenham and Others on the State of Ireland." *Edinburgh Review* 24 (July 1808): 336–55.

———. "Newenham on the State of Ireland." *Edinburgh Review* 14 (April 1809): 151–70.

———. "Population." In *Supplement to the Fourth, Fifth and Sixth Editions of the Encyclopaedia Britannica*, edited by M. Napier, 306–33. London: Hurt Robinson, 1824.

Mangan, James Clarence. *The Collected Works of James Clarence Mangan. Poems: 1838–1844*. Blackrock, County Dublin: Irish Academic Press, 1994.

Marcus, Steven. *Engels, Manchester and the Working Class*. New York: Norton, 1974.

Mauss, Marcel. *The Gift: The Form and Reason for Exchange in Archaic Societies.* New York: Norton, 2000.

Michaels, Walter Benn. "'You Who Never Was There': Slavery and the New Historicism, Deconstruction and the Holocaust." *Narrative* 4, no. 1 (January 1996): 1–17.

Mitchel, John. *The Last Conquest of Ireland (Perhaps).* Glasgow: Author's Edition, 1876.

Mitchell, Frank G. *Reading the Irish Landscape.* Dublin: Town House and Country House, 1997.

Mokyr, Joel. *Why Ireland Starved: A Quantitative and Analytical History of the Irish Economy, 1800–1850.* London: Allen and Unwin, 1981.

Moran, Michael. "Thomas Carlyle." In *The Encyclopedia of Philosophy*, edited by Paul Edwards, 2:23–25. New York: Macmillan and the Free Press, 1967.

Moran, Sean Farrell. *Patrick Pearse and the Politics of Redemption: The Mind of the Easter Rising, 1916.* Washington, DC: Catholic University of America Press, 1994.

Morash, Christopher. *Writing the Irish Famine.* Oxford: Clarendon Press, 1994.

Morash, Cristopher, ed. *The Hungry Voice: The Poetry of the Irish Famine.* Blackrock, County Dublin: Irish Academic Press, 1989.

Morash, Christopher, and Richard Hayes, eds. *Fearful Realities: New Perspectives on the Famine.* Blackrock, County Dublin: Irish Academic Press, 1998.

Morgan, Hiram. *Tyrone's Rebellion: The Outbreak of the Nine Years War in Tudor England.* Rochester, NY: Boydell Press, 1993.

Morris, Henry. "Irish Wake Games." *Béaloideas* 8 (1938): 123–41.

Murphy, Denis. *Cromwell in Ireland: A History of Cromwell's Irish Campaign.* Dublin: M. H. Gill, 1902.

Nagy, Joseph Falaky. *Conversing with Angels and Ancients: Literary Myths of Medieval Ireland.* Ithaca, NY: Cornell University Press, 1997.

———. "Liminality and Knowledge in Irish Tradition." *Studia Celtica* 16–17 (1981–1982): 135–43.

———. "The Wisdom of the Geilt." *Éigse* 19 (1982–1983): 44–60.

Neumann, Klaus. *Not the Way It Really Was: Constructing the Tolai Past.* Honolulu: University of Hawaii Press, 1992.

Ní Bhrolcháin, Muireann. "Women in Early Irish Myths and Sagas." In *The Crane Bag Book of Irish Studies (1977–1981)*, edited by Mark Patrick Hederman and Richard Kearney, 525–32. Dublin: Blackwater Press.

Ní Cheannain, Áine. *The Heritage of Mayo.* Dublin: Foilseachain Naisunta Tearanta, 1982.

Nicholson, Asenath. *Annals of the Famine in Ireland.* Dublin: Lilliput Press, 1998.

Nietzsche, Friedrich. *The Use and Abuse of History.* Translated by Adrian Collins. New York: Liberal Arts Press, 1957.

Nowlan, Kevin B. *The Politics of Repeal: A Study of the Relations Between Britain and Ireland, 1841–50.* London: Routledge and Keegan Paul, 1965.

Ó Catháin, Séamas. *The Festival of Brigit: Celtic Goddess and Holy Woman.* Blackrock, County Dublin: DBA Publications, 1995.

Ó Cathaoir, Brendan, ed. *Famine Diary.* Blackrock, County Dublin: Irish Academic Press, 1999.

Ó Ciosáin, Niall. "Boccoughs and God's Poor: Deserving and Undeserving Poor in Irish Popular Culture." In *Ideology and Ireland in the Nineteenth Century,* edited by Tadgh Foley and Sean Ryder, 93–99. Dublin: Four Courts Press, 1998.

O'Connor, Anne. "The Placeless Dead." *Sinsear: The Folklore Journal* 1 (1979): 33–41.

O'Connor, John. *The Workhouses of Ireland.* Minneapolis: Irish Books and Media, 1995.

O'Connor, Sinead. "Famine." From *Universal Mother.* Capitol Records, 1994.

Ó Crualaoich, Gearoid. "The Primacy of Form: A 'Folk Ideology' in de Valera's Politics." In *De Valera and His Times,* edited by J. P. O'Carroll and John A. Murphy, 47–61. Cork: Cork University Press, 1983.

Ó Danachair, Caoimhín. "The Progress of Irish Ethnology, 1783–1982." *Ulster Folklife* 29 (1983): 3–17.

Ó Duilearga, Séamus. "Editorial Address." *Béaloideas* 1, no. 1 (1928): 3–6.

———. "Volkskundliche Arbeit in Irland von 1850 bis zur gegenwart mit besonderer Berücksichtigung der Irischen Volkskunde Kommission." *Zeitschrift für keltische Philologie und Volksforschung* 23 (1943): 136–41.

Ó Duilearga, Séamus, ed. *Leabhair Sheáin Í Chonaill: Sgéalta agus seanchas ó Íbh Ráthach.* Dublin: Comhairle Bhéaloideas Éireann, 1981.

O'Farrell, Patrick. "Millenialism, Messianism and Utopianism in Irish History." *Anglo-Irish Studies* 2 (1976): 45–68.

O'Ferrall, Fergus. *Catholic Emancipation: Daniel O'Connell and the Birth of Irish Democracy, 1820–1830.* Dublin: Gill and Macmillan, 1985.

Ó Giolláin, Diarmuid. *Locating Irish Folklore: Tradition, Modernity, Identity.* Cork: Cork University Press, 2000.

Ó Gráda, Cormac. *An Drochshaol: Béaloideas agus Amhráin.* Dublin: Coiscéim, 1994.

———. *Black '47 and Beyond: The Great Irish Famine in History, Economy and Memory.* Princeton, NJ: Princeton University Press, 1999.

———. *The Great Irish Famine.* Basingstoke: Macmillan Education, 1989.

————. *Ireland Before and After the Famine: Explorations in Economic History.* New York: St. Martin's Press, 1988.

————. *Ireland: A New Economic History, 1780–1939.* Oxford: Clarendon Press, 1994.

————. "Making History in Ireland in the 1940s and 1950s: The Saga of *The Great Famine.*" In *Interpreting Irish History: The Debate on Historical Revisionism, 1938–1994,* edited by Ciaran Brady, 269–73. Blackrock, County Dublin: Irish Academic Press, 1994.

O'Hara, Bernard, ed. *Mayo: Aspects of Its Heritage.* Galway: Archaeological, Historical and Folklore Society, 1982.

Ó hÓgáin, Dáithí. *Myth, Legend and Romance: An Encyclopaedia of Irish Folk Tradition.* London: Ryan Publishing, 1990.

Ó Máille, Tomás S. *Seanfhocla Chonnacht.* Dublin: Oifig an tSoláthair, 1952.

Ó Muimhneacháin, Aindreas. "An Cumann le Béaloideas Éireann, 1927–1977." *Béaloideas* 45–47 (1977–1979): 1–6.

O'Neill, Aine. "Peig Sayers and Need Foods." *Sinsear: The Folklore Journal* 6 (1980): 75–82.

O'Neill, T. "Poverty in Ireland 1815–45." *Folk Life* 11 (1973): 22–33.

Ong, Walter J. *Orality and Literacy: The Technologizing of the Word.* London: Methuen, 1982.

O'Rahilly, Thomas F. *Early Irish History and Mythology.* Dublin: Institute for Advanced Studies. Dublin, 1946.

Ó Riain, Padraig. "A Study of the Irish Legend of the Wild Man." *Éigse* 14 (1971–1972): 179–206.

O'Ryan, Jeremiah. *The Tipperary Minstrel.* Dublin: Marcus Maddigan, 1861.

Ó Súilleabháin, Seán. *A Handbook of Irish Folklore.* Dublin: Educational Council, 1942.

————. *Irish Wake Amusements.* Dublin: Mercier Press, 1967.

Ó Tuama, Seán. *The Gaelic League Idea.* Cork: Mercier Press, 1972.

Ó Tuama, Seán, and Thomas Kinsella, eds. *An Duanaire 1600–1900: Poems of the Dispossessed.* Dublin: Dolmen Press, 1994.

Pandolfo, Stefania. *Impasse of the Angels: Scenes from a Moroccan Space of Memory.* Chicago: University of Chicago Press, 1997.

Piña-Cabral, Joao de. "The Gods of the Gentiles Are Demons: The Problem of Pagan Survivals in European Culture." In *Other Histories,* edited by Kirsten Hastrup, 45–61. New York: Routledge, 1992.

————. "Paved Roads and Enchanted Mooresses: The Perception of the Past Among the Peasant Population of the Alto-Minho." *Man* 4 (n.s., December 1987): 715–35.

Póirtéir, Cathal. *Famine Echoes.* Dublin: Gill and Macmillan, 1995.

————. *Glórtha ón Ghorta: Béaloideas na Gaeilge agns an Gorta Mór*. Dublin: Coiscéim, 1995.

Póirtéir, Cathal, ed. *The Great Irish Famine*. Dublin: Mercier Press, 1995.

Polanyi, Karl. *The Great Transformation*. New York: Farrar and Rinehart, 1944.

Prakash, Gyan. Introduction to *After Colonialism: Imperial Histories and Postcolonial Displacements*, edited by Gyan Prakash, 3–17. Princeton, NJ: Princeton University Press, 1997.

Pringle, Dennis, Jim Walsh, and Mark Hennessy, eds. *Poor People, Poor Places: The Geography of Poverty and Deprivation in Ireland*. Dublin: Oak Tree Press, in association with the Geographical Society of Ireland, 1999.

Rees, Jim. *A Farewell to Famine*. Arklow, County Wicklow: Arklow Enterprise Center, 1994.

Rofel, Lisa. *Other Modernities: Gendered Yearnings in China After Socialism*. Berkeley: University of California Press, 1999.

Ronell, Avital. *Stupidity*. Urbana: University of Illinois Press, 2002.

Ryder, Séan. "Reading Lessons: Famine and the *Nation*, 1845–1849." In Morash and Hayes, *Fearful Realities*, 151–63.

Sagnol, Marcel. "La Méthode Archaeologique de Walter Benjamin." *Les Temps Modernes* 40, no. 444 (July 1983): 143–63.

Sahlins, Marshall. *Historical Metaphors and Mythic Realities: Structure in the Early History of the Sandwich Islands Kingdom*. Ann Arbor: University of Michigan Press, 1981.

————. *Islands of History*. Chicago: University of Chicago Press, 1985.

Salaman, Redcliffe N. *The History and Social Influence of the Potato*. Cambridge: Cambridge University Press, 1985.

Scally, Robert. *The End of Hidden Ireland: Rebellion, Famine and Emigration*. New York: Oxford University Press, 1995.

Schechner, Richard. *The Future of Ritual: Writings on Culture and Performance*. New York: Routledge, 1992.

Scheper-Hughes, Nancy. *Saints, Scholars and Schizophrenics: Mental Illness in Rural Ireland*. Berkeley: University of California Press, 2001.

Schneider, Jane. "Spirits and the Spirit of Capitalism." In *Religious Regimes and State Formation: Perspectives from European Ethnology*, edited by Eric R. Wolf, Adrianus Koster, and Daniel Meijers, 181–220. Albany, NY: State University of New York Press, 1991.

Scott, David. "Colonial Governmentality." In *Refashioning Futures: Criticism After Postcoloniality*. Princeton, NJ: Princeton University Press, 1999, 23–52.

Scott, Thomas Colville. *Connemara After the Famine: Journal of a Survey of the Martin Estate*. Dublin: Lilliput Press, 1995.

Sen, Amartya. *Poverty and Famines: An Essay on Entitlements and Deprivation*. Oxford: Clarendon Press, 1981.

Senior, Nassau. "Ireland." *Edinburgh Review* 79 (January 1844): 189–266.

———. *Journals, Conversations and Essays Relating to Ireland*. 2 vols. London: Longmans, Green, 1868.

———. "Proposals for Extending the Irish Poor Law." *Edinburgh Review* 84 (October 1846): 267–314.

Shapin, Steven, and Simon Schaffer. *Leviathan and the Air Pump: Hobbes, Boyle and the Experimental Life*. Princeton, NJ: Princeton University Press, 1985.

Silver, Carole G. *Strange and Secret Peoples: Fairies and Victorian Consciousness*. New York: Oxford University Press, 1999.

Silverman, Marilyn, and P. H. Gulliver, eds. *Approaching the Past: Historical Anthropology Through Irish Case Studies*. New York: Columbia University Press, 1992.

Silverstein, Michael. "Whorfianism and the Lingusitic Imagination of Nationality." In *Regimes of Language: Ideologies, Polities and Identities*, edited by Paul V. Kroskrity, 35–84. Santa Fe: School of American Research Press, 2000.

Sloan, Robert. *William Smith O'Brien and the Young Irelander Rebellion of 1848*. Dublin: Four Courts, 2000.

Somerville, Alexander. *Letters from Ireland During the Famine of 1847*. Edited by K. D. M. Snell. Blackrock, County Dublin: Irish Academic Press, 1994.

Spaan, David Bruce. "The Otherworld in Early Irish Literature." PhD diss., University of Michigan, 1969.

Spence, Lewis. *British Fairy Origins: The Genesis and Development of Fairy Legends in British Tradition*. Wellingborough: Aquarian Press, 1981.

Spenser, Edmund. *A View of the Present State of Ireland*. London: E. Partridge, at the Scholartis Press, 1934.

Stengers, Isabelle, and Ilya Prigogine. "The Reenchantment of the World." In *Power and Invention: Situating Science*, translated by Paul Bains, 33–58. Minneapolis: University of Minnesota Press, 1997.

Stepan, Nancy. *The Idea of Race in Science: Great Britain 1800–1960*. Hamden, CT: Archon Books, 1982.

Stephens, Walter. *Giants in Those Days: Folklore, Ancient History and Nationalism*. Lincoln: University of Nebraska Press, 1989.

Stocking, George W. *Victorian Anthropology*. New York: Free Press, 1987.

Stüssi, Anna. *Erinnerung an die Zukunft: Walter Benjamin's "Berliner Kindheit im Neunzehnhundert."* Gottingen: Vandenhoeck and Ruprecht, 1977.

Synge, John Millington. *The Aran Islands*. Evanston: Northwestern University Press, 1999.

Taussig, Michael. "The Construction of America: The Anthropologist as Columbus." In *Culture/Contexture: Explorations in Anthropology and Literary Studies*, edited by E. Valentine Daniel and Jeffrey M. Peck, 323–56. Berkeley: University of California Press, 1996.

———. *The Magic of the State*. New York: Routledge, 1997.

———. *Mimesis and Alterity: A Particular History of the Senses*. New York: Routledge, 1993.

———. *Shamanism, Colonialism and the Wild Man: A Study in Terror and Healing*. Chicago: University of Chicago Press, 1987.

Taylor, Lawrence J. "Bas InÉirinn: Cultural Constructions of Death in Ireland." In *The Uses of Death in Europe*, edited by Lawrence J. Taylor. Special edition, *Anthropological Quarterly* 62, no. 4 (October 1989): 175–88.

———. *Occasions of Faith: An Anthropology of Irish Catholics*. Philadelphia: University of Pennsylvania Press, 1995.

Trevelyan, Charles Edward. "The Irish Crisis." *Edinburgh Review* 87 (January 1848): 229–320.

Tyler, Stephen A. "On Being Out of Words." In *Rereading Cultural Anthropology*, edited by George E. Marcus, 1–7. Durham, NC: Duke University Press, 1993.

Van der Kolk, Bessel, Alexander C. McFarlane, and Lars Weisath. *Traumatic Stress: The Effects of Overwhelming Experience on Mind, Body and Society*. New York: Guilford Press, 1996.

Vida, Elizabeth M. *Romantic Affinities: German Authors and Caryle*. Toronto: University of Toronto Press, 1993.

Vries, Hent de. "In Media Res." In *Religion and Media*, edited by Hent de Vries and Samuel Weber, 3–42. Stanford, CA: Stanford University Press, 2001.

Vries, Hent de, and Samuel Weber, eds. *Religion and Media*. Stanford, CA: Stanford University Press, 2001.

Waters, John. "Confronting the Ghosts of Our Past." In *Irish Hunger: Personal Reflections on the Legacy of the Famine*, edited by Tom Hayden, 27–31. Dublin: Wolfhound Press, 1997.

Weber, Max. *The Protestant Ethic and the Spirit of Capitalism*. London: Harper Collins, 1991.

———. "Science as a Vocation." In *From Max Weber: Essays in Sociology*, edited by H. H. Gerth and C. Wright Mills, 129–56. New York: Oxford University Press, 1949.

Weber, Samuel. *Mass Mediauras: Form, Technics, Media*. Stanford, CA: Stanford University Press, 1996.

Weigel, Sigrid. *Body and Image Space: Re-Reading Walter Benjamin*. New York: Routledge, 1996.

Wellek, Rene. "Carlyle and the Philosophy of History." *Phililogical Quarterly* 23 (1944): 55–76.

Whelan, Irene. "The Stigma of Souperism." In In *The Great Irish Famine*, edited by Cathal Póirtéir, 135–54. Dublin: Mercier Press, 1995.

Whelan, Kevin. *Fellowship of Freedom: The United Irishmen and 1798.* Cork: Cork University Press, 1998.

Whelan, Kevin, and T. Power, eds. *Endurance and Emergence: Catholics in Ireland in the Eighteenth Century.* Blackrock, County Dublin: Irish Academic Press, 1990.

Wilde, William. *Irish Popular Superstitions.* Dublin: Irish Academic Press, 1979.

Wilson, William A. *Folklore and Nationalism in Modern Finland.* Bloomington: Indiana University Press, 1976.

Witoszek, Nina. "Ireland: A Funerary Culture?" *Studies* 76, no. 301 (Spring 1987): 206–15.

Witoszek, Nina, and Pat Sheeran. *Talking to the Dead: A Study of Irish Funerary Traditions.* Amsterdam: Rodopi, 1998.

Woodham-Smith, Cecil. *The Great Hunger: Ireland 1845–1849.* Harmondsworth: Penguin Books, 1991.

Woolf, S. *The Poor in Western Europe in the Eighteenth and Nineteenth Centuries.* London: Methuen, 1986.

Young, Arthur. *A Tour in Ireland, with General Observations as to the State of that Kingdom.* 2 vols. Dublin: G. Bonham for Whitestone, 1780.

Žižek, Slavoj. "Enjoy Your Nation as Yourself." In *Tarrying with the Negative: Kant, Hegel, and the Critique of Ideology,* 200–238. Durham, NC: Duke University Press, 1994.

———. *The Sublime Object of Ideology.* London: Verso, 1989.

———. "Taking Sides: A Self-Interview." In *The Metastases of Enjoyment: Six Essays on Woman and Causality,* 167–217. London: Verso, 1994.

Zonabend, Francoise. *Memoire Longue: Temps et Histoires au Village.* Paris: Presses Universitaires de France, 1980.

Index

Mahony, James, 75–77, 115

Malthus, Thomas, 53–57, 63–68 *passim*

Manchester, Irish in, 51–52, 177n4. *See also* Emigration

Mangan, James Clarence, 13, 169n50

Marcus, Steven, 177n4

Marx, Karl, 52, 112, 191n37

Materiality: of corpse, 1, 95, 113; of famished body, 115, 122–26 *passim*, 161f; of specter, 122, 128, 191n37. *See also* Death; Prehistory; Spectrality

Mauss, Marcel, 66, 109, 180n54, 188–89n57

Meagher, Thomas Francis, 87–91 *passim*, 184n69

Michaels, Walter Benn, 196n21

Mimetic faculty, 15, 143–44, 149, 194n43. *See also* Benjamin, Walter; Performance; Prehistory; Women

Mitchell, John, 6, 71, 87–90 *passim*, 183–84n57, 184n69

Modernity: concepts of, 3–5, 158–63 *passim*, 165–66n13, 167n13; critiques of, 4–5, 148–50; 158–63; 166–67n13; invocation of premodern past, 5–12 *passim*, 17–19, 29–33 *passim*, 44–45, 68–69, 101, 108–9, 121–22, 148–50, 158–63 *passim*. *See also* Disenchantment; Historiography; Nature; Prehistory; Progress

Moran, Michael, 173n6

Morash, Christopher, 14, 168n25, 169n50

Morgan, Hiram, 175n24

Morris, Henry, 186n26

Mouffe, Chantal, 176n46

Murphy, Denis, 175n25

Nagy, Joseph Falaky, 171n32

Nation (journal), 35, 87–94 *passim*, 119–20, 183–84n57. *See also* Young Ireland

Nationalism, Ireland, cultural politics of:

folklore, 20–25 *passim*, 29–30, 71, 87–93 *passim*; gender, 130–34, 149–50, 161, 192n9; historiography, 6–7, 71, 92, 167n21; language, 20, 23, 30–31, 172–73n48; state-building, 20–25 *passim*, 29–32 *passim*, 131, 149, 160. *See also* O'Connell, Daniel; United Irishmen; Young Ireland

Nation-state: relationship to past, 19–20, 26–32 *passim*, 155–56, 172nn37, 42; national time, 7, 12, 26, 31

Natural history (*Naturgeschichte*), 14–15, 169n54

Nature: disenchantment of, 3–9 *passim*, 16–17, 148; reawakening of, 15–16, 162, 197n30

Nature/society binary, 70–72, 131–32, 181n5

Ní Cheannain, Aine, 182n34

Nicholls, George, 57–59

Nicholson, Asenath, 195n3

Nietzsche, Friedrich, 8, 12, 19

Nine Years War, 40, 174–75n24

Nowlan, Kevin B., 179n35

Oedipus, as prototype of modern subject, 8

Ó Cadhain, Mairtín, 30–31, 172–73n48

Ó Catháin, Séamas, 194n45

Ó Ciosáin, Niall, 182n20

Ó Conaill, Seán, 32–33, 173nn51, 52

O'Connell, Daniel, 62, 84, 87, 89, 183n45

O'Connor, Sinead, 154

Ó Crualaoich, Gearoid, 171n22

Ó Duilearga, Séamus (James Hamilton Delargy), 21–25 *passim*, 31f, 167n18, 170n10, 171n18

O'Ferrall, Fergus, 178n17

O'Flaherty, Liam, 140–42, 193–94n38

Ó Giolláin, Diarmuid, 20

Ó Gráda, Cormac, 168n22, 195n2

Cultural Memory | in the Present

Martin Stokhof, *World and Life as One: Ethics and Ontology in Wittgenstein's Early Thought*

Gianni Vattimo, *Nietzsche: An Introduction*

Jacques Derrida, *Negotiations: Interventions and Interviews, 1971–1998*, ed. Elizabeth Rottenberg

Brett Levinson, *The Ends of Literature: Post-transition and Neoliberalism in the Wake of the "Boom"*

Timothy J. Reiss, *Against Autonomy: Global Dialectics of Cultural Exchange*

Hent de Vries and Samuel Weber, eds., *Religion and Media*

Niklas Luhmann, *Theories of Distinction: Redescribing the Descriptions of Modernity*, ed. and introd. William Rasch

Johannes Fabian, *Anthropology with an Attitude: Critical Essays*

Michel Henry, *I Am the Truth: Toward a Philosophy of Christianity*

Gil Anidjar, *"Our Place in Al-Andalus": Kabbalah, Philosophy, Literature in Arab-Jewish Letters*

Hélène Cixous and Jacques Derrida, *Veils*

F. R. Ankersmit, *Historical Representation*

F. R. Ankersmit, *Political Representation*

Elissa Marder, *Dead Time: Temporal Disorders in the Wake of Modernity (Baudelaire and Flaubert)*

Reinhart Koselleck, *The Practice of Conceptual History: Timing History, Spacing Concepts*

Niklas Luhmann, *The Reality of the Mass Media*

Hubert Damisch, *A Childhood Memory by Piero della Francesca*

Hubert Damisch, *A Theory of /Cloud/: Toward a History of Painting*

Jean-Luc Nancy, *The Speculative Remark (One of Hegel's Bons Mots)*

Jean-François Lyotard, *Soundproof Room: Malraux's Anti-Aesthetics*

Jan Patočka, *Plato and Europe*

Hubert Damisch, *Skyline: The Narcissistic City*

Isabel Hoving, *In Praise of New Travelers: Reading Caribbean Migrant Women Writers*

Richard Rand, ed., *Futures: Of Derrida*

William Rasch, *Niklas Luhmann's Modernity: The Paradox of System Differentiation*

Jacques Derrida and Anne Dufourmantelle, *Of Hospitality*

Jean-François Lyotard, *The Confession of Augustine*

Kaja Silverman, *World Spectators*

Samuel Weber, *Institution and Interpretation: Expanded Edition*